TEACH YOURSELF BOOKS

ARABIC

NTC *NTC Publishing Group*

TEACH YOURSELF BOOKS

ARABIC

J. R. Smart

 NTC Publishing Group

To my Mother and Father

This edition was first published in 1992 by NTC Publishing Group,
4255 West Touhy Avenue, Lincolnwood (Chicago), Illinois 60646 –
1975 U.S.A. Originally published by Hodder and Stoughton Ltd.
Copyright 1986 by J. R. Smart.

Printed in England by Clays Ltd, St Ives plc.

Contents

(A reference guide to the structure of the course and the grammatical content of the units)

Acknowledgments

I should like to acknowledge with gratitude the help and encouragement over the years of all my teachers, colleagues and friends who have contributed indirectly to the writing of this book.

In particular I should like to thank the Professor and staff of the Department of Arabic and Islamic Studies at the University of Exeter, especially Dr R. el-Enany who spent many patient hours in discussion, made innumerable valuable suggestions and checked all the Arabic texts.

My special thanks are also due to my wife Frances and daughters Mairi and Kirsty for their unfailing support and encouragement while this book was being written.

JRS

Introduction

The Arabic taught in this book is the written and officially spoken means of communication between over 100 million Arabs of some twenty nations stretching from the Atlantic coast of North Africa in the west to the Sultanate of Oman in the east and from Syria in the north to Sudan in the south. It has existed without major change since the seventh century AD and the continuous literary output of this long period is one of the greatest achievements of civilised man.

This is a self-teaching book, not an Arabic grammar in the traditional sense, and the aim throughout has been to bring the student up to the standard where he or she will be able to read a newspaper with the aid of a dictionary and converse with educated Arabs in the literary language which serves as a *lingua franca* between Arabs from different countries.

To make this task easier, some liberties have been taken with traditional Arabic grammar which may alarm the purists, both Arab and European.

As you will soon be learning, Arabic is written in a so-called 'defective' script. This means (among other things) that the short vowels are not written. Now many of the grammatical endings of the noun and the verb are, in fact, short vowels and consequently do not appear in print. Knowing what they are is, therefore, an academic exercise for, being absent, they cannot contribute to the meaning.

Feeling that Arabic is difficult enough for the beginner without his being asked to learn unnecessary rules and facts, I have ruthlessly pruned all such grammatical paraphernalia from the text of this book and mentioned them only in passing in footnotes. Once the basic structures of the language have been learned from this book, the full grammatical apparatus can easily be tacked on by the student with academic leanings. Reference to two excellent traditional grammars is given in the hints for further study in Appendix Four.

How to use this book

You will find that the Units in this book vary considerably in length. This is because the material has been arranged logically, each unit up to Unit 10 dealing with a specific compartment of Arabic grammar and sentence construction. By the end of Unit 10, all the basic constructions of the language have been taught, and Units 11 to 18 fill in the gaps by means of illustrative texts dealing with various aspects of Arab life, new grammatical points being picked out in analyses and special sections. Vocabulary is kept to a minimum in the earlier lessons, and there is much repetition of words in the exercises. Note that these exercises have been introduced at specific points within the units, and they should be done *as and when instructed*. Do not attempt to get through a whole unit at a time; rather, read the material and do the exercises for each section, then review the whole unit when you have finished. This is a self-teaching course, and *it is essential that each unit is thoroughly mastered before you go on to the next.* Although full cross-references are given, nothing is repeated.

Your plan of study should go something like this:

The Arabic Script and Pronunciation   This introduces the Arabic script, which is much simpler than it first looks. Obviously you will have to learn this thoroughly before proceeding, and many practice exercises are given. Pronunciation is dealt with, but of course this is much easier to pick up if you have access to a native speaker. If you can get hold of one, listen to him and ignore the written instructions which are at best a poor substitute for the real thing.

Units 1–10   These are all structured in the same way:
First, there is a set of sentences and/or phrases which illustrate the material for the whole unit. Reference is made back to these in the grammar section, which should be read very carefully along with these examples, and the exercises completed as they occur. There is a key to the exercises at the end of the book, and you should check each of your exercises on completion and *try to find out where you went wrong* (if you did!). It is emphasised again that you should have a good grasp of each unit before going on to the next.

New vocabulary is given with each unit and this should obviously be learned. The lists include all new words introduced in the unit, and not just those in the initial text. Since Arabic is almost never printed with the vowel signs, the policy of this book has been to give them only in the vocabularies (and in a few difficult situations within the texts). What you do about this is up to you (bearing in mind that you will eventually *have* to read unvowelled Arabic). If you can read the vowelled vocabularies and then memorise the sound of the words, so much the better. If not, pencil in the vowels of words you do not know in the text, and gradually wean yourself away from them as you learn the words. After the first few units, transliterations of the texts are given in the Key at the end of the book.

Units 11–18 These are set out differently, as it is assumed that you now have a firm grasp of the basic structures of the language. Each of these units begins with a text, followed by a list of new vocabulary. The next section is a literal translation of the text into a sort of pidgin English which follows the Arabic word for word as far as possible. You are asked as an exercise to convert this into normal idiomatic English, and a version is given in the Key.

Minor grammatical points occurring in the texts are then picked out in the analysis, and special sections are devoted to completely new or important features. Some information about Arab life and society are given in the Background to Text sections.

Appendices The appendices deal with matter which would have occupied too much space within the units, or which could not be learned inductively. The most conspicuous example is the Arabic verb. I have found that most traditional grammar books cover the rest of Arabic grammar in the first half, then have to devote the whole of the second half to the verb. This is obviously not much fun, and very restrictive on the choice of texts, so here the verb has been relegated to separate tables, each with its own set of explanatory notes. The basic rules for forming the two tenses are, of course, given within the units, and the recommendation is that each new type of verb encountered should be looked up in the tables (references are given), and time devoted to learning the conjugations by heart as you go along.

Other topics covered in the appendices are the numerals, which are difficult to use correctly, and the internal plural and its most common patterns. There is also a section recommending dictionaries and books for further study.

The Arabic Script and Pronunciation

Basic characteristics

1   Arabic, whether handwritten, typed or printed, is *cursive*, i.e. the letters (with certain exceptions noted below) are joined to each other by means of ligatures. There is no equivalent in Arabic of the separate, independent letters used in European type-faces. There are no capital letters, and punctuation presents no difficulties as the conventions have been borrowed from European sources.

2   The **script** is written *from right to left*, and consequently books and magazines begin on what looks like the back page. The **numerals**, on the other hand, are written *from left to right*, in the same way as European numerals (which are derived in varying forms from the Arabic signs).

3   In learning the script, it would be very helpful to appreciate the underlying principle that each letter has what we shall call a *nucleus form*, i.e. an essential basic stem. This nucleus form is a concept useful only in learning the script, as in practice it only occurs in the case of six specific letters which by convention do not join to the letter which follows them. The rest of the letters always appear with one or more of the following features:

(*a*)   a ligature joining them to the preceding and/or following letter
(*b*)   if at the end of a word, a final 'flourish'.

This is best illustrated by an example, for which we shall take the letter which has the sound of English *s* in 'sit':

> Nucleus form   س
> With both preceding and following ligatures   ـسـ
> With one ligature and final flourish   سـ
> Separate (after a non-joining letter)   س

From the above it should be obvious that the basic part of the letter, the nucleus which represents the sound 's', is the basic three-pronged form س, so the ligatures and final flourish are extraneous.

It is quite easy to draw a parallel with European handwriting:

Nucleus form *d*   *d*
With both ligatures   *d*
With one ligature and final flourish   *d*

The only difference is that in the European system the nucleus forms occur quite freely in print and typescript, while in Arabic they do not, as even type-face is only an adaptation of the handwritten form and still cursive.

4   With the exception of the first letter *alif*, all the Arabic letters are *consonants*. *Alif* and the vowels (which are not considered as letters of the alphabet) are discussed separately on pp. 13–15 and 18. The Arabic alphabet is given in its traditional order, which should eventually be learned so that dictionaries may be consulted.

Alphabet table

Note that transliterations are English letters, combinations of letters or special signs used to represent Arabic sounds for learners. These are fully discussed in the section on pronunciation on pages 9–12. To simplify the table, a separate form is given for each letter, showing the final flourish, if any. This may, when required, be joined to a preceding letter with the same ligature which is used on the nucleus form.

Arabic name	Separate form	Nucleus form showing both ligatures	Transliteration
alif	ا	*ا	(See page 18)
baa'	ب	ب	**b**
taa'	ت	ت	**t**
thaa'	ث	ث	**th**
jiim	ج	ج	**j**
Haa'	ح	ح	**H**

Arabic name	Separate form	Nucleus form showing both ligatures	Transliteration
khaa'	خ	خ	**kh**
daal	د	* د	**d**
dhaal	ذ	* ذ	**dh**
raa'	ر	* ر	**r**
zaay	ز	* ز	**z**
siin	س	س	**s**
shiin	ش	ش	**sh**
Saad	ص	ص	**S**
Daad	ض	ض	**D**
Taa'	ط	ط	**T**
DHaa'	ظ	ظ	**DH**
:ayn	ع	ع [2]	**:**
ghayn	غ	غ [2]	**gh**
faa'	ف	ف [3]	**f**
qaaf	ق	ق [3]	**q**
kaaf	ك	ك	**k**
laam	ل	ل	**l**
miim	م	م	**m**

Arabic name	Separate form	Nucleus form showing both ligatures	Transliteration
nuun	ن	ڔ	**n**
haa'	ه	ﻫ [2]	**h**
waaw	و	و [*]	**w**
yaa'	ى [4]	ي	**y**
(*hamza*)	ء	(See page 18)	(')

Notes to alphabet table:

1   The letters marked with an asterisk (*) do not, by convention, join to the letter which follows them.

2   The letters :*ayn*, *ghayn* and *haa'* present some difficulty in isolating a nucleus form. In the former two (which are identical except for the dot), the 'gap' between the horns of the letter by convention is closed up when it is joined to a preceding letter. The forms given in the table are (from right to left): initial, medial, final joined, separate. In the case of *haa'* the extra form given is medial, i.e. for use in the middle of a word.

3   In material printed in North Africa, you will sometimes find the *faa'* with one dot *below*, and the *qaaf* with *one* dot above.

4   The separate/final form of the *yaa'* can be written with or without the two dots (see page 21).

As in any cursive writing system, slight variations in the ligatures and the position of the letters relative to the line of script occur in various type-faces and even more so in handwriting. None of these should present any difficulty, but the following standard combination of *laam* and *alif*, which is always used, should be learned:

Separate	**Joined** (to preceding letter only)
لا	لا

Pronunciation of the consonants

Some of the Arabic consonants are very difficult for Europeans to pronounce, but it is essential to attempt accurate pronunciation, otherwise you will be unable to distinguish between words whose difference in meaning depends, for instance, on the distinction between **H** and **h**, **D** and **d** etc. Obviously, as in all languages, the best thing to do is enlist the aid of a native speaker. If his pronunciation varies from the instructions given below, as it may well do, depending on which part of the Arab world he comes from, adopt *his* system and imitate *his* sounds. The ear, in this case, is much more useful than the eye.

Some reference has been made in the following notes to English dialects and the more familiar European languages. This is done in the hope that you might find it easier to get hold of a Scotsman or a Spaniard than a Lebanese or a Libyan!

Group One
The following are pronounced more or less as in English:

ب	**b**	ز	**z**	ل	**l**	ى	**y** (*y*es)
ت	**t**	ش	**sh** (*sh*oe)	م	**m**		
ج	**j**	ف	**f**	ن	**n**		
د	**d**	ك	**k**	و	**w** (*w*as)		

Group Two
These occur in English, but care must be taken:

ث   **th** as in 'think', 'through', etc. (*not* as in 'this', 'these').

ذ   **dh** as the English *th* in 'the', 'that', 'then'. The **dh** transliteration has been used to distinguish this sound from the preceding one (**th**). This is important in Arabic.

س   **s** as in 'sip', 'pass', etc. – *not* the *z*-sound of *s* in 'these', 'pins', 'feeds' and so on.

ه   **h** is the ordinary English *h*-sound in 'house', 'behind'. In English this sound often disappears ('vehicle', 'vehement'), but in Arabic it must *always* be sounded, even in such positions as **sahm** (sah-m), **shibh** (shib-h).

Group Three

These occur in English dialects, and in other European languages.

خ   **kh** is the sound at the end of Scottish 'loch' and German 'doch', and also occurs in Dutch, Spanish and Russian. The Arabic version is a strong rasping sound, produced by closing the back of the tongue against the palate as in pronouncing the letter *k*, then forcing the breath through the constriction.

ر   **r** is the sound in Spanish 'pero', Italian 'parlare', and the *r* of Scottish dialects. It is produced by applying the tip of the tongue to the gum ridge behind the upper front teeth and expelling air to cause it to flap or trill rapidly. This should be a *pronounced* trill, not like the sound in the standard English pronunciation of 'furrow'. (Not to be confused with the French *r* pronounced at the back of the palate.)

غ   **gh** The only European language with an approximation of this sound is Dutch ('morgen', 'negen'). It is vaguely similar to the French (Parisian) *r*, but with more of a scrape than a trill. It is produced by pronouncing the **kh** described above and activating the vocal chords (say 'Ah' at the same time).

Group Four

These sounds do not occur in other familiar languages.

ص ، ض ، ط ، ظ   **S, D, T** and **DH** form a group in that they are articulated more or less like their 'regular' equivalents (س ، د ، ت ، ذ **s, d, t** and **dh**) but with different acoustic conditions obtaining inside the mouth cavity. Pronounce the four regular sounds and you will find that the tip of your tongue will touch in the region of the upper front teeth/gum. Now pronounce the sounds again and at the same time depress the *middle* of the tongue. This has the effect of creating a larger space between the tongue and the roof of the mouth and gives the sound produced a distinctive 'hollow' characteristic, which also affects the surrounding vowels. It is difficult to find a parallel in English, but the difference between 'Sam' and 'psalm' (standard English pronunciation) gives a clue. Tense the tongue muscles in pronouncing 'psalm' and you are nearly there. Now pronounce the a-vowel of 'psalm' before and after each of the four letters, saying **aSa, aDa, aTa** and **aDHa**, keeping the tongue tense, and that's as near as we can get to describing it in print. The effort expended in depressing the middle of the tongue means that these four consonants are pronounced more forcefully, hence they are often known as the 'emphatics'.

ق **q** Although not normally grouped with the above four dental (pronounced against the teeth) consonants, **q** has a somewhat similar acoustic effect. First forget any connection with English *q* or *qu*. The **q** is merely a handy spare symbol, and the sound is pronounced by closing the back of the tongue on the palate, like *k*, but much further back, and then releasing it to produce a click. The nearest sound we have is *c* in standard English 'calm'. Pronounce 'calm' over and over again, trying to force the point at which tongue meets palate further back into the throat. The mouth should be well open, again causing an open-vowel effect like that described above.

ح **H** is probably the most difficult sound of all, and it *must* be distinguished from the ordinary *h*-sound. It is pronounced very deep down in the throat, and if you try a very deep and forceful sigh, with mouth wide open, and at the same time try to constrict your throat in the region of the Adam's apple, you should achieve an approximation. The tongue is slightly tensed and its tip tucked down behind the bottom teeth. This contributes to the effect.

ع **:** is also difficult. The only English non-technical description which can be applied to it is 'a violent, tense glottal stop' (a glottal stop being the sound a Cockney or a Glaswegian substitutes for the *tt* in 'bottle'). The breath passage is blocked deep down in the throat by constricting the muscles near the Adam's apple, then suddenly opened under pressure and with the vocal chords in action (give a grunt). The only time English speakers use these muscles is in vomiting, so if the action brings back unhappy memories, you have probably got it right. (Note that the *ordinary* glottal stop also occurs in Arabic as a different sign: see page 18.)

That concludes the rather difficult range of Arabic consonant sounds. These are very difficult to put down on paper without resort to phonetic terminology, and even more difficult to recreate following a written description, so the aid of a native speaker is invaluable. Accurate pronunciation of Arabic is very important, as certain of the consonants form correlative pairs **h-H**, **d-D**, etc. The similarity in print, of course, only occurs in transliteration, and the Arabic characters for these pairs are not in the least similar, nor are the sounds to an Arab. Failure to distinguish between these sounds can be very misleading, as illustrated by the following pairs of words:

فهم	**fahm**	*understanding*	فحم	**faHm**	*coal, charcoal*
درب	**darb**	*path, track*	ضرب	**Darb**	*a blow, striking*

Arabs know their language is difficult to pronounce, and will be highly delighted if you make the effort and achieve even a modest success. Note that the letter *alif* and the *hamza* will be dealt with later (see page 18).

Doubled consonants

It is a feature of the Arabic language that consonants are sometimes doubled to effect a change in meaning. Obviously this must be reflected by the pronunciation, otherwise the altered significance of the word will be lost. The so-called doubling is effected by *lengthening* the consonant rather than trying to pronounce it twice separately. The phenomenon can be heard frequently in Italian ('riso*tt*o', 'Giova*nn*i'). The special orthographic sign for doubling a consonant is given on page 17.

EXERCISE 0.1 Transliterate the following series of Arabic consonants (without vowels):

برك — فقد — لمس — شذذ — عفو — طلب — خزن — ثغر —

هلك — صيت — بهل — كره — مضي — لغم — فهم — برقوق —

بغل — خرج — جرح — حمد — مدح — ضغط — برنج —

جمهور — ظنن — شكك — حملق — بربر — نبت — ثقف —

زلزل — حمض — غرنط — ربل — بغض — نعس — طلسم —

هبب — عدو — ومض — سيطر — حزن — بلغ — ثلث —

مكن — ريص — زندق — سكن — نهض — ذلل — بدر —

بذر — رحم — برطم — غمض — لستك — تلفن — خلخل —

رعد — درع — حشي — طحن — قفز .

EXERCISE 0.2 Write the following consonant series in joined Arabic characters. (Two-letter transliterations have been underlined to avoid confusion.)

qrd – mmkn – DbT – <u>dh</u>ll – dhn – mktb – rmy – sqT – b:D –
b<u>gh</u>D – whm – srTn – <u>sh</u>ms – <u>gh</u>fl – byrm – wrwr – rTn – <u>th</u>ny –
rb:– tl<u>gh</u>rf – ktbn – Hjj – <u>kh</u>lf – rjz – fDD – DfD: – <u>kh</u>nfs –
<u>sh</u>k<u>h</u>r – <u>sh</u>kl – mzgh – zmrd – <u>gh</u>ly – <u>th</u>wr – <u>sh</u>bb – qlql – THn –
<u>sh</u>ghl – bnfsj – twt – Hrmn – <u>th</u>wb – fndq – nzk – Srm – mrD –
ylzm – <u>kh</u>rb<u>sh</u> – jhnm – mHll – Dmn – DHhr – jrjyr – Dnq –
frwl – :nkbwt – zm<u>kh</u> – <u>sh</u>m<u>kh</u> – HDrmwt – n:n: – br<u>gh</u>t<u>h</u>

The vowels and vowel signs

It is a very important feature of Arabic that the meaning of words depends to a large extent on the *consonants* and the *long vowels*, while the short vowels play a secondary role. Hence the language shows only the consonants and long vowels in the script, and indicates the short vowels and some other features by means of orthographic signs placed above and below the consonants. So fundamental is this feature that *the short vowels are not marked at all*, except in the Koran, some difficult older texts and children's school books. This is one of the most difficult aspects of the language, but one has to get used to it. There is no point in learning to read vowelled texts and then having the vowels suddenly taken away. The policy of this book has therefore been to give the vowelling of words in the vocabularies, but in the sentences and texts to give no more information than an Arab printer would. The reader is at liberty to pencil in his own vowel signs, but is advised to learn the sounds of words so that he can recognise them on sight without the vowel signs.

Fortunately, the Arabic vowel system is very simple. Although they vary somewhat in different phonetic environments, only three vowels are recognised, each occurring in long or short forms. The orthographic system for writing vowels is as follows:

Short vowels
a is indicated by placing a short oblique stroke above the letter. (This sign is called *fatHa* by the Arabs.) Thus:

لَكَ   **laka**   كَتَبَ   **kataba**

u is a miniature *waaw* (like a comma) placed above the letter (Arabic name *Damma*):

تُ   **tu**   مُ   **mu**

i is a short oblique stroke like the *fatHa*, but placed *below* the letter (Arabic name *kasra*):

لِ   **li**   بِهِ   **bihi**

(See also page 17.)

Long vowels
The long vowel equivalents are expressed by using the same signs in combination with the letters *alif, waaw* and *yaa'* respectively written into the word. Thus, to make all the vowels in the above examples long, we would write:

لَاكَا   **laakaa**   كَاتَابَا   **kaataabaa**
تُو   **tuu**   مُو   **muu**
لِي   **lii**   بِيهِي   **biihii**

Note that when the letters *waaw* and *yaa'* are preceded by an a-vowel, they keep their full consonantal values of w and y, for example:

بَيْت   **bayt** (like English 'bite')

دَوْن   **dawn** (like English 'down')

(For the sign ° see next section.)

Consonants without a following vowel
When a letter has no following vowel, it is marked with a small
circle above, called a *sukuun*:

مَكْتَب **maktab**   نَفْس **nafs**

In this book *sukuun* has not normally been written on letters at the
end of words.

Pronunciation of the vowels

The distinction between long and short vowels is very important
and major (often ridiculous) changes in meaning can occur if
vowels are not given their correct length. *So keep long, long and
short, short.*

The a-vowels are usually pronounced much as in English 'man',
'ban', extended accordingly for the long variety which does not
occur in English. Before or after the letters **S, D, T, DH, gh, q** and
sometimes **kh, r** and **l** the a-vowel takes on a character somewhat
like the vowel in standard English 'calm', 'far' – again adjusted for
length.

The short u-vowel is very like the English 'put' and the long u-
vowel resembles 'plume'. They are never pronounced as in 'cut' or
'up'. The short *i* is as in 'stick', long *i* as in 'marine'.

The u- and i-vowels also vary in proximity to the consonants
listed above, but perhaps not quite so obviously as the a-vowel. In
practice you will find that if you get the consonant right, the vowel
will also be correctly shaped.

In certain foreign words, the vowels written **-uu** and **-ii** are
pronounced more like *o* in 'more' in the first case, and *a* in 'fate' in
the second. This is not usually important, but when it needs to be
pointed out, the transliterations used will be **-ee** and **-oo**, for
example:
     sikriteer *secretary*   **banTaloon** *trousers*

EXERCISE 0.3 Transliterate and read aloud the following words:

صَرْفْ — صَفَرْ — ثُلْثْ — هَمَجْ — قِفْلْ — فَرْغْ — مَرْكَزْ — زَمْزَمْ —

وَقْرْ — ثَرْثَرَ — بَلَحْ — نَهْرْ — مَرْحَبْ — غَرِقَ — ظَهَرَ — شَرْطْ —

— سِجْنْ — جَحْشْ — بَغْلْ — طَرَدَ — مَيْسَرْ — يَمَنْ — نَحْو — فِقْه

— بُلْبُلْ — مَكَثَ — نَتِنْ — قُدْسْ — صِدْقْ — صَدَفْ — جُنْدْ

شَخْصْ .

EXERCISE 0.4   Pronounce the following words and write them out in Arabic characters. (Note that the *sukuun* – no-vowel sign – may be left out on the final letters of words.)

baTal – nakhl – minbar – burj – Hajar – naqada – Hanbal – la:iba – raqam – Husiba – rub: – gharz – laqab – baqar – rakiba – habaTa – shibshib – bashar – fils – rabaTa – Tursh – ghazl – sahm – makr – milH.

EXERCISE 0.5   Transliterate and pronounce the following words:

— كَرِيم — رَخِيص — صَغِير — فَصِيح — صَالِح — طَاهِر — رَاغِب

— قَابُوس — مِنْكَار — فَانُوس — صَنْدُوق — غَفُور — كُلَيْب — بَصِير

— رُكُوب — فَوْر — غَيْر — فَنَادِق — مِيزَان — مُلِيق — بَيْرَم

— بَلِيد — تَعْبَان — رِيحَان — صَمِيم — مَرْحُوم — لَبِيد — صَوْت

— دِين — ذَيْل — بَيْت — يَاسِر — مُنِير — نَطْرُون — نَظِير — فَيْرُوز

مِصْبَاح — بَارُود — مَوْسِم — سَمِير .

EXERCISE 0.6   Pronounce the following words and write them out in Arabic. (Note that the signs for the short vowels may be omitted before the 'lengthening letters' *alif*, *waaw* and *yaa*', but should be put in before the diphthongs *aw* and *ay*.)

baaTin – jamiil – kaamil – SaHiiH – jawaab – riiH – salaam – haarib – miithaaq – hilaal – DaabiT – maDbuuT – DHaahir – ghuraab – qindiil – Saaruukh – talkhiiS – jaaz – bahluul – mawj – fii – yuqiim – safiir – fiil – qayd – quyuud – diik – khurTuum.

The doubling sign *shadda*

The importance of pronouncing doubled consonants correctly was discussed on page 12, and the sign used to indicate this feature is ٝ (a nucleus form *shiin* for *shadda*, without the three dots) written above the letter.

رَتَّبَ **rattaba**   دَلَّ **dalla**

Note that when a letter marked with this sign is followed by an i-vowel, the common practice is to place the *kasra* (the i-vowel sign) below the *shadda* instead of below the letter. Thus:

قَبِّلْ **qabbil**   نَزِّل **nazzil**

EXERCISE 0.7 Read aloud and transliterate the following words illustrating the doubling sign *shadda*:

مَرَّ — مُعَلِّم — مُدَرِّس — صَرَّاف — تَمَزَّق — حَادّ — مُمَيِّزَات —

دَبَّاغ — خَيَّام — حَمَّال — سُوَّاح — رُكَّاب — خَبَّاز — رَتَّبَ —

سَتَّار — فَنَّان — دُبُّور — دَلَّ — ضَلَّ — حَقّ .

Unfortunately, the *shadda* is not marked consistently in Arabic printing, a practice which, for authenticity, has been adopted in this book.

Nunation

In Classical Arabic indefinite nouns and adjectives were marked by a final n-sound, called by the Arabs *tanwiin* and translated into English as 'nunation' (from Arabic *nuun* – n). This is written in the case of final u- and i-vowels simply by doubling the vowel sign:

جَبَلٌ or جَبَلٌ **jabalun**   قَلَمٍ **qalamin**

These endings are no longer used in ordinary printed matter, so will concern us little. However, on words ending in an a-vowel, not only was the vowel sign doubled, but an extra *alif* was added at the end of the word, and this is retained in print, so has to be recognised and reproduced:

كِتَابًا **kitaaban**   فَرَسًا **farasan**

The practice today is to omit the doubled vowel sign, but to keep the *alif*. The pronunciation of the ending **-an** is also retained in many words. Note that this *alif* is not written after words which have the feminine ending and some other suffixes. This feature will be pointed out as it occurs.

EXERCISE 0.8   Read aloud and transliterate the following words. (These are words which retain in pronunciation the Classical *-an* ending of the indefinite accusative.)

جِدًّا — مَرْحَبًا — مَثَلاً — طَبْعًا — فِعْلاً — سَهْلاً — رَغْمًا — كَثِيرًا —
يَوْمِيًّا — سَنَوِيًّا .

The letter *alif*

It should be noted that the first letter of the alphabet, *alif*, has no sound of its own. Its main uses in Arabic orthography are:

1   As a lengthening sign for the a-vowel (see page 14).
2   As a carrier letter for the *hamza* (see pp. 19–20).

It also has one or two other minor functions, such as in writing the *-an* ending discussed on page 17, but appears most often in the above two roles.

The glottal stop – *hamza*

By some accident of history, the glottal stop – which is a meaningful sound in Arabic – has come down to us not as a letter of the alphabet, but as an orthographic sign. The Arabs call this sign *hamza* and it is usually written over one of the 'carrier' letters *alif*, *waaw* or *yaa*'. It can take any of the three vowels, long or short, just like any consonant.

Pronunciation
As already mentioned, the glottal stop is the sound substituted by Cockneys and Glaswegians for the *tt* in 'butter', 'bottle'. In standard English it is heard as the initial or attacking sound in the emphatic and deliberate pronunciation of such phrases as '*A*bsolutely *a*wful'. *Hamza* should not be confused with the much stronger sound *:ayn* (see page 11).

Transliteration

Hamza is transliterated by the apostrophe ('), except when it occurs at the beginning of words where it is not marked unless for special reasons (e.g. **sa'al**, **ghinaa'**, but **'intikhaab**).

Orthography

Classical Arabic recognises two types of *hamza*, which it calls the 'cutting *hamza*' and the 'joining *hamza*'. 'Cutting' in this context means basically that this variety of *hamza* is always pronounced, and 'joining' means that it is frequently elided (omitted in pronunciation). In an attempt at simplification, the joining *hamza* has largely been ignored, since it is of no practical importance in modern Arabic pronounced without the old case endings. The cutting *hamza* is noted and commented upon where it occurs. In modern printed Arabic, *hamza* is rarely shown when it occurs at the beginning of a word, but to aid the learner, such *hamzas*, when they are of the 'cutting' (i.e. pronounced) variety, have been marked in the Arabic texts. The rules for writing *hamza* in Arabic are very complicated, but for practical purposes it is sufficient to note the following basic principles and to learn by observing the spelling of words in the texts and vocabularies. You will probably find this confusing, so do not attempt to learn it thoroughly now; rather, refer back to it when you encounter words containing *hamza*.

1 At the beginning of a word, *hamza* is always written on an *alif* carrier, no matter which of the three vowels it takes:

أَحمد **'aHmad**   أُريد **'uriid**

When it takes an i-vowel, it is written *below* the *alif*:

إكرام **'ikraam**

The sign which indicates a 'joining' *hamza* (which can only occur at the beginning of a word) is called a *waSla* and is written like this:

ٱ — ٱسم

This is included here only for completeness, and will not be used in this book. It is never printed in modern Arabic texts.

2 In the middle of a word, *hamza* is almost always written above one of the three carrier letters *alif, waaw* or *yaa'*. Which one is used depends on the vowels preceding and following the *hamza*, and the rules are complicated (a common source of spelling errors among Arabs themselves). The best way is to learn by observation, but here are a few examples:

سَأَل **sa'al**   مُؤْمِن **mu'min**   نَائِم **naa'im**

Note that when the *yaa'* is used as a carrier for the *hamza* in the middle of a word, it loses its two dots.

3 At the end of a word it is written above one of the carrier letters after a short vowel, or alone on the line after a long vowel or a *sukuun* (vowelless letter):

قَرَأ **qara'**   خَطِيء **khaTi'**   جُزْء **juz'**   بِنَاء **binaa'**

EXERCISE 0.9 Read aloud and transliterate the following words which contain *hamza*. (For the sake of the exercise, all *hamzas* should be transliterated.)

سُؤَال — رَئِيس — أَمَل — بِئْر — جُزْء — إِلْهام — مَلَأَ — مَمْلُوء —

رُؤَساء — قائِل — رَأْس — أَسْنان — أَرْبَعاء — ضَئِيل — رَؤُوف —

إِسْلام — أَغْنِياء — يَأْس — بَأْس — إيمان — أُدَبَاء — مِثْناث —

أَسَد — رَدِيء — مُتَأَسِّف — أَحْدَاث — أَحاديث — أُنْس — خُنْفُساء .

The sign *madda*

The sign *madda*, which is still very often shown in print, is used when either of the following two combinations of *hamzas* and a-vowels occur in a word:

1 **'a'** (*hamza* – short *a* – *hamza*), e.g. آثار for **'a'thaar**

2 **'aa** (*hamza* followed by long *a*), e.g. قرآن for **qur'aan**

Normal pronunciation in *both* cases is **'aa** (**'aathaar, qur'aan**).

EXERCISE 0.10 Read aloud and transliterate these words with the sign *madda*:

آداب — آبار — آخَذَ — آلاف — آكَلَ — شُطآن — آماد —
آمال — آحاد .

Special spellings

Contrary to the impression you may have gained over the last few sections, Arabic spelling is, within its own system, fairly phonetic. In the case of the vast majority of words, if you can say them, you can spell them. However, there are a few irregularities and special conventions.

1 The long a-vowel at the end of many words is written with a *yaa'* instead of an *alif*, for example:

مَعْنَى **ma:naa**   رَمَى **ramaa**

To avoid confusion, there is a convention of printing final *yaa'*s in such words without the two dots (see examples above), but *with* the dots when the sound is **-ii**:

فِي **fii**   بَيْتِي **baytii**

This convention is by no means universally adopted throughout the Arab world, but has been used in this book as far as possible to assist the learner.

Note that the above spelling occurs only in certain words, and can *only occur when the **aa** sound is final*. If any suffix is added to such words, the spelling reverts to the normal *alif*:

مَعْنَاهُم **ma:naa-hum**   رَمَاهَا **ramaa-haa**

EXERCISE 0.11 Read aloud and transliterate the following exercise, being careful to distinguish between **-aa**'s and **-ii**'s:

فُصْحَى — غَضْبَى — بِلادِي — لِي — إِلَى — كِتَابِي — لَدَى —

مَنْزِلِي — كُبْرَى — وُسْطَى — مَرْسَى — دَرْسِي — عَلَى —

أُخْرَى — يُمْنَى — مَبْنَى — مَبْنِي .

2   The most usual feminine ending in Arabic is, in pronunciation,
-**a**. Again for historical reasons, this is written with a special hybrid
letter which has the body of a *haa'* (final form ﻪ), and the two dots
above borrowed from the letter *taa'* (ﺕ). The whole letter is
ignored in pronunciation, only the preceding a-vowel being pronounced except in specific grammatical contexts where the ending
is pronounced -*at*. This will be explained in the grammar lessons.

مَدْرَسَة **madrasa**   سَيَّارَة **sayyaara**

Notes:

(*a*) As in the case of the final long **aa** discussed above, the hybrid
feminine ending letter can only occur finally. If any suffix is added,
the ending is spelled with an ordinary *taa'*:

مَدْرَسَتَنا **madrasat-naa**   سَيَّارَتْكُم **sayyaarat-kum**

(*b*) In modern Arabic it is not uncommon to find the two dots of
this letter omitted. Printers seem especially reluctant to put them
on masculine proper names which happen, for linguistic reasons, to
have the feminine ending, for example:

طلبه **Tulba**   جمعه **jum:a**

EXERCISE 0.12   Read out and transliterate these words with the
feminine ending.

سَيَّارَة — مَكْتَبَة — مَجَلَّة — جَرِيدَة — وِزَارَة — تَرْبِيَّة — نَمْلَة —

نَخْلَة — قَرْيَة — تَرْجَمَة — صَغِيرة — اِشْتِراكِيَّة — دِيمُوقْراطِيّة —

مِرْوَحَة — طائِرة — رِوَاية — مَسْألة — أَصْلِيَّة — مَكَّة .

(Note that the vowel sign before the feminine ending can be
missed out, because it is always 'a'.)

3 Certain parts of the Arabic verb end in a long u-vowel, and this is conventionally written with a following *alif*. This *alif* has no effect on the pronunciation, and again is omitted if any suffix is added:

كَتَبُوا **katabuu** *they wrote*   كَتَبُوهَا **katabuu-haa** *they wrote it*

4 In a number of words, the archaic practice of expressing the long a-vowel by means of a miniature *alif* placed *above* the letter is preserved, for example:

هٰذَا **haadhaa**   رَحْمٰن **raHmaan**

This, of course, does not appear in unvowelled texts, nor should the practice be extended to other words.

EXERCISE 0.13 Transliterate these examples of the superscript *alif*:

ذٰلِك — هٰذا — اَللّٰه — هٰذِهِ — هٰذان — هٰؤُلاء .

5 The male proper name Amr **:amr** is written with an unpronounced final *waaw*, thus عَمْرو to distinguish it from the consonantally identical name Umar, Omar (**:umar** عُمَر).

Writing words which consist of only one Arabic letter

Quite a few Arabic words consist of only one Arabic consonant and a short vowel (**bi**, **la**, **ka**, etc.). These are never written alone, but must be joined to the following word, for example:

li + rajul is written لِرَجُل

When such words must be given separately (as happens in grammar books such as this) the convention used has been to use the hyphen in transcription (**li-**, **ka-**, etc.) and to use the initial form of the letter in Arabic with an extended ligature, thus لِـ ، كَـ .

Stressed syllables

When an Arabic word has more than one syllable, one of these must be stressed or accented in pronunciation, exactly as in English. Fortunately many Arabic words have only one closed syllable with a long vowel (*vvC*), and if this is pronounced with its correct length, you will find that the stress falls naturally (and correctly) on this syllable:

كريم **kariím**   راكب **ráakib**   مناسبة **munaásaba**

However, by no means all words fall into this convenient pattern, and in a self-teaching book such as this, some guidance must be given. If you have access to a live teacher, ignore the rest of this section and learn by ear.

Otherwise, you will have to learn to analyse consonant-vowel series in words, and will undoubtedly find this easier to do in transliteration. The two series which we must learn to recognise are long vowels followed by a consonant (shorthand *vvC*) and short vowel followed by two successive consonants (i.e. without a vowel between them – *vCC*). Remember that doubled consonants count as two single ones. The procedure is as follows:

1   Transliterate the word.
2   Eliminate any single-consonant words which may have been tacked on to the beginning (see page 23), and also the definite article *al-* (see page 29).
3   *Starting at the end of the word*, look for either of the series *vvC* or *vCC* mentioned above, and the first one will be the stressed syllable. Here are some examples:

يكتب	**yáktub**	حمار	**Himaár**	تحبّ	**tuHíbb**
يقرّب	**yuqárrib**	جردل	**járdal**	يستحقّ	**yastaHíqq**
صناديق	**Sanaadííq**	تلميذ	**tilmiídh**	ينظّف	**yunáDHDHif**

(Beware of single Arabic consonants which happen to be transliterated by two English letters. These obviously count as only one.)

4   If there is no such series in the word, then the stress will fall on
the first syllable:

رجل	**rájul**	حكمت	**Húkimat**	درسوا	**dárasuu**
متى	**mátaa**	كلمة	**kálima**	كرها	**kárihaa**

Note that this system is designed for the analysis of literary
Arabic as taught in this book (i.e. without the Classical case
endings). It works for most words, but there are certain exceptions,
for example Forms VII and VIII of the verb (where the first
syllable has to be ignored to make it work), and pronoun suffixes
preceded by single-consonant words (which in these cases have to
be included). However, it is hoped that it will be generally useful for
the self-taught student until he gains a feel for the language.

If the aid of a native speaker is enlisted, it may be found that he
uses the stress pattern of his own dialect. Egyptians, for instance,
have a strong tendency to stress the penultimate syllable where the
rules given above indicate otherwise. This will do no harm as long
as you are consistent in which method you follow.

EXERCISE 0.14 Transliterate the following words, identify and
mark the accented syllable.

جِبَال — خَبِير — اِزْدِهار — أَرْقام — مُسْتَعِدّ — مُتَنَوِّعَة — أَرانِب —

عَصافِير — يَمَرّ — يَمْسِك — مَنْشورات — كائِن — بارِز — فَتيلة —

أَصْدِقاء — كُتِبَت — كَتَبْنا — سافَروا — ذِكْرُى — قاتَلوني — تَجْرِبة —

طاوِلة — اِسْتَعْلَمَت — فَناجين — زُمُرُّد — بَنَفْسَج — ذَلِك —

موسيقَى — قَنابِل — مَرْحوم — مَعْلوم — مَعْلومات — مُعَلِّمُون —

تَلامِذة — فَتَحَ — صَبِيّ — تَقَدُّم — مَشَت — قُمْنا — تَعَشَّى —

صَدَقَتْ — لَعِبُوا — فَقَط — لَمّا .

Unit One

Text and translations

Transliteration and literal translation	Idiomatic Translation	Arabic
bayt kabiir *house big(-one)*	A big house.	١ بيت كبير
rajul Tawiil *man tall(-one)*	A tall man.	٢ رجل طويل
al-bayt al-kabiir *the-house the-big(-one)*	The big house.	٣ البيت الكبير
ar-rajul aT-Tawiil *the-man the-tall(-one)*	The tall man.	٤ الرجل الطويل
bayt kabiir waasi: *house big(-one) spacious(-one)*	A big spacious house.	٥ بيت كبير واسع
ar-rajul aT-Tawiil an-naHiif *the-man the-tall(-one) the-thin (-one)*	The tall thin man.	٦ الرجل الطويل النحيف

Literal translation system

The literal translation is a word-for-word rendering of the Arabic in English, given so that Arabic constructions may be seen immediately for what they are. It is obvious that in two languages as far apart as Arabic and English, structure, word order, etc., will be widely different. The literal translations will enable you to see at once how Arabic expresses an idea, and how the words and phrases are arranged.

To attain this end, three devices have been used. These are:

1. The placing of ordinary brackets round words which are either necessary to the sense in English but do not occur in Arabic, or are superfluous in English but help to explain the Arabic concept. For example, (-*one*) is added to all the adjectives, which are regarded almost as nouns in Arabic grammar.
2. The use of oblique signs (/) round words which are necessary in

26

Arabic, but are either unnecessary or would distort the sense in English. No examples occur in this unit.

3   The use of the hyphen where it is either necessary or desirable for the sake of clarity to translate one Arabic word by more than one English word, for example *big*(-*one*), *tall*(-*one*), etc. The hyphen is also used when Arabic writes as one word what English writes as two, for example the-man, the-house.

This system has been adopted so that you can follow the Arabic *word-for-word* in the Arabic word order and so learn by study and observation how the language works. Idiomatic translations are given either with the unit or in the key to the exercises at the end of the book.

Vocabulary

Note that although not used in this unit, the plurals of Arabic nouns are very varied and difficult, and the best way to learn them is to memorise them along with their singulars. In the vocabularies they are given in brackets after the singular.

Nouns

بَيْت (بُيُوت)	*house*	شَارِع (شَوَارِع)	*street*
رَجُل (رِجَال)	*man*	وَلَد (أَوْلَاد)	*boy*
كِتَاب (كُتُب)	*book*	مَكْتَب (مَكَاتِب)	*desk, office*
بَاب (أَبْوَاب)	*door*	شُبَّاك (شَبَابِيك)	*window*
مُدِير (مُدِيرُون)	*manager*	مَطَار (مَطَارَات)	*airport*

Adjectives

طَوِيل	*long, tall*	كَبِير	*big; old (of people)*
قَصِير	*short*	صَغِير	*small; young (of people)*

مَشْغُول	busy	نَحِيف	thin
وَاسِع	spacious	بَعِيد	far, distant
نافِع	useful	عَرِيض	wide
مَشْهُور	famous	نَظِيف	clean

Nouns and adjectives

It will be a great help in learning Arabic if you can come to look on nouns and adjectives as virtually the same thing. Nouns are the names of objects, living beings or ideas (*house, man, justice*) and adjectives are usually defined as words which describe nouns (*good, bad, big, small*).

In English – although not very frequently – adjectives can be used as nouns, as in the sentence 'The wicked shall be punished'. More commonly, however, the helping word 'one' is used: 'Which book do you want?' 'The green *one*'. Arabic grammar will be made much easier for you if you can get into the habit of always thinking of Arabic adjectives as implying this -*one*, thus effectively equating themselves with nouns. For instance, in Arabic our answer to the question above would be simply 'The green'.

Definites and indefinites

The question of whether a noun/adjective in a particular context is definite or indefinite is of great importance in Arabic.

Indefinites do not refer to any specific object or person. In English the indefinite article *a* or *an* is usually used, for example: 'A cat ran across the road', 'A lady phoned this morning'. We do not specify any particular cat or lady in these sentences.

Definites specify the particular, and are of three different types:

(a) Words preceded by the definite article *the*. 'The cat', 'the lady' in the above sentences would indicate a *particular* cat or lady known to both the speaker and the listener.

(b) Proper nouns (written in English with a capital). These are the names of *specific* people or places (e.g. Margaret, Mr Smith, Kuwait, Germany).

(c) Pronouns such as *I*, *you*, *she*, etc., which again obviously refer to one *specific* person. This category also includes the demonstrative pronouns *this*, *these*, etc. (see Unit 4).

Indefinites in Arabic

There is *no* indefinite article equivalent to English 'a' or 'an' in Arabic, e.g. in phrases 1 and 2 in the text at the beginning of the unit:

بيت · means *a house*   كبير means *a big one* (thing)

رجل means *a man*   طويل means *a tall one* (person)

Definites in Arabic

Here we deal with nouns preceded by the definite article. Proper nouns and pronouns will be discussed later.

The definite article in Arabic is ال (**al-**) and is always attached to the word it qualifies. If immediately preceded by a word ending in a vowel, the *a* of **al-** is omitted in pronunciation, but the *alif* is retained in writing.

Written	Pronounced
البيت	**al-bayt** after a preceding consonant
البيت	**l-bayt** after a preceding vowel

The definite article is always written ال, but there is a convention of pronunciation which must be observed when the word to which it is attached begins with one of the following consonants:

n	l	DH	T	D	S	sh	s	z	r	dh	d	th	t
ن	ل	ظ	ط	ض	ص	ش	س	ز	ر	ذ	د	ث	ت

In these cases, the *l* of the article is *omitted* in pronunciation, and the following letter *clearly doubled*. Thus:

Written	**Pronounced**
الرجل	**ar-rajul** after a preceding consonant
الرجل	**r-rajul** after a preceding vowel

Do not be careless about pronouncing this doubled consonant, as the meaning may be affected.

The easiest way to remember which letters show this feature is to pronounce them and note the position of the tip of your tongue while doing so. You will find that it is always in the region of the front teeth/upper gum – which is where the letter *l* is pronounced – which is why the assimilation occurs. No other Arabic consonant is pronounced in this area.

The Arabs call these the Sun Letters, because the Arabic word for sun, **shams**, begins with one of them, *shiin*. The rest of the letters, which do not assimilate, are called the Moon Letters (Arabic **qamar** *moon*, beginning with the non-assimilating *q*).

EXERCISE 1.1

A Pronounce the following aloud, transliterate and check against the key to the exercises.

١ المدير	٢ الواسع	٣ الشبّاك	٤ المطار	٥ النظيف
٦ الصغير	٧ الكتاب	٨ النافع	٩ القصير	١٠ الرجل

B In transliteration, add the definite article to the following words. Pronounce and check your answers.

١ نحيف	٢ بعيد	٣ بيت	٤ طويل	٥ شارع
٦ عريض	٧ مشغول	٨ رجل	٩ مطار	١٠ ولد

Phrase/sentence construction

Indefinite noun with adjective

Examine phrases 1 and 2 in the text on page 26. Here an indefinite noun is *followed by* an indefinite adjective and parallels the English construction

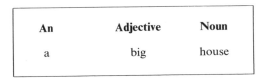

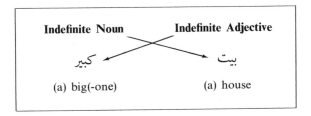

There is nothing complicated about this. Arabic has no equivalent of *a/an*, and the English word order adjective ——→ noun becomes noun ——→ adjective, as it does in many languages (e.g. French *vin blanc*). Again, try to think of the adjective as implying a noun, a member of the class of things described by the adjective. Compare the English construction 'He's bought a house, a big one'.

Note that the reverse order – adjective followed by noun – is *not* possible in Arabic.

EXERCISE 1.2 Translate into Arabic:

1 A busy man. 2 A small book. 3 A wide door.
4 A tall boy. 5 A long street. 6 A clean window.
7 A distant airport. 8 A famous man. 9 A spacious office.
10 A young manager.

Definite noun with adjective

Examine phrases 3 and 4. This construction is identical to the previous one, except that both noun and adjective have the definite article. This type of phrase is equivalent to English:

The	**Adjective**	**Noun**
the	big	house

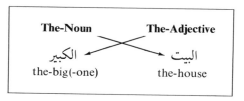

Again there are only two rules to remember:

(*a*)   Word order is *noun first, adjective second*;
(*b*)   *Both* must have the definite article.

Compare English 'The officer, the handsome one, danced with her all night'.

EXERCISE 1.3   Change your answers to Exercise 1.2 into definite phrases following the model:

>   A busy man ⟶ The busy man

Additional adjectives

Examine phrases 5 and 6. In Arabic, additional adjectives are simply added after the first one with *no* punctuation or joining word. If the noun is definite, all adjectives are definite and must carry the definite article.

EXERCISE 1.4   Transliterate and then translate into English:

٢ الشبّاك العريض النظيف	١ مطار كبير واسع
٤ رجل مشغول مشهور	٣ الولد الطويل النحيف
٦ شارع طويل نظيف	٥ الباب الكبير العريض

Summary

The principles involved in the two types of noun/adjective phrase described above are quite simple and can be summarised as follows:

(a)   Adjective *follows* noun;
(b)   Adjective agrees with noun in *definition*.

Study both phrase types thoroughly and make sure you can distinguish between them.

Numerals

Learn the Arabic numerals, which will be used in the exercises. Remember that they are written *from left to right*, in the opposite direction to the script.

1	2	3	4	5	6	7	8	9	10
١	٢	٣	٤	٥	٦	٧	٨	٩	١٠

Examples:

٢٦   26   ٣٩   39   ٦٠   60   ١٧٢   172   ٤٥٨   458

Numerals 1 to 10: pronunciation

The grammar of the Arabic numbers is somewhat complicated and will be dealt with later. Here are the forms which the Arabs usually use in speech:

sitta	ستّة	٦	waaHid	واحد	١
sab:a	سبعة	٧	ithnayn	اثنين	٢
thamaaniya	ثمانية	٨	thalaatha	ثلاثة	٣
tis:a	تسعة	٩	arba:a	اربعة	٤
:ashara	عشرة	١٠	khamsa	خمسة	٥

(For ة see page 22.)

Word shape

As will be explained in detail in Unit 6, most Arabic words are built up around a three-consonant root which contains the nucleus of meaning, and it is important to get used to recognising the *shapes* of words – that is, how the long and short vowels are arranged around the root consonants. This is helpful both in understanding grammar and in learning to read unvowelled texts. Examples of the most common shapes are given in the first ten units.

Schematic	Arabic example	English sound-alike
CaCiiC	كبير	'*marine*'

In the schematic, *C* represents any consonant, and the vowels are given as they occur. This is a very common pattern for *adjectives* in Arabic. Pick out examples from the vocabulary for this unit.

Unit Two

Text and translations

al-bayt kabiir
the-house (is a) big(-one)
The house is big.

١ البيت كبير

ar-rajul Tawiil
the-man (is a) tall(-one)
The man is tall.

٢ الرجل طويل

muHammad naHiif
Muhammad (is a) thin(-one)
Muhammad is thin.

٣ محمّد نحيف

ana mariiD
I (am an) ill(-one)
I am ill.

٤ أنا مريض

hal al-kitaab naafi:
/?/ the-book (is a) useful(-one)
Is the book useful?

٥ هل الكتاب نافع ؟

a-huwa mashghuul
/?/ he (is a) busy(-one)
Is he busy?

٦ أهو مشغول ؟

Vocabulary

Nouns

طَالِب (طَلَبَة ، طُلَّاب)	student	كَلْب (كِلَاب)	*dog*
كَاتِب (كَتَبَة ، كُتَّاب)	clerk	حَاكِم (حَاكِمُون ، حُكَّام)	*ruler (of a country)*
صُنْدُوق (صَنَادِيق)	box, trunk	صَحْن (صُحُون)	*plate, dish*
دَوْلَاب (دَوَالِيب)	cupboard	تَاجِر (تُجَّار)	*merchant, shopkeeper*
سَائِق (سُوَّاق ، سَائِقُون)	driver	مَتْحَف (مَتَاحِف)	*museum*
سِكْرِتَيْر	secretary	مُوَظَّف (مُوَظَّفُون)	*official, employee*

35

Adjectives

عَادِل	just, honest	شَاطِر	clever
جَمِيل	beautiful, handsome	سَمِين	fat
غَائِب	absent	قَرِيب	near
حَاضِر	present	مَمْلُوء	full
ثَقِيل	heavy	خَفِيف	light
فَارِغ	empty	مَكْسُور	broken

Names (male)

سَلِيم	Salim	أَحْمَد	Ahmad
عُمَر	Omar	جُون	John
رَشِيد	Rashid	رُوبَرْت	Robert

Other words

نَعَم	yes	لَا	no

(Personal pronouns are given on page 39)

Grammar and sentence construction

Equational sentences

Re-examine the phrases given in Unit 1 and you will find that we have dealt with two types of noun/adjective combination:

Indefinite + Indefinite which gives the meaning 'An X Y' (e.g. *a big house*)

Definite + Definite which gives the meaning 'The X Y' (e.g. *the big house*)

We now turn to a third possibility:

Definite + Indefinite

which results in what is called an equational sentence, the term presumably borrowed from algebra, $X = Y$.

Definite Noun		Indefinite Adjective
X	=	Y
X	*is*	Y

So in other words, when we say in Arabic 'something *is* something' (or use other parts of the English verb 'to be', such as *am*, *are*, etc.), we do not use a verb at all, but simply state a definite concept followed by an indefinite one. (This idea is not unique to Arabic, but happens elsewhere, for instance in Russian and Hebrew. In the authorised version of the Bible, italics are used to indicate words which are not present in the original Hebrew, e.g. Gen. XXVII, 11: 'Esau my brother *is* a hairy man, and I *am* a smooth man'.)

The first part of such sentences is called the *subject* (i.e. what or who you are talking about) and the second part the *predicate* (the information you are giving about the subject). The only rule is that *the subject must be definite and the predicate indefinite.*

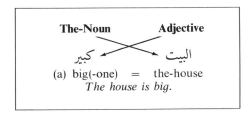

(a) big(-one) = the-house
The house is big.

EXERCISE 2.1

A Translate into Arabic.

1 The box is heavy.   2 The plate is broken.
3 The ruler is just.   4 The clerk is busy.
5 The dog is fat.   6 The merchant is absent.
7 The museum is near.   8 The secretary is here (present).
9 The cupboard is roomy.   10 The student is clever.

B Translate the following noun/adjective phrases into English, then change them into equational sentences like those above:

رجل نحيف ←——*A thin man*——← نحيف الرجل (*The man is thin*)

٢ الموظّف المشغول   ١ السائق السمين

٤ متحف جميل   ٣ الحاكم الحاضر

٦ صندوق خفيف   ٥ التاجر العادل

Proper nouns

These are the names of people or places (see page 28), written in English with a capital letter. Since they refer to specific persons or places, they are by nature *definite*, and thus may be used as the subjects of equational sentences without further ado, e.g. sentence 3 on page 35:

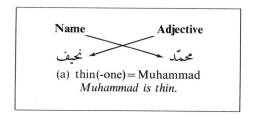

(a) thin(-one) = Muhammad
  Muhammad is thin.

EXERCISE 2.2 Translate into Arabic:

1 Omar is handsome.   2 Ahmad isn't here (is absent).
3 Salim is fat.   4 Robert is young (small).
5 Rashid is clever.   6 John is honest.

Pronouns

These also refer to specific persons and are therefore definite.

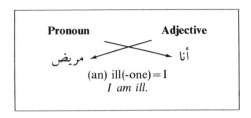

The singular personal pronouns in Arabic should now be learned. They are:

أنا	**ana**	*I*
أنت	**anta**	*you* (m)
أنت	**anti**	*you* (f)
هو	**huwa**	*he*
هي	**hiya**	*she*

Notes:
(*a*) The final *alif* of أنا is there to distinguish it from other similarly spelled words. Pronounce it short, and accent the first syllable.
(*b*) The male and female forms of *you* are identical in unvowelled writing. The context usually makes it clear which is intended.
(*c*) Since – as in French – all Arabic words are either masculine or feminine, English *it* must be translated *he* or *she* as required.

EXERCISE 2.3 Translate into Arabic:

1 He is thin.
2 I am busy.
3 You are fat.
4 He is famous.
5 You are ill.
6 I am tall.

Question-mark words

Arabic has two words which are used *in written Arabic only* to indicate that what follows is a question. Since the fact that a question is being asked has already been indicated by prefixing one of these words, the *word order of the sentence does not change,* but remains in the form of a statement. Study sentences 5 and 6 on page 35 carefully.

هل الكتاب نافع ؟   *Is the book useful?*

Delete the question-mark word هل and you are left with

الكتاب نافع   *The book is useful.*

The same applies to أ in sentence 6.

Both هل and أ serve exactly the same purpose. A good general rule is to use هل before words with the definite article, and أ before pronouns and proper names without the article. Note also the following section on one-letter words. The question mark ؟ , although technically redundant, is usually used in modern Arabic.

One-letter words

Remember that Arabic words which consist of only one letter of the alphabet, plus a short vowel, must *not* be written alone, but always attached to the following word (see page 23). Note the question-mark word أ in sentence 6, and also the very common وَ meaning *and*:

الرجل والولد   *The man and the boy.*

EXERCISE 2.4 Translate the following questions, then provide negative answers on the pattern:

Is the man old?   No, he is young.

لا ، هو صغير   هل الرجل كبير ؟

1 Is the cupboard full?	2 Is Muhammad present?	3 Is the museum far?
4 Is the box light?	5 Is the street long?	6 Is the boy tall?
7 Is the office small?	8 Is Salim thin?	9 Is the driver present?
	10 Is he old?	

Additional adjectives in equational sentences

In English we require at least one *and* in such a series of adjectives. In Arabic the general practice is not to use a joining word:

الرجل طويل نحيف   *The man is tall and thin.*

Word shape

Schematic	Arabic example	English sound-alike
CaaCiC	نافع	'varnish'

(The English sound-alikes are of course only approximate. In standard English pronunciation, the *r* in 'varnish' effectively lengthens the vowel, cf. 'vanish'.)

This type of word is technically the active participle of a verb, i.e. the noun/adjective which refers to someone or something which is *carrying out the action of the verb*. Adjectivally, we have in English 'a *going* concern', 'a *moving* performance'. For nouns, English usually uses the suffix *-er*, or a variant of it – e.g. *painter* (a painting person), *actor* (an acting person).

We have already had two Arabic examples, نافع and واسع, which really mean '*being* useful/spacious'. Pick out examples from the vocabulary and pronounce them aloud so that you get used to the sound of Arabic.

Unit Three

Text and translations

madrasa jayyida	١ مدرسة جيّدة
(*a*) *school* (*a*) *good*(-*one*)	A good school.
al-bint al-jamiila	٢ البنت الجميلة
the-girl the-beautiful(-*one*)	The beautiful girl.
ash-shams Haarra	٣ الشمس حارّة
the-sun (*is a*) *hot*(-*one*)	The sun is hot.
buyuut kabiira	٤ بيوت كبيرة
houses big(-*ones*)	Big houses.
al-kitaab :ala r-raff	٥ الكتاب على الرفّ
the-book (*is*) *on the-shelf*	The book is on the shelf.
as-sikriteera fi l-maktab	٦ السكرتيرة في المكتب
the-secretary (*is*) *in the-office*	The secretary is in the office.
hunaaka zaa'ir fi l-ghurfa	٧ هناك زائر في الغرفة
there (*is a*) *visitor in the-room*	There is a visitor in the room.

Vocabulary

Nouns

سِكْرِتَيرة (ـات) *	*secretary* (f)	بِنْت (بَنات)	*girl*
خَيّاط (ـون) *	*tailor*	رَفّ (رُفوف)	*shelf*
زائِر (زُوّار)	*visitor*	مَدْرَسة (مَدارِس)	*school*
غُرْفَة (غُرَف)	*room*	كَلِمة (ـات)	*word*

---

*The abbreviations ـات-**aat** and ـون-**uun** represent the suffixes which are added to these words to form the plural, e.g. سكرتيرات (the feminine singular suffix is dropped), and خيّاطون. (See pp. 101–2.)

42

سَيّارة (ـات) *car*	اِشْتِراكِيّة *socialism*
كِتابة *writing*	مَكْتَبة (ـات) *library, bookshop*
أُمّ (أُمَّهات) *mother*	أُخْت (أَخَوات) *sister*
شَمْس (شُموس) *sun* (f)	يَد (أَيادٍ) *hand* (f)
حَرْب (حُروب) *war* (f)	سُوق (أَسْواق) *market* (f)
مَشْروع (ـات) *project*	مَنْدُوب (ـون) *delegate*
أَرْض (أَراضٍ) *ground* (f)	طَاوِلة (ـات) *table*
كُرْسِيّ (كَراسي) *chair*	مَدينة (مُدُن) *town, city*
مَسْجِد (مَساجِد) *mosque*	جامِع (جَوامِع) *large mosque*

Adjectives

جَيِّد *good*	حارّ *hot, burning*
مَجْنون *mad*	مَبْسوط *pleased*
مَجْروح *wounded, injured*	مَقْفول *closed*
مَفْتوح *open*	وَسِخ *dirty*

Prepositions

في *in*	عَلَى *on*
مِن *from*	فَوْقَ *above, on top of*
عِنْدَ *near, with ('chez')*	مَعَ *together with*

Gender and sex

Gender means whether a word which refers to a non-living object, or an abstract concept, is regarded in the grammar of a language as masculine or feminine.

Sex means what it says, the sex – male or female – of a human being or a higher animal (i.e. one whose sex is normally distinguished, for example bull/cow, etc.).

As English speakers, we are not used to dealing with grammatical genders since our system is completely logical: males are masculine, females are feminine, and inanimates and abstracts are neuter. In any case, English words, except for the pronouns, do not in general change their shapes or endings according to whether they refer to a male or a female.

However, most of us will know that in French, for example, every word has to be masculine or feminine, and Arabic follows the same system. All nouns/adjectives are *he* or *she*: there is no *it*.

It is important from the outset that you understand the distinction between sex and gender. An Arabic word referring to a male will always be masculine, and a word referring to a female will always be feminine regardless of any grammatical endings or trappings it may have.

Words referring to inanimates generally show their grammatical gender in the following way:

Masculines	No ending
Feminines	The ending ة

The feminine ending

Refer to phrases 1 and 2, also page 22.

The feminine ending used on the vast majority of Arabic words is the hybrid letter ة which (*a*) is always preceded by an a-vowel, and (*b*) is ignored in pronunciation except in special cases which will be described later.

Effectively, therefore, the Arabic feminine ending is **-a**, the same as in Italian and Spanish.

It is found in two main situations:

A Distinguishing males from females in words referring to human beings and some animals, for example:

Male		**Female**	
خَيّاط	*tailor*	خيّاطة	*tailoress*
مُدير	*manager*	مديرة	*manageress*
كَلْب	*dog*	كلبة	*bitch*

B In words referring to inanimates which are grammatically feminine, for example:

سيّارة *car* إِشْتِراكِيّة *socialism*

Note that sometimes pairs of words occur, one with and one without the feminine ending, and with different meanings:

كِتاب *book* كتابة *writing*

مَكْتَب *office, desk* مكتبة *library, bookshop*

Exceptions
The rule given about sex of human beings on page 44 takes care of such comparative rarities as:

خَليفة *Caliph*, historical head of the Islamic community (always male), and the common words for females which dispense with the ending:

أُمّ *mother* أُخْت *sister*

There are, however, quite a few endingless words which are feminine by convention, for example:

شَمْس *sun* حَرْب *war*

يَد *hand* سُوق *market*

Such words, and others showing rarer feminine endings, are marked feminine in the vocabularies.

Plurals of inanimates
It is as well to try to get used to the bizarre fact that in Arabic *plurals of inanimates are regarded as feminine singulars.* Study the agreement in phrase 4 on page 42:

Feminine Singular Adjective	Plural Noun Inanimate
كبيرة	بيوت

Agreement of words

Obviously there is no point in having a masculine/feminine gender distinction if you don't use it. The Arabic system is much like the French:

> Masculine noun takes masculine adjective.
> Feminine noun takes feminine adjective.

This also applies to equational sentences such as sentence 3 on page 42:

الشمس حارّة   *the sun* (f noun) *is hot.*

EXERCISE 3.1
A   Combine the following nouns and adjectives to form definite phrases on the pattern:

مدرسة ، كبيرة ←——— المدرسة الكبيرة   *The big school*

Look out for plurals.

٢ سيّارة ، سريع	١ سائق ، مشغول
٤ أرض ، نظيف	٣ مكاتب ، واسع
٦ أمّ ، حاضر	٥ غرفة ، مقفول
٨ مسجد ، بعيد	٧ كتابة ، جميل
١٠ طاولة ، ثقيل	٩ حرب ، طويل

B   Read your answers aloud, then translate them into English.

C Rewrite them as indefinite phrases: مدرسة كبيرة *A big school.*

D Rewrite them as equational sentences: المدرسة كبيرة *The school is big.*

Prepositions

Prepositions are, as their name suggests, words which tell you the *position* or *place* of something, in either space or time: *In* the house, *Under* the table, *At* school, *On* Saturday. Many sentences can be formed by using *prepositional phrases* (such as the above English examples) as the predicate.

Study carefully sentences 5 and 6.

Note on pronunciation Some of these prepositions end in long vowels, e.g. في *in* and على *on* (for the special spelling of this final long a-vowel, see page 21).

These vowels are pronounced *short* when followed by the definite article (which of course loses its a-vowel according to the rule given on page 29). This is one of the reasons why it is so important to pronounce doubled consonants clearly. The only difference between على الرفّ **:ala r-raff** 'On *the* shelf', and على رفّ **:ala raff** 'On *a* shelf', is the doubled *r*.

EXERCISE 3.2 Translate into English:

٢ الكرسي في الغرفة	١ الصحن على الطاولة
٤ الشمس فوق الأرض	٣ سليم في الجامع
٦ أحمد من المدينة	٥ السكرتيرة مع المدير
٨ المدير والسكرتيرة في المطار	٧ الكتب في المكتبة
١٠ الخيّاطة في السوق	٩ المندوب عند المدير

'There is' and 'There are'

When the subject of a sentence such as those we have been studying is indefinite, we tend to use the prefix 'there is/there are' in English. The Arabic construction is exactly parallel, using the word هناك *there*, and of course omitting the verb *is/are* as usual. Look at sentence 7 on page 42.

There	(*is a*)	*visitor*	*in*	*the-room*
hunaaka		**zaa'ir**	**fi**	**l-ghurfa**

هناك زائر في الغرفة

Another possible way of expressing the same thing is to reverse the subject/predicate order of the sentence:

In	*the-room*	(*is a*)	*visitor*
fi	**l-ghurfa**		**zaa'ir**

في الغرفة زائر

EXERCISE 3.3 Translate into Arabic:

1 There is a book on the desk.
2 There are large houses in the town.
3 There is a bookshop in the market.
4 The new car is in the street.
5 The student is from the school.

Word shape

Schematic	**Arabic example**	**Sound-alike**
maCCuuC	مكتوب	'mad fool'

Note that the **ma-** here is a standard prefix. No other letter can be substituted for the *m*.

This is the passive participle of the verb, expressing as a noun/adjective *something to which the action of the verb has been done*. The Arabic example comes from the root k-t-b, which has, as we know, to do with writing. مكتوب therefore means 'written' (as an adjective) or 'something which has been written', i.e. a letter, document, etc.

The connection with the action of a verb is not always so easy to spot, but note the examples we have had (مشغول *occupied, busy*, and مشهور *famous*) and pick out the new ones from the vocabulary.

Unit Four

Text and translations

haadha l-qalam wa-haadhihi
  l-waraqa
*this(-thing) the-pen and-this
  (-thing) the-paper*

١ هذا القلم وهذه الورقة

This pen and this paper.

dhaalik al-walad wa-tilka l-bint
*that(-person) the-boy and-that
  (-person) the-girl*

٢ ذلك الولد وتلك البنت

That boy and that girl.

haadha   l-muwaDHDHaf
  al-jadiid
*this(-person)   the-employee   the
  new (-one)*

٣ هذا الموظّف الجديد

This new employee.

haadhihi l-kutub thaqiila
*these(-things) the-books (are)
  heavy(-ones)*

٤ هذه الكتب ثقيلة

These books are heavy.

tilka l-karaasii maksuura
*those(-things) the-chairs (are)
  broken(-ones)*

٥ تلك الكراسي مكسورة

Those chairs are broken.

tilka nukta qadiima
*that(-thing) (is a) joke (an)
  old(-one)*

٦ تلك نكتة قديمة

That is an old joke.

haadha huwa l-muwaDHDHaf
  al-jadiid
*this(-person) he (is) the-employee
  the-new(-one)*

٧ هذا هو الموظّف الجديد

This is the new employee.

Vocabulary

Nouns

وَرَقة (ـات) sheet of paper — قَلَم (أَقْلام) pen, pencil

مَصْنَع (مَصانِع) factory — نُكْتة (نُكَت) joke

نِصْف (أَنْصاف) half — ساعة (ـات) hour, clock, watch

رُبْع (أَرْباع) quarter — ثُلْث (أَثْلاث) third

مَنْزِل (مَنازِل) house, dwelling — عامِل (عُمّال) worker

إِعْلان (ـات) announcement — مَجْلِس (مَجالِس) council

مَجَلّة (ـات) magazine — جَريدة (جَرائِد) newspaper

مَصْدَر (مَصادِر) source — طائِرة (ـات) aeroplane

مَطْبَعة (ـات) printing house — مِنْطَقة (مَناطِق) area, zone

ماء (مِياه) water — شَجَرة (أَشْجار) tree

حُكومة (ـات) government — سينما (سينِمات) cinema (f)

قِسْم (أَقْسام) department, section — وِزارة (ـات) ministry

Adjectives

جَديد new

هامّ important — مُجْتَهِد diligent, hard working

ثَقافيّ cultural — أُسْبوعيّ weekly

يَوْميّ daily — حَديث modern

رَئيسيّ main, principal — عامّ general

خاصّ special — كَسْلان lazy, idle

Other words

إِلَّا   *except*   كَمْ   *how many?*

Demonstratives

To demonstrate is to show or to indicate, therefore demonstratives are words which indicate the particular person or object you are talking about. The demonstratives in English are *this*, *that*, *these* and *those*. They can be either adjectives with a following noun, 'This cake is good', or pronouns with no following nouns, and meaning really 'this thing' or 'this person':

'This is good' i.e. This object, cake or whatever it may be is good.

'That's my brother over there' i.e. That person ... , and so on.

In Arabic, the demonstratives always function as *pronouns*, never as adjectives, and it will be a great help if you always think of them as implying a *person* or a *thing*.

Singular demonstratives
In the singular these are:

This		**That**
هٰذَا	(m)	ذٰلِك
هٰذِهِ	(f)	تِلْكَ

Notes:
1   For the spelling of the long a-vowel in three of these, see page 23.
2   The final a-vowel of هذا is usually pronounced short.

Demonstratives with nouns
Study phrases 1–3 on page 49.

As noted above, the Arabic demonstrative is always a pronoun, implying with it an object or a person. What we are really saying, therefore, in phrase 1 is:

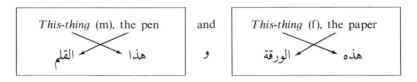

Note that the demonstrative must agree in gender – masculine or feminine – with its noun, and that the noun, since it always refers to a specific thing, takes the *definite* article.

The equivalent construction occurs in English when we say things like 'Mr Jones, the postman, came this morning', as 'Mr Jones' and 'the postman' are one and the same person.

Adjectives with demonstrative-noun phrases
Adjectives follow the noun in the usual way. Analyse phrase 3 on page 49:

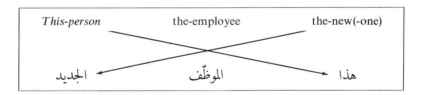

We simply have a series of three nouns referring to the same object.

EXERCISE 4.1
A Apply the word 'this' to the following nouns:

بيت ← هذا البيت *this house*

١ مجلّة ٢ مجلس ٣ أقلام ٤ مصنع ٥ ماء

٦ منطقة ٧ سينا ٨ وزارة ٩ جامع ١٠ شوارع

B In the same way, apply 'that' to the following:

٥ كاتب   ٤ متحف   ٣ مدن   ٢ مدينة   ١ مدينة

١٠ يد   ٩ طاولة   ٨ مشروع   ٧ دواليب   ٦ سائق

C Translate your answers to both A and B.

D Translate into Arabic:
1 That important announcement. 2 This new government.
3 Those weekly magazines. 4 This general council.
5 These modern aeroplanes. 6 That main department.

Equational sentences
Examples 4 and 5 on page 49 are equational sentences. Their subjects are the definite concepts 'These books' and 'These chairs'.

There is nothing new here, except another reminder that *plurals of inanimate objects* are regarded as *feminine singulars*!

EXERCISE 4.2
A From the words given, form sentences of the type:

هذا ، بيت ، كبير ⟶ هذا البيت كبير *this house is big.*

٢ ذلك ، عامل ، مجتهد   ١ هذا ، شجرة ، صغير

٤ هذا ، منازل ، واسع   ٣ هذا ، جريدة ، قديم

٦ ذلك ، مصانع ، كبير   ٥ ذلك ، سكرتيرة ، كسلان

٨ هذا ، باب ، مقفول   ٧ هذا ، صندوق ، فارغ

١٠ ذلك ، شارع ، عريض   ٩ ذلك ، بنت ، جميل

B Translate your answers.

'This is a ...' and 'This is the ...' type sentences
Examine carefully sentences 6 and 7. Apart from the change in the gender of the subject, there is one important difference between the

two – the presence of the word هو *he* in sentence 7. A little closer examination will show why this is necessary.

The easiest way is to remove the هو and see what remains:

هذا الموظّف الجديد ←——— هذا ⊠ الموظّف الجديد

Now look back at example 3, and compare the two:

3 هذا الموظّف الجديد　　　7 هذا الموظّف الجديد

They are identical – but example 3 had a different meaning: 'This new employee'. In other words, the هو is used to separate the demonstrative هذا from the definite noun-adjective phrase الموظّف الجديد (which it would otherwise qualify).

The rule is that in sentences which have a nounless demonstrative as their subject, and a predicate qualified by the definite article, the 'separating pronoun' of the appropriate gender must be placed between the two. (The rule does in fact apply to all sentences with such a predicate, but those with demonstratives as subjects are perhaps the most common.)

In sentence 6 there is no problem, as the predicate نكتة قديمة has no definite article, and could not therefore be read as being immediately qualified by the demonstrative تلك .

EXERCISE 4.3

A　Form 'This/that is a...' type sentences:

هذا بيت كبير ——→ هذا—بيت—كبير　*this is a big house*

١ ذلك — مطبعة — قديم　　　٢ هذا — منطقة — كبير

٣ ذلك — قسم — خاصّ　　　٤ هذا — جرائد — أسبوعي

٥ ذلك — شبابيك — وسخ　　٦ هذا — يد — نظيف

٧ ذلك — رجل — عادل　　　٨ ذلك — متاحف — هامّ

٩ هذا — حكومة — حديث　　١٠ ذلك — مصادر — رئيسي

B Change the sentences in **A** into 'This/that is *the* ...' sentences by inserting the appropriate pronoun:

This is the big house. هذا هو البيت الكبير ← هذا بيت كبير

C Translate your answers to **A** and **B**.

Word shape

Schematic	Arabic example	Sound-alike
maCCaC	مكتب	'madman'

The **ma-** is, again, a set prefix and does not change.

This word shape is not quite so stable as the others we have looked at so far, and has two main variations: the substitution of *i* for the second *a*, and the addition of the feminine ending.

Words of this shape are nouns of place; that is, they express the *place* where the action of the root verb is carried out. We have already noted that the root k-t-b means 'to write', hence:

مكتب place of writing *office, desk*

We also know مدرسة, from the root d-r-s *to study*, hence 'place of study, school', and an example of the *i*-form is مَنْزِل from n-z-l *to live, dwell*, hence 'a place of dwelling, a house, a home'.

It is impossible to predict which of the three forms the derivative from a given root will take, but the order of frequency is certainly *maCCaC*, then *maCCaCa* (with a feminine ending), then *maCCiC*.

Sometimes more than one form exists, with a difference in meaning:

مكتب *an office, desk*   مكتبة *a library, bookshop*

Telling the time

(Since in practice this will be of more use in speech than in reading, the colloquial forms of the numbers are given. For the numbers 1–10 see page 33.)

11   **iHda:shar**   12   **ithna:shar**

Question

| | **as-saa:a kam** | the-hour (is) how-many | *What time is it?* |

Answer

| | **as-saa:a ...** | the-hour (is) ... | *It is ...* |

Follow **as-saa:a** with:

On the hour ....(number alone)
               thamaaniya, tis:a   *eight o'clock, nine o'clock*
Five past.................(number) **wa-khamsa**
               arba:a wa-khamsa *five past four*
Ten past ....(number) **wa-:ashara**
               sitta wa-:ashara   *ten past six*
Quarter past ....(number) **wa-rub:**
               khamsa wa-rub: *quarter past five*
Twenty past..............(number) **wa-thulth***
               sab:a wa-thulth   *a third,* i.e.
                                   twenty past seven
Half past..................(number) **wa-niSf***
               :ashara wa-niSf   *half past ten*

*(In colloquial Arabic nearly always pronounced **thilth** and **nuSS**.)

Watch the next two carefully:

Twenty-five past ... (number) **wa-niSf illa khamsa** *Lit. and a half except for five*
    tis:a wa-niSf illa khamsa *twenty-five past nine*
Twenty-five to ... (number) **wa-niSf wa-khamsa** *Lit. and a half and five*
    sitta wa-niSf wa-khamsa *twenty-five to seven*

The rest of the times are expressed by taking the *next hour on* and using the terms given above preceded by **illa** *except for*, instead of **wa-** *and*:

khamsa	**illa thulth**	*a third*, i.e. twenty to five
	illa rub:	*quarter to* . . .
	illa :ashara	*ten to* . . .
	illa khamsa	*five to* . . .

Note that when they are written out in full in Literary Arabic, the expressions of time take a different form. The exercise on times is therefore to be answered in transliteration.

EXERCISE 4.4 Translate the following times into Arabic, writing your answers in transliteration:

1	6.45	2	10.20	3	4.15	4	8.35	5	7.05
6	11.40	7	3.10	8	9.25	9	11.50	10	8.30

Unit Five

Text and translations

Transliterations of the texts for Units 5–10 are given in the key to the exercises at the end of the book. It is essential that you get used to reading unvowelled Arabic.

book-(of)-you	١ كتابك
	Your book
room-(of)-her	٢ غرفتها
	Her room
office (of) the-manager	٣ مكتب المدير
	The manager's office
ministry (of) the-interior	٤ وزارة الداخليّة
	The Ministry of the Interior
house (of) Peter	٥ بيت بُطْرسُ
	Peter's house
university (of) Cairo	٦ جامعة القاهرة
	The University of Cairo, Cairo University
shirt-(of)-me the-new(-one)	٧ قميصي الجديد
	My new shirt
car (of) the-minister the-large (-one)	٨ سيّارة الوزير الكبيرة
	The minister's large car
piece (of) meat	٩ قطعة لحم
	A piece of meat
novel of novels (of) Thomas Hardy	١٠ رواية من روايات توماس هاردى
	A novel of Thomas Hardy; one of Thomas Hardy's novels

58

result (*of*) this (-*thing*)
the-policy

١١ نتيجة هذه السياسة
The result of this policy

government-(*of*)-us, this-one

١٢ حكومتنا هذه
This government of ours

Vocabulary

Nouns

قَميص (قُمْصان) shirt   جامعة (ـات) university

وَزير (وُزَراء) minister   الداخِليّة interior (political)

لَحْم (لُحوم) meat   قِطْعة (قِطَع) piece

نَتيجة (نَتائِج) result   رواية (ـات) novel, story

دُخول entering, entrance   سِياسة (ـات) policy

كيلوغرام (ـات) * kilogram   حَديقة (حدائِق) garden

خُبْز bread   دَقيق flour

حَرْف (حُروف) letter (alphabet)   وَظيفة (وظائِف) job, function

بَنْك (بُنوك) bank   رَأْس (رُؤوس) head

خُروج exit   طَرْد (طُرود) parcel

رُجوع return   فَرْع (فُروع) branch (all senses)

فُسْتان (فَساتين) dress (lady's)   بَذْلة (بِذَل) suit (of clothes)

بِتْرول oil (crude)   شَرِكة (ـات) company

---

*Sometimes spelled with a *jiim* كيلوجرام .

Adjectives

غَرِيب	strange	عَجِيب	wonderful
صعب	difficult	سَهْل	easy
مَرْكَزِيّ	central	رَخِيص	cheap
مَحَلِّيّ	local	أَجْنَبِيّ	foreign

Possessive constructions

Possessive constructions contain two elements: the possessor or *owner*, and the thing possessed or *property*. In 'the doctor's car' the doctor is the *owner*, and the car is his *property*.

The most usual way to express possession in English is by the use of 'apostrophe *s*' as in the example above (also: Jack's house, *his* wife) in which the order is owner *before* property. In certain circumstances, however, we use the word 'of' and reverse this order, for example 'The *title of the book* is "*The Dogs of War*"'

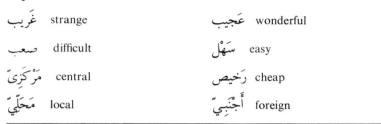

The Arabic construction is similar to the above, except that no word for *of* is used and the definite article *the* is omitted before the first element (*Title, Dogs*). Remember, the order is always:

> **Property   (of)   Owner**

The Arabic construction depends on the fact that the property and owner are placed next to each other in that order and, with the one exception noted below, *no other word may come between them.*

Pronoun suffixes

When the owner is a pronoun, as in 'his house', 'my book' (owners *he* and *I* respectively), Arabic uses a special set of suffixes tacked directly on to the *property* noun. (These suffixes are also used with verbs to supply the object, the separate pronouns given on page 39 being reserved for use as the *subject* of a sentence.) The pronoun suffixes are as follows:

	Singular			Plural
me, my	ـنِي ، ـِي		ـنَا	*us, our*
you, your (m)	ـكَ		ـكُمْ	*you, your* (m)
you, your (f)	ـكِ		ـكُنَّ	*you, your* (f)
him, his	ـهُ		ـهُمْ	*them, their* (m)
her, her	ـهَا		ـهُنَّ	*them, their* (f)

1   In this table, the suffixes have been given with a preceding ligature to emphasise the fact that they join on to the property word. However, if this word ends in one of the non-joining letters such as و and ر , the suffixes are not actually joined, but still written as part of the same word, e.g. سكرتيره *his secretary*.

2   The second form given for the first person singular pronoun suffix, ـِي *me* is used only after verbs and will be dealt with later. All the other suffixes retain the same form after both verbs and nouns.

3   ـهُ ، ـهُمْ and ـهُنَّ change their u-vowels to i-vowels when they follow long or short -i or the combination -ay (e.g. فِيهِ *in him, it*).

4   In spoken Arabic -ka and -ki are pronounced -ak and -ik (after words ending in vowels, -k and -ki), and -hu is -uh (and a scarcely detectable -h after vowels).

The feminine ending

The hybrid letter ة of the feminine ending is *always* pronounced *t* when it occurs in the first (property) element of a possessive construction. (This is also true in spoken Arabic.)

Since this letter can *only* occur at the end of a word (see page 22), it changes into an ordinary ـت when a suffix is added, for example:

غرفتها   *her room* (pronounced **ghurfat-haa**).

Simple possessives

Study carefully phrases 1–6 on page 58. 1 and 2 show the simple possessive with the pronoun suffixes, 2 illustrating the pronunciation (and writing) of the feminine marker as 't'. 3 and 4 show the most frequent type of possessive found in Arabic, noun plus noun. The second of these reminds us to pronounce (but not to write, as it is still at the end of a word) the *t* of the feminine ending. (Note also that it is *not* pronounced at the end of the second element, **ad-daakhiliyya**). 5 and 6 show the use of proper (personal or place) names as *owner* elements, the first having no definite article.

EXERCISE 5.1

A   Translate into Arabic:

1   The manager of the bank.

2   The announcement of the council.

3   Your (m, sing.) garden.

4   The minister of the Interior.

5   His magazines.

6   Our mother.

7   Omar's car.

8   The branches of the company.

9   The government('s) printing house.

10   Her head.

B   Read aloud, then change the masculine suffix into a feminine one, or vice versa:

بيته *his house* ⟷ بيتها *her house*

٣ طرودهم	٢ سيارتها	١ منزلكَ
٦ ساعتكم	٥ روايتكِ	٤ أختهنّ

C   Read aloud, then change both the nouns (or noun and pronoun suffix) from plural to singular or vice versa:

بيوت الرجال *the men's houses* ⟷ بيت الرجل *the man's house*

٣ وظيفة الوزير	٢ حدائق البيوت	١ فستان البنت
٦ قصانكم	٥ رأسه	٤ نتيجة السياسة
	٨ مكتب السكرتيرة	٧ روايتها

Adjectives with possessive constructions

Examine phrases 7 and 8. Because of the rule that nothing may intervene between property and owner (see page 60), another place must be found for adjectives qualifying one of the two elements. Since adjectives *never* come before their nouns in Arabic, they must be placed *after the completed possessive construction*.

Phrase 7 in the text on page 58 gives an example with a pronoun suffix, and phrase 8 one with two nouns. If you look at phrase 8 carefully, you will see that there is no possibility of mistaking which noun is qualified by the feminine adjective كبيرة. Since وزير *minister* is a masculine noun, it must apply to the feminine noun سيّارة *car*.

Since the Arabs regard *both* elements of a possessive construction as definite, all adjectives applying to either element *must have the definite article* (*and* come after the completed construction). It therefore follows that بيت الوزير الجديد can mean either '*The minister's new house*' or '*The new minister's house*' (both nouns being masculine). In practice, when the meaning is not obvious from the context, such ambiguities are avoided by the use of alternative constructions.

Contrast also بيت الوزير جديد *The minister's house is new*. In this example, since the adjective جديد is *indefinite*, it cannot refer to either element of the possessive, and must therefore be the predicate of a sentence, the subject of which is the compound definite 'The minister's house'.

EXERCISE 5.2

A Read aloud, then translate:

١	ساعتي الرخيصة	٢	سيارة المدير الجديدة
٣	طرد سليم الثقيل	٤	بذلته الوسخة
٥	اعلان الجرائد الهامّ	٦	مدير البنك المجتهد
٧	سائق السيارة السمين	٨	نكتها القديمة
٩	مصنع الحكومة الجديد	١٠	غرفتنا الواسعة

B Change the phrases in A into sentences of the type:

بيت الرجل كبير *The man's house is big.*

Indefinite possessives
Study phrases 9 and 10 carefully.

Although not all that common in practice, it is sometimes necessary to express indefinite possessives, such as these two phrases.

In example 9, the owner-word is simply written without the definite article, and the whole construction regarded as *indefinite*, '*a* piece of meat'. (Note that the *t* of the feminine ending must still be pronounced.)

If the owner-word is definite by nature (such as proper names and pronoun suffixes) a construction using the plural must be used, as illustrated by example 10. This sounds clumsy in English, but occurs quite frequently in Arabic. An example with a pronoun suffix is بيت من بيوته *One of his houses*. (Note that there is an alternative construction, using a preposition. See page 135.)

EXERCISE 5.3   Read aloud, then translate:

۳ رجوع رجل	۲ قطعة خبز	۱ كيلوغرام لحم
	٥ كيلوغرام دقيق	٤ فرع شركة

Demonstratives with possessives
Refer to examples 11 and 12.

The demonstratives are the only kind of words which are allowed to come between the two elements of a possessive construction. This should not surprise us if we recall that all Arabic demonstratives imply with themselves a noun – a thing or a person (see page 51). Explained in this way, example 11 does not really break the 'non-intervention' rule at all, since what we are really saying is 'The result of this thing, the policy'. The two elements of the possessive are interpreted as being 'result' (property) and 'this thing' (owner), the following noun 'policy' being added by way of explanation.

When, as in example 12, the demonstrative qualifies the property-word and not the owner-word, it is placed after the completed construction:

حكومتنا هذه government-(of)-us, this-one.

EXERCISE 5.4

A Apply the correct part of هذا to the owner-word in the following and translate your answers.

٣ دخول المندوب		٢ رأس الولد		١ فروع البنك	
٦ سيارة السائق		٥ أخت البنت		٤ سياسة الشركة	
٩ يد الرجل		٨ قلم السكرتيرة		٧ باب الطائرة	
				١٠ غرفة الزائر	

B Apply the correct part of ذلك to the property-word and translate your answers.

٣ باب الجامعة	٢ مشروع الحكومة	١ مدينتنا
	٥ مصدر البترول	٤ كتابه

Summary

The possessive in Arabic is undoubtedly tricky. What you have to look out for is the placing together of two nouns (or a noun and a pronoun suffix). You should learn to recognise the latter fairly quickly, and in practice the noun-noun possessive usually looks like this:

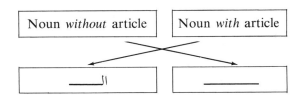

Try and remember this visual picture and it will help you to spot these constructions. Remember, too, *property* before *owner*.

Word shape

Schematic	Arabic example	Sound-alike
CuCuuC	بيوت	Toulouse

This is a fairly common noun-shape in Arabic, having the two basic functions:

1 To form the plural of words whose singular shape is usually *CaCC*, e.g. بيت **bayt** takes plural بيوت **buyuut**.

2 To form the verbal noun from simple verbs, that is the word which means 'the action of doing'. For example, from the root d-kh-l which has the basic meaning of 'entering', we get دخول **dukhuul** which means 'the act of entering; entrance'.

Note that, as is unfortunately the case with many shapes, *CuCuuC* cannot be formed in an arbitrary manner from any noun or verb root. The benefit of learning the shapes is in recognition, not formation. Any word which you come across in the form *CuCuuC* will be *either* a plural or a verbal noun.

Unit Six

Unit 6 contains no new grammatical material. Units 1 to 5 contain most of the basic groundwork of Arabic grammar, apart from the verb, so take the opportunity to revise these and make sure you have mastered them thoroughly.

Study the words overleaf and read them *aloud*, taking special care to give full value to *all* consonants (including doubled ones) and *all* vowels (especially long ones). The root consonants are given after each word.

Root consonants and word shapes

We have already learned a few Arabic word-shapes in the previous units. Now it is time to take a closer look at the structure of the language. Overleaf is an incomplete list of word shapes which occur in Arabic, and you will benefit greatly if you read these words aloud several times and try to tune your ear to the cadences of the language.

The reason that Arabic is able to use a defective script which omits all short vowels (among other things) is that it is primarily a language of patterns. These patterns are in the vast majority of cases based on what we shall call the *three-consonant root system.* This means that the framework of most Arabic words is a series of three consonants which carry the basic meaning. This framework is filled in with vowels and other additions to produce an actual word. For instance, in the familiar word **kitaab** *book* the consonant series k-t-b suggests the basic idea of 'writing', and the short *i* and long *a*-vowels then produce the word **kitaab** which has the accepted meaning 'book'.

The first thing to note is that the consonant series (in this case k-t-b) remains in fixed order and there is no question of altering the position of any of these consonants. This would cause a complete change in meaning. The body of the word is constructed by applying one of a complex but limited set of variations in internal vowelling, and/or using certain prefixes and suffixes. Root consonants − usually the middle one − can be doubled, and occasionally other consonants can be introduced between those of the root series.

A

ضَرْب	(D-r-b)	*a blow, hit*
رِبْح	(r-b-H)	*profit*
رُكْن	(r-k-n)	*corner*
بَطَل	(b-T-l)	*hero*
وَسِخ	(w-s-kh)	*dirty*
فُرْشة	(f-r-sh)	*brush*
تاج	(t-w-j)	*crown*
مَرَّة	(m-r-r)	*time, occasion*

B

رَتَّب	(r-t-b)	*arrange*
صالِح	(S-l-H)	*righteous*
شُجاع	(sh-j-:)	*brave*
كَلام	(k-l-m)	*speech*
كَرِيم	(k-r-m)	*generous*
رَؤُوف	(r-'-f)	*compassionate*

C

أَصْلَع	(S-l-:)	*bald*
صَحْراء	(S-H-r)	*desert*
أَصْدِقاء	(S-d-q)	*friends*
أَطِبّاء	(T-b-b)	*doctors*
طَيَران	(T-y-r)	*aviation*

D

تِمْثال	(m-th-l)	*statue*
تَعْلِيم	(:-l-m)	*education*
تَقَدُّم	(q-d-m)	*progress*
مِنْبَر	(n-b-r)	*pulpit*
مَطار	(T-y-r)	*airport*
مِكْنَسَة	(k-n-s)	*broom*
مِفْتاح	(f-t-H)	*key*
مُحاسِب	(H-s-b)	*accountant*
مُدَرِّس	(d-r-s)	*teacher*
مُدِير	(d-w-r)	*manager*
اِسْتِعْلام	(:-l-m)	*enquiry*
اِمْتِحان	(m-H-n)	*exam*
اِنْقِلاب	(q-l-b)	*coup d'état*

E

| يَد | (y-d) | *hand* |
| دَم | (d-m) | *blood* |

F

زَلْزَلة	(z-l-z-l)	*earthquake*
صَنْدوق	(S-n-d-q)	*box*
زُمُرُّد	(z-m-r-d)	*emerald*
شَطْرَنْج	(sh-T-r-n-j)	*chess*
بَنَفْسَج	(b-n-f-s-j)	*violet*
تِلِفِزْيون	(t-l-f-z-y-n)	*television*

Being able to recognise word shapes is important for two main reasons:

(a) Obviously, in the usual sort of unvowelled text, the recognition of a known word shape will enable you to pronounce the particular word and learn it without puzzling out which vowels go where.

(b) In many cases, the pattern of a word will suggest its function within the sentence and help you to determine its meaning.

Neither of these principles works all the time, but every little guidance helps.

The three-consonant root

We have already learned that these fixed series of three Arabic consonants form the basic nucleus of most Arabic words. It is important to note that the sign *hamza* is, for these purposes, *regarded as a consonant*, although it unfortunately crops up in prefixes and suffixes as well.

Let us take a few more examples of k-t-b and look at a few ways in which this root-series can be used to give different words and meanings. (For the sake of clarity in the following examples, the root letters are given in capitals. This does not in this case indicate any change in pronunciation.)

كتاب **KiTaaB**	*book* (simply a choice of internal vowelling, with no prefixes or suffixes)	
كتابة **KiTaaBa**	*writing* (feminine suffix added to the previous word to change its meaning)	
كاتب **KaaTiB**	*a writer, clerk* (change of internal vowelling: this shape should already be familiar to you as the 'doing' pattern)	
مكتب **maKTaB**	*office, desk* (the very common prefix **ma-** here, plus another change in vowelling. This is the 'place of' pattern, which you should also recognise)	
مكتبة **maKTaBa**	*library, bookshop* (same as above, but again the feminine ending is used to change the meaning)	
مكاتبة **muKaaTaBa**	*correspondence* (another common prefix **mu-** plus another change in vowelling)	

In addition, if you look back in the vocabulary lists, you will find that more internal vowel-changes and suffixes are used to form the plurals of these words (e.g. مَكْتَبات and مَكاتِب, كَتَبة or كِتاب, كُتُب).

The concept of the three-consonant root is, therefore, a very useful and important one in Arabic. Remember that a root is an *idea*, not a word. To become that, it needs the application of *vowels*, and sometimes prefixes and/or suffixes.

Roots, word shapes and meaning

In an ideal world

(a) Each Arabic root would have one specific meaning assigned to it;

(b) Each word-shape derived from it would alter or extend that meaning in a specific way;

(c) Each Arabic root would utilise all the patterns available to it.

If all these were true, we would have the world's finest natural computer language, and you could throw this book away and start pressing buttons. Now for the reality.

(a) While it is true that most roots retain some semblance of their basic meaning throughout their derivatives, there are quite a few exceptions. For instance, returning to k-t-b, مكتوب **maKTuuB** means, as you know, 'written', and مكتتب **muKtaTiB** means a 'subscriber' (the first **t**, incidentally, being an added letter, not part of the root), but كتيبة **KaTiiBa** means 'a battalion'. The connection in this last with writing is certainly not immediately clear. The root D-:-f vacillates between the rather contrasting meanings 'weakness' and 'doubling', and dh-h-b hovers between 'going away' and 'gold'. This problem (although fortunately rarely) extends as far as the archaic poetic word جون **jawn**, for which one dictionary gives the entry 'Black, white. Light red'. However, in the majority of cases the roots are quite stable, and their study provides a very useful tool in learning Arabic.

(b) Many derived word shapes *do* change the application of the root meaning in a reasonable specific way, but there are unfortunately many alternatives, and some of the connections with the root may be clear to the Arab mind, but not to ours. Again, however, it is in general well worth paying attention to the system and making the best of it.

(*c*)   Some word shapes are very common, others quite rare. In any case, words should not be coined without resort being made to a dictionary to see if they exist, until some basic rules have been learned.

Notation of the roots

The system used in this book is that already familiar from the word-shape sections, i.e. *C* for the consonants (numbered *C¹*, *C²*, etc., if necessary), and *v* for a short vowel, *vv* for a long vowel. If these vowels are invariable within a certain pattern, the actual vowel (**a**, **ii**, **uu**, etc.) is given, and similarly standard prefixes and suffixes, again not subject to change, are spelled out (e.g. **ma-** and **mu-** above). Doubled consonants are noted twice (*C²C²*).

The point of the exercise is to develop a sense of how Arabic words *sound* and, where possible, English words which more or less 'rhyme' with the Arabic example are given.

Phonetic nature of the roots

Most roots contain three distinct consonants, such as k-t-b, d-r-s and so on. Quite a few, however, have identical second and third radicals, and this causes some problems in the derivation of certain patterns. Examples are m-r-r, f-n-n. More rarely the first and third consonants are the same (e.g. th-l-th) but this causes no problems.

The greatest nuisances are the so-called 'weak' consonants ي and و (ا *alif* does *not* count as a consonant *at all*) which can occur in any position in a root. These vacillate between being elided and reappearing, and we shall need to say much more about them later.

Analysis of the word list (p. 68)

Group A   All these words are very simple, basic derivatives formed from the root without the use of any long vowels, the only extraneous feature being the feminine ending. Worthy of note are مرّة, derived from a root with identical second and third consonants, and تاج, which is from the root t-w-j, the *w* having been in this case elided. Although simple in form, the vowelling of these basic nouns is difficult to predict.

Group B This group shows the second stage of internal change. رتّب has a doubled middle consonant, and all the other examples make use of long vowels. These are mostly adjective shapes, but of course can be used as nouns too.

Group C These words show the introduction of prefixes (اِ) and suffixes (اِن and اِء) without internal additions to the root. أطبّاء again illustrates a 'doubled' root (i.e. with C^2 and C^3 the same).

Group D This is a *pot pourri* of more complex shapes, mainly using both prefixes *and* internal changes. They are all common derivatives and will be dealt with later. For now, try to get used to the sound of the words – *remembering to keep your long vowels long and to pronounce the doubled consonants*.

Group E Here are two examples of roots which have only *two* consonants. There are not many of these, and they are mainly basic primitive nouns.

Group F This group consists of roots whose radicals exceed three in number. There are quite a few four-consonant roots in Arabic, many of them repeating two pairs of consonants as in زلزلة, *earthquake*. The remainder of the list, extending to five or even six consonants (if you count 'television') are all words of foreign origin and are included only for interest. They have few derivatives, except their plurals.

Using a dictionary

Another very good reason for developing the ability to determine the root consonants of an Arabic word is that all currently available Arabic–English dictionaries are arranged by *roots*, not words. (There is one exception to this, but the dictionary is Arabic–German: see Appendix 4). Therefore, to look up an Arabic word, you must first isolate the root consonants (usually three), then look up this root, and finally seek the word required among the derivatives listed after the root entry. For instance, all the derivatives we have mentioned – such as مكتوب ، مكتبة ، كتاب and so on – will be listed in the entry كتب k-t-b.

This obviously presents problems, and really the only way to overcome them is to study the shape of Arabic words and thus gain experience in distinguishing roots from extraneous letters. In fact the number of letters which occur 'non-radically' is fairly limited, and you will soon get used to them by conscientiously learning the word shapes given. For instance, you may already have noticed that **mu-** and **ma-** are very common prefixes, which should be ignored when looking up a word.

Apart from long vowels (ا ، و and ى) and the doubling of root letters (usually the middle one), the following are the most common Arabic letters added to roots to form derivatives:

ة م ء ت ن س and ى (used as a consonant). Of these, س is the least common, being used only in certain types of verbs.

EXERCISE 6.1   Read the following words *aloud*, trying to get the feel of their shape, then try to isolate and write down their root consonants. (The words have all been given in the vocabularies of preceding units.)

٤	وزارة	٣	مجنون	٢	كبير	١	دقيق
٨	حكومة	٧	مشغول	٦	شارع	٥	شجرة
١٢	سيّارة	١١	موظّف	١٠	حاضر	٩	بعيد
١٦	دخول	١٥	فروع	١٤	حارّ	١٣	مشروع
٢٠	صندوق	١٩	خفيف	١٨	رواية	١٧	حديقة
٢٤	مملوء	٢٣	سوّاق	٢٢	شاطر	٢١	أحمد
						٢٥	مجلس

Unit Seven

Text and translation

He travelled to Kuwait, then returned to Bahrain.	سافر الى الكويت ثمّ رجع الى البحرين	١
She opened the door and went in.	فتحت الباب ودخلت	٢
Did you pay the money? No, I refused.	هل دفعت الفلوس ؟ لا رفضت	٣
We have eaten and drunk.	أكلنا وشربنا	٤
The driver spoke to the boss.	كلّم السائق الرئيس	٥
My wife cooked the food.	طبخت زوجتي الطعام	٦
The newspapers announced the result of the election.	أعلنت الجرائد نتيجة الانتخاب	٧
The workmen refused the raise and went on strike.	رفض العمّال العلاوة وأضربوا	٨
The secretaries met and elected their delegate.	اجتمعت السكرتيرات وانتخبن مندوبتهنّ	٩
I put it in my briefcase in the morning.	وضعته في شنطتي في الصباح	١٠
The girl admitted me and sat me down.	أدخلتني البنت وأجلستني	١١
The Prime Minister arrived in Riyadh yesterday.	قد وصل رئيس الوزراء الى الرياض أمس	١٢
We didn't find the report in the file.	ما وجدنا التقرير في الدفتر	١٣

74

Vocabulary

Verbs (past stems given)[1]

(III) *travel* سافَر		رَجَع	*come back, return*	
فَتَح *open*		دَخَل	*enter*	
دَفَع *push, pay*		أَدْخَل	(IV) *admit, cause to enter*	
رَفَض *refuse*		أَكَل	*eat*	
شَرَب *drink*		كَلَّم	(II) *address someone, speak to*	
طَبَخ *cook*				
أَضْرَب (IV) *strike; go on strike*		أَعْلَن	(IV) *announce*	
اِنْتَخَب (VIII) *to elect*		اِجْتَمَع	(VIII) *meet, hold a meeting*	
وَصَل *arrive (at -* إلى)		وَضَع	*put, place*	
وَجَد *find*		أَجْلَس	(IV) *seat someone, cause to sit*	
		كَتَب	*write*	

Nouns

الكويت *Kuwait*		البحرين	*Bahrain*
الرياض *Riyadh*		فُلوس	*money (f)*[3]
زَوْجة (ـات) *wife*		طَعام (أَطْعِمة)	*food*
اِنْتِخاب (ـات) *election*		عَلاوة	*raise (in pay)*
شَنْطة (شُنَط) *case, briefcase*[2]		صَباح	*morning*
رَئيس (رُؤَساء) *boss, chief*		تَقْرير (تَقارير)	*report*
رَئيس الوُزَراء *Prime Minister*		دَفْتَر (دَفاتِر)	*file, dossier*

[1] Roman figures with verbs indicate that they are *derived forms*, whose parts are given in Table 2 of Appendix 1. This is for reference only, and makes no difference to how the past tense of these verbs is formed.

[2,3] More literary words for these are حَقيبة (حَقائِب) and نُقود respectively.

Other words

ثُمَّ　*then*

إِلَى　*to, towards* (*pronounced* **'ilaa**)

مَا　*not*

أَمْس　*yesterday*

قَدْ ، لَقَدْ　*particle said to emphasise
the past tense*

The Arabic verb

The Arabic verb differs from its English counterpart in two important ways:

1　It has only two tenses (i.e. ways to express *when* the action takes place), which we shall call *past* and *present*. The past tense is used for all actions which are already *completed*, and the present tense for all actions *not yet complete*.

2　As we shall see shortly, most verbs can be reduced to a *past stem* and a *present stem*, and a standard set of prefixes and suffixes can be added to these stems (which are not actual words, but 'tools' of grammar) to form meaningful words. The main problem with these stems is that they are frequently distorted by the occurrence of the weak letters *waaw* and *yaa'* as one of the radicals, or the fact that the second and third radicals are identical. *Verbs with such features will not be used yet.* Also, Arabic has a system by which the stem of a verb may be altered in a series of nine specific ways to vary the meaning. These modified stems are traditionally numbered II-X in Roman numerals, and will be introduced now to increase our scope in vocabulary, the Roman numeral of the stem type being given for reference. These so-called Derived Forms of the verb form the tenses in the same way as the simple verb (referred to as Form I).

Because of its complexity and the fact that there is no shortcut to learning it, the section on the verb has been separated from the main body of this book and is given in the form of a general description and a series of tables in Appendix 1. All verb types must obviously be learned eventually, so start now and learn by heart the past-tense suffixes in Table 1. These are used with only very slightly varying forms on all Arabic verbs.

Talking about verbs
Verbs are 'doing words', words which refer to actions, and in English we usually talk about them as 'to do, to find, to speak' etc. This 'to – ' part of the verb is called the *infinitive*. Arabic has no infinitive, and the usual practice is to give Arabic verbs in the *he-form of the past tense*. The reason for this is that this part of the verb has no written prefixes or suffixes, and is thus regarded as the most basic part of the verb. In many verbs it also constitutes the *past stem*, from which all other parts of the past tense can be formed. So remember that when we give a verb as, say كتب **katab** *to write*, the part we give actually means 'he wrote'.

The past tense

Study Table 1 thoroughly, as it forms the basis for forming the past tense of all Arabic verbs.

Since this is our first attempt at the verb, here is the past tense of **katab** *to write* given in transliteration:

Singular		Plural	
katab	*he wrote*	**katabuu**	*they* (m) *wrote*
katabat	*she wrote*	**katabna**	*they* (f) *wrote*
katabt(a)	*you wrote* (m)	**katabtum**	*you* (m) *wrote*
katabti	*you wrote* (f)	**katabtunna**	*you* (f) *wrote*
katabt(u)	*I wrote*	**katabnaa**	*we wrote*

Notes:
1 Arabic distinguishes the sex of the person carrying out the action of the verb more precisely than English. English once had 'thou dost' and 'ye do' instead of the singular and plural 'you', but never distinguished between the sexes. You have to be more careful of whom you are speaking to or about in Arabic.
2 The dual forms given in Table 1 are used when talking to or about *two* people or things. They are not too common in practice, so you can reduce your burden by omitting them here, though always bearing them in mind for future reference.

Translation of the past tense
Since Arabic has very few tenses in comparison to English, the Arabic past tense has to be translated in a variety of ways, according to context. **Katab** can mean 'he wrote; he has written; he had written', i.e. anything that indicates that the action of writing is complete, over and done with.

Subject pronouns
In English we have to say '*he* wrote', '*you* wrote', etc., to clarify who performed the action. This is because the English verb has no varying forms in the past tense, but is always 'wrote' no matter what the subject. Arabic, on the other hand, carefully distinguishes exactly who has carried out the action of the verb, and consequently *subject pronouns are not normally stated*. To go back to pidgin English, if you like:

كتبوا wrote (-they, m) *they* (m) *wrote.*

كتبت wrote (-she) *she wrote.*

كتبنا wrote (-we) *we wrote.*

Study the examples 1–4 on page 74, where the subject of the verb (i.e. the person carrying out the action) is expressed by the verb-suffix, and there is *no need* to supply a separate pronoun.

EXERCISE 7.1 Read aloud and translate:

رفضن ٤	انتخَبَتْ ٣	وصلوا ٢	كتبنا ١
دفعوا ٨	شربتنّ ٧	أضربتم ٦	طبخ ٥
أعلنوا ١٢	دخلنا ١١	أكلتم ١٠	وضعتُ ٩
وصلتَ ١٦	كتبتِ ١٥	كلّمتم ١٤	اجتمعن ١٣
أكل ٢٠	شربَتْ ١٩	وصلنا ١٨	وضعوا ١٧

Word order and agreement

On page 78 we dealt with sentences in which the subject (do-er) of the verb is a pronoun like 'he', 'I' or 'you'. When the subject of a verb is actually specified, like 'the driver' (example 5), 'my wife' (example 6) and so on, two important points arise:

1   *The verb comes first,* followed by the subject.
2   *The verb is always in the he- or she-form.*

The verb coming first is merely a fact of (Arabic) life, about which little can be said. Other word-orders are possible, but this is the most common, so if you are using a verb remember this order:

1 Verb	**2** Subject	**3** The rest.

The fact that the verb in these cases is either in the he- or the she-form, i.e. *always singular, never plural,* is unusual to say the least, and should be noted carefully. You will remember that the plural of *things* (inanimate objects or abstracts) is regarded in Arabic as *feminine singular,* so the rule for verbs which precede their subjects looks like this:

Verb	**Subject**
he-form for	1 One male being.
	2 Two or more male beings.
	3 One object of grammatically masculine gender.
she-form for	1 One female being.
	2 Two or more female beings.
	3 One object, grammatically feminine.
	4 *Two or more of any object.*

Examples 5–7 in the text on page 74 illustrate this important point, so study them carefully.

EXERCISE 7.2

A Apply the correct part of the verb in brackets to the following sentences:

وصلت البنت الى المدينة ← ⟶ (وصل) البنت الى المدينة

٢ (شرب) السكرتيرة الماء		١ (أكل) الولد الخبز	
٤ (أعلن) الجرائد النتيجة		٣ (كلّم) الخيّاطة السائق	
٦ (سافر) الأمّ من المطار		٥ (دفع) العمّال الفلوس	
٨ (فتح) الطالبة الباب		٧ (وجد) البنت شنطتها	
١٠ (وضع) التجّار الصناديق في البيت		٩ (كتب) زوجته التقرير	

B Translate your answers.

Agreement of verbs coming after their subjects
Study examples 8 and 9 on page 74 carefully. Sometimes a subject has more than one verb, and in these cases the word-order is:

1 First Verb	**2** Subject	**3** Object (if any)	**4** Second Verb

In such sentences the second verb, which comes after its subject, has to *agree fully* with it, that is, to reflect exactly its number and gender (masculine or feminine). The reasoning is something like this (in sentence 8):

Refused   the workers   the raise   and *they* struck

The second verb needs to be given its full form, so the suffix conveys the exact nature of its subject – in this case *male* and *plural*. In any case, the rule is that verbs which for any reason come after their subjects *must agree fully in gender and number*.

EXERCISE 7.3

A Apply the correct part of *both* verbs to the following sentences.

١ (شرب) البنت الماء ثمّ (أكل) اللحم

٢ (اجتمع) الوزراء و(انتخب) مندوبهم

٣ (دخل) الموظّفون و(كلّم) المدير

٤ (سافر) البنات الى الرياض ثمّ (رجع) الى الكويت

٥ (دخل) التاجر الغرفة و(وجد) زوجته

٦ (اجتمع) العمّال و(رفض) العلاوة

B Translate your answers.

The verb with pronoun suffixes

Study examples 11 and 12 on page 74. The basic idea of the use of
the pronoun suffixes which we have already looked at on page 60 is
to connect two concepts. When we connect a noun with a person,
the result is a *possessive*:

| Idea of book | connected with | Idea of him | ⟶ | *his book* كتابه |

From this it is simple to connect ideas of action to persons or
objects. Since, as we have seen on p. 78, Arabic verbs already
imply the tense and the doer of the action, we have a more complex
first idea (example 10):

| Idea of me having put | connected with | Idea of him (it) | *I put it* (past tense) ⟶ وضعَته |

In other words, pronoun suffixes attached to verbs express the
object of the verb, that is, the person or thing directly affected by
the verb.

The only pronoun suffix which has a special different form when

82 *Arabic*

attached to verbs is the 'me' suffix which is ـنِي -nii instead of ـِي -ii.

Verbs having pronoun suffixes added to them remain themselves unaffected, with the following exceptions:

(*a*) the *alif* written after all verb forms ending in -**uu** is omitted (see Table 1, note 3).

(*b*) the 'you' plural masculine ending -**tum** adds a *waaw* before the pronoun suffix, e.g.

وجدتموها *you found* + ها *her* ⟵ وجدتم

EXERCISE 7.4

A Form one-word sentences on the following pattern (as there is no 'it' in Arabic, 'him' or 'her' has been given):

They (m) — *me* (وجد) ⟶ وجدوني ⟶ *They found me.*

1 He — her (أدخل) 2 She — him (كلّم) 3 We — her (طبخ) 4 They (f) — him (رفض) 5 You (m,s) — her (شرب) 6 I — him (أكل) 7 You (m,pl) — them (m) (كلّم) 8 You (f,s) — him (كتب) 9 He — her (دفع) 10 We — her (أجلس)

B Read aloud and translate your answers

Particles used with the past tense

'Particles' is a handy term for the odds and ends of a language which do not fit into any of the main categories (verb, noun, etc.). Arabic has many such short words, some virtually meaningless (but habitually used), and others which affect the meaning of a phrase or sentence quite significantly. Here are two examples used with the past tense of the verb:

1 قد **qad**, often strengthened to لقد **laqad**. Placed before the verb, as in example 12 on page 74, it emphasises the completeness of the action, i.e. that it is really and truly over and done with. However, its use is mainly stylistic, although it is very common.

2 ما **maa**. This can be placed before the past tense verb, to negate it, as in example 13 on page 74. Watch out for this word in Arabic, because it has several meanings apart from the one given here.

EXERCISE 7.5   Read aloud and translate:

١   وضع المدير الدفتر في الدولاب

٢   كلّم الوزير زوجته ثمّ سافر الى المطار

٣   ما كلّمنا الرئيس أمس

٤   قد شربوا الماء وأكلوا اللحم

٥   أدخلَتْ أمّها وأجلسَتها

٦   وجدن بيتها في الرياض

٧   اجتمعت الموظّفات أمس في المصنع

٨   هل سافرتَ الى البحرين ؟

٩   كتبت السكرتيرة التقرير الطويل ووضعته في الدفتر

١٠   قد سافروا الى الكويت وما رجعوا منها

Words beginning with vowels

The Arabs refuse to accept words beginning with two consonants (i.e. without a vowel between them, as in English *stop, cliff*). They get round the problem by writing an *alif* on the front of such words and giving this *alif* a vowel, usually *i*. The process is very like the English use of 'Spain', while the Spanish say 'España' (as they don't like two initial consonants either). However, the Arabs, having produced an initial vowel, then insist that it is elided (missed out) *unless* the word occurs at the beginning of an utterance or after a pause in speech. This can cause a great deal of bother, especially if such words occur after another word ending in a consonant, in which case the Arabs supply a vowel on the end of the previous word, so they can still elide the vowel of the *alif*.

اجتمع **ijtama:** *to meet, hold a meeting* is such a word. If this occurs after a natural pause, you are supposed to pronounce it as it stands **ijtama:** but if, for example, it is preceded by **wa** *and*, you are supposed to say, **wa jtama:**, dropping the initial i-vowel. Furthermore, if it is preceded by the question-mark word **hal**, you are supposed to supply an i-vowel on the end of this and say **hali jtama:**.

This is all too much – and has little practical meaning. In English we frequently glide over such junctures as in 'I saw Priscilla in the shop' (said quickly), and this is equally acceptable in Arabic.

More important, some Arabic words like **'aDrabuu** أضربوا in example 8 on page 74 which *look* as if they begin with vowels, actually begin with a glottal stop (*hamza*) which ought to be retained in pronunciation. **wa + 'aDrabuu** is pronounced **wa 'aDrabuu**, *not* **wa Drabuu**. To save ourselves a lot of trouble, words where the glottal stop has to be retained will be written in Arabic with the *hamza*, and in transliteration with the apostrophe (') representing it, e.g. أَضْرَبُوا **'aDrabuu**. Words which elide will be written without the appropriate sign in either alphabet, e.g. اِجْتَمَع **ijtama:**.

Unit Eight

Text and translation

Gamal Abdul Nasser was a great leader.	كان جمال عبد الناصر قائدا عظيما	١
The engineer was busy.	كان المهندس مشغولا	٢
His mother was ill.	كانت أمّه مريضة	٣
I was in Dubai on Thursday.	كنت في دبي يوم الخميس	٤
We were at the theatre.	كنّا في المسرح	٥
This programme is not suitable for children.	ليس هذا البرنامج مناسبا للاطفال	٦
Her sister is not beautiful.	ليست أختها جميلة	٧
The king became a tyrant.	صار الملك جبّارا	٨
Matters became complicated.	أصبحت الامور معقّدة	٩
The man is ignorant!	إنّ الرجل جاهل	١٠
This policy is futile.	إنّ هذه السياسة لفاشلة	١١
Muhammad is a good worker (diligent).	إنّ محمّدا عامل مجتهد	١٢
He is shrewd!	إنّه ذكي	١٣
The delegation had (already) arrived.	كان الوفد قد وصل	١٤
They had (already) eaten.	كانوا قد أكلوا	١٥

Vocabulary

Nouns

مَسْرَح (مسَارِح) theatre	يَوْم (أَيَّام) day
قَائِد (قُوَّاد ، قادة) leader	يوم الأَحَد Sunday

85

مُهَنْدِس (ـون)	engineer	يوم الاثْنَيْن	Monday
بَرْنامَج (بَرامِج)	programme	يوم الثَّلاثاء	Tuesday
طِفْل (أَطْفال)	child, baby	يوم الأَرْبَعاء	Wednesday
مَلِك (مُلوك)	king	يوم الخَميس	Thursday
جَبّار (جَبابرة)	tyrant	يوم الجُمْعة	Friday
أَمْر (أُمور)	matter, affair	يوم السَبْت	Saturday
وَفْد (وُفود)	delegation	مُحَرِّر (ـون)	editor
تَرْتيب (ـات)	arrangement	مُمَثِّل (ـون)	representative, actor
تَعْليم	education	دُبَيْ	Dubai
تَمْرين (تَمارين)	exercise	مُحَمَّد	Muhammad
مُدَرِّس (ـون)	teacher	مُنَظِّم (ـون)	organiser
مُفَتِّش (ـون)	inspector	جَمال عَبْد الناصِر	Gamal Abdul Nasser

Adjectives

عَظيم	great, mighty	مُعَقَّد	complicated
ذَكِي	clever, intelligent	مُناسِب	suitable, fitting
فاشِل	futile, a failure	جاهِل	ignorant

Verbs

كان	was, were	لَيْسَ	is/are not
أَصْبَح (IV) become		دَرَّس (II) teach	
صار	become	وَظَّفَ (II) appoint, employ	
رَتَّب (II) arrange		أَخَذَ	take

Other words

اِنَّ word introducing a type of equational sentence

لَ .. word used before the predicate of the above, lending some emphasis.

Grammar and sentence construction

So far we have learned how to write simple equational sentences (X is/are Y) and sentences with a verb. This unit gives a few more basic techniques to help us understand other types of sentence.

The verb 'was/were'

We have already learned that no verb is used in Arabic to translate *is/are* in simple equational sentences (see page 37). However, when talking about past time, a verb for *was/were* is necessary.

The verb used is a rather difficult one, having an original middle radical *waaw*, which is elided in the past tense. This type of verb will be discussed later (see page 251), but meanwhile, let us learn the past tense of this important verb **kaan**. Note that it is the *stem* of the verb which is difficult, having two separate forms. The endings are the standard ones used on all Arabic verbs.

Singular			**Plural**		
he was	كان	**kaan**	*they* (m) *were*	كانوا	**kaanuu**
she was	كانت	**kaanat**			
			they (f) *were*	كنّ	**kunna**
you (m) *were*	كنت	**kunt(a)**	*you* (m) *were*	كنتم	**kuntum**
you (f) *were*	كنت	**kunti**	*you* (f) *were*	كنتنّ	**kuntunna**
I was	كنت	**kunt(u)**	*we were*	كنّا	**kunnaa**

Notes

1   There are two stems, **kaan** used in the *he, she* and *they* (m) forms, and **kun** used in the rest. If it helps you to remember, note that the second, shortened stem **kun** is used before *suffixes which begin with a consonant*.

2   Note the spelling of the *they* (f) and the *we* forms, where the *nuun* of the verb and that of the suffix are united and written with a *shadda* (doubling sign). Except for certain cases involving the letter l (*laam*), this is a general rule in Arabic, where an *unvowelled* letter is immediately followed by its twin.

Learn the parts of this verb thoroughly.

The accusative marker (See also page 17)

If you have ever learned Latin or German, you will know that nouns can take certain special endings to show their function in a sentence. The only such ending to survive in English is the apostrophe *s* which indicates possession: 'the manager's office'. Such endings are called 'case' endings, the 'case' being the function the noun has in the sentence.

Classical Arabic has a system of (usually) three case endings to mark the three cases of the noun:

1   Nominative,   2   Accusative,   3   Genitive

The use of these three cases in Arabic differs so much from the general application of the terms in European languages that it is not really worth while explaining the terms. We shall simply use them as a method of labelling.

Now, in modern written Arabic – with the exception of a few special types of noun which will be dealt with later – the only case ending which is indicated in print is the accusative case of indefinite nouns and adjectives, singular or plural, *which do not have a suffix* (e.g. the feminine ending, etc.). This ending is written by placing an *alif* after the noun/adjective, e.g. قائدًا عظيمًا (example 1), and its correct pronunciation is **-an**.

In spoken Arabic this ending is ignored, except in many common expressions where it is given its full value, e.g.

أهلا وسهلا	pronounced	**ahlan wa sahlan**	*Hello*
مرحبا	or	**marHaban** **marHab**	*Hello, Welcome*
شكرا		**shukran**	*Thanks*
عفوا		**:afwan**	*Don't mention it*
جدّا		**jiddan**	*Very*
أبدا		**abadan**	*Never*
طبعا		**Tab:an**	*Naturally*

Note that this is an indefinite ending and must *not* be used on words which have the definite article. Remember it is also *not* used after words which have other suffixes, such as the feminine ending. A few other nouns of a specific phonetic nature do not use it, but these will be pointed out as they arise.

Simple 'X was/were Y' sentences

Examine examples 1–3 on page 85. The structure of these sentences should be familiar, the pattern being the usual Verb – Subject – The Rest order.

The important thing to remember is that in the *X was/were Y* type of sentence, the *Y* must be in the *accusative case* in Arabic grammar. This is marked in examples 1 and 2 by the use of the accusative marker *alif*, but not in example 3, because the feminine ending is present. If we change example 1 into 'Gamal Abdul Nasser was *the* great leader...', the accusative marker will also disappear, because it is *not* used on words which have the definite article '*the*':

كان جمال عبد الناصر القائد العظيم . . .

Examples 4 and 5 show the use of the verb was/were with prepositional phrases. The intervention of the preposition (in both cases **fii** *in*) eliminates the possibility of an accusative, with or without marker. The question of accusatives only arises in *simple* equational type sentences in the past, when we say X *was/were* Y (i.e. was the same thing as Y, not *in* Y, or *at* Y, or the like).

EXERCISE 8.1

A   Change the following sentences into the past tense, using the verb **kaan**, for example:

المدير مشغول ◄——— كان المدير مشغولا

٢ السياسة فاشلة		١ البنت جميلة	
٤ هذا صعب		٣ الصندوق الكبير ثقيل	
٦ ذلك المهندس أجنبي		٥ فستانها جميل	
٨ هي من دبي		٧ بذلته رخيصة	
١٠ الوفد عند الوزير		٩ البنت مع أمّها	
١٢ التمرين سهل		١١ هي ذكية	

B   Read aloud and translate your answers.

The negative verb *laysa* – 'is/are not'

Think back to the simple equational sentence in the present tense, X is/are Y. As you already know, no verb is used in such sentences. However, when we wish to negate them, the special verb **laysa**, meaning is/are *not*, is used.

This is rather a peculiar verb. Not only does it have this strange negative meaning, but it also takes the form of a *past* verb, but with a *present* meaning; 'is/are not', not 'was/were not'. There are some peculiarities about its conjugation, so study the following table carefully. **Laysa** has two stems **lays** and **las** used in the same way as those of **kaan**, and in addition it preserves the full terminations of Classical Arabic, including the original **-a** suffix of the he-form.

Singular		**Plural**	
he is not ليس **laysa**		*they* (m) *are not* ليسوا **laysuu**	
she is not ليست **laysat**			
		they (f) *are not* لسن **lasna**	
you (m) *are not* لست **lasta**		*you* (m) *are not* لستم **lastum**	
you (f) *are not* لست **lasti**		*you* (f) *are not* لستنّ **lastunna**	
I am not لست **lastu**		*we are not* لسنا **lasnaa**	

The verb **laysa** is used in exactly the same way as **kaan**, and takes its predicate (the 'Y' in X is/are not Y) in the accusative case, shown by the marker when the word does not have the definite article. Examples 6 and 7 on page 85 illustrate its use.

EXERCISE 8.2

A Negate the following sentences, using **laysa** for equational sentences and **maa** (see page 82) to negate **kaan** sentences.

٢ السكرتيرة في المكتب		**١** الولد جاهل	
٤ هذه المجلّة جديدة	**٣** كانت في البحرين يوم السبت		
٦ كنّا عند أختنا		**٥** باب البنك مقفول	
٨ كانت الأرض وسخة		**٧** الكتاب على الرفّ	
١٠ محمّد مدرّس في المدرسة الجديدة		**٩** هذا الكرسي ثقيل	

B Read aloud and translate your answers.

'X became Y' sentences
Arabic has several verbs meaning 'to become', all of which share with **kaan** and **laysa** the feature that their *predicate* ('Y') *is in the accusative*, again shown by the marker as required. The most common of these verbs are **'aSbaH**, which is perfectly regular in the past tense, and **Saar**, which has two past stems **Saar** and **Sir**, used in exactly the same way as the two stems of **kaan** (**kaan** and **kun**). Refer to page 87. The stem **Saar** is used above the line in the box, and **Sir** below it (i.e. where the verb suffixes begin with a *consonant*). This type of verb is called a 'Hollow Verb' (because its middle radical drops out, leaving it hollow), and has three types which are given in Table 5 in Appendix 1. Have a look at this now, for future reference. Examples 8 and 9 on page 85 illustrate the use of these verbs.

EXERCISE 8.3 Translate into Arabic, using either of the verbs 'to become':

1 The sun became hot.   2 (The) meat became cheap.
3 His shirt got (became) dirty.
4 She became famous in Kuwait.
5 The exercise became easy.   6 His job became difficult.

7   He became a great leader.
8   She became a secretary in the government.
9   That new newspaper has become (=became) famous.
10   Their policy became strange.

Equational sentences with 'inna

Apart from learning some new basic verbs and generally expanding
our powers of recognition and expression, this unit has really been
concerned with the use of the accusative case in Arabic. The
accusative is the only case in Arabic which is ever marked in
everyday print (on unsuffixed nouns which do not carry the definite
article). It also has some rather strange uses, as we shall now see.

To review matters, *nothing* was in the *accusative* in ordinary
equational sentences of the type

| X | is/are | Y |

With the three types of sentence using the verbs just dealt with, i.e.

X	was/were	Y
X	is/are not	Y
X	became	Y

the *predicate* (or Y-part) of the sentence was *accusative*.

Now, while it is perfectly adequate to express 'The man is
ignorant' by saying جاهل الرجل there is an alternative, of which
Arab writers are very fond, which is to use the particle 'inna at the
beginning of the sentence and say جاهل الرجل إنّ . Traditional
grammar books used to say that this 'inna meant 'Indeed' or the
Biblical 'Verily', but its common use today does not really suggest
much emphasis. It is more a matter of style.

Anyhow, the important and rather odd thing about 'inna is that
it puts the *subject* (X-part) of the equational sentence *in the
accusative*, again marking this accusative according to the rules
given above. Examples 10–13 show usages of 'inna, so let us analyse
them one by one.

10   There is no *marked* accusative here, because the X-part **ar-rajul**
     has the definite article.

11   Again there is no marked accusative, but note the particle
     word **la-** attached to **faashila** (the Y-part of the sentence). This
     is a fairly common practice, and may give extra emphasis to
     the sentence.

12   Here the accusative marker goes on the subject 'Muhammad',
     as this is a word with no suffix and without the definite article.

13   Watch this one carefully. Because the subject of the sentence
     should technically be accusative, the separate subject
     pronouns cannot be used. We therefore use the suffix
     pronouns, attached directly to **'inna**.

EXERCISE 8.4

A   Rewrite the following sentences, introducing them with **'inna**.
(The use of emphatic **la** is optional, but use it sometimes for
practice.)

٢ المهندس المشهور أجنبي	١ هذا الولد ذكي
٤ البنك المركزي في المدينة	٣ الجامعة بعيدة
٦ هذه الرواية غريبة	٥ وظيفة المفتّش سهلة
٨ تلك الشركة محلّية	٧ المحرّر رجل ذكي
١٠ المدير مبسوط	٩ هو من الكويت

B   Read aloud and translate your answers.

kaan with other verbs – 'He had done ....'
Although the Arabic verb has only two tenses, *past* and *present*, the
verb **kaan** *was* can be used to give a more precise sense of time.
When it is used with another past verb (e.g. **waSal** and **'akaluu** in
examples 14 and 15), it usually gives the meaning in English of '*had*
done something' (called the pluperfect tense). Again there is the
optional – but common – particle **qad** which can be placed directly
before the *main* verb of the sentence. This is said to stress the

finality of the action, that it is completely over and done with, but again its use is mainly a matter of style.

The word order in such sentences is always:

1 **kaan**	2 Subject	3 **qad** (optional)	4 Main Verb	5 The Rest

Note that the agreement of verb and subject follows the normal rules given on pp. 79–80, depending on whether the verb comes before or after its subject. If no subject is stated (as in example 15) both verbs must obviously carry their subject marker suffixes.

EXERCISE 8.5

A   Read aloud and translate the following sentences.

١   وصل المندوب الى مطار البحرين

٢   شربت البنت الماء

٣   أكلنا اللحم

٤   أخذ المهندس التقرير من السكرتير

٥   وضعت الطالبة كتابها في الشنطة

٦   أخذ التاجر الفلوس يوم الاثنين

٧   رفضت الحكومة التقرير

٨   كلّمت السكرتيرة مدير الشركة الجديدة

٩   سافر رئيس الوزراء الى الرياض يوم الأحد

١٠   أصبحت أمور هذه الحكومة الفاشلة صعبة ومعقّدة

B   Change them into the pluperfect tense (had arrived, had drunk, etc.) using the auxiliary verb **kaan** and the particle **qad**, e.g.

Sentence 1 above   ⟶   كان المندوب قد وصل الى مطار البحرين

Word shapes

Schematic	Arabic example	Sound-alike
1 $muC^1aC^2C^2iC^3$	ممثّل	MacAskill; demanded
2 $taC^1C^2iiC^3$	ترتيب	tartine (Fr.); canteen

1   This is the active participle of Verb Form II (see Table 2 and later), indicating the person who carries out the action of that verb. The verb مثّل **maththal** means 'to represent', so ممثّل is 'a representative', also 'an actor'. The form occurs also with an a-vowel instead of an *i* between C^2 and C^3, in which case it means the person who has had the action of the verb *done to him* (passive participle). We have already had موظّف **muwaDHDHaf** *an official, employee* from وظّف *to appoint, employ*; note also the adjective معقّد *complicated, having been complicated*.

2   This is the verbal noun (that which expresses the action of the verb) from the same Verb Form (II). رتّب means 'to put in order, arrange', thus ترتيب **tartiib** is 'arranging', 'arrangement', 'organisation'.
   Remember the point of learning word shapes is to be able to read and know something about Arabic words. It is not always easy to get an exact English sound-alike, but the cadence of the pattern is usually easy to imitate, e.g. **mumaththil** *demanded*. Say these aloud one after another until they become familiar.

Unit Nine

Text and translation

Large towns	مدن كبيرة	١
The new engineers	المهندسون الجدد	٢
The new teachers (f)	المدرّسات الجديدات	٣
The drillers arrived yesterday.	وصل الحفّارون أمس	٤
The customs official searched the departing travellers.	فتّش موظّف الجمارك المسافرين المغادرين	٥
The students (f) entered many universities.	دخلت الطالبات جامعات كثيرة	٦
They are workers in the car factory (factory of the cars).	هم عمّال في مصنع السيّارات	٧
We are merchants in the capital (city).	نحن تجّار في العاصمة	٨
Are you (m) Egyptians?	أأنتم مصريّون ؟	٩
These boys are not from those schools.	ليس هؤلاء الأولاد من تلك المدارس	١٠
Those women are skilled tailoresses.	أولائك النساء خيّاطات ماهرات	١١
The two friends (m) came out of the cinema.	خرج الصاحبان من السينما	١٢
He read two long articles in the magazine.	قرأ مقالتين طويلتين في المجلّة	١٣

96

Vocabulary

Nouns

مُسافِر (ـون) traveller

حَفّار (ـون) driller

عاصِمة (عَواصِم) capital (city)

جُمرُك (جَمارك) customs

صاحِب (أَصْحاب) friend

اِمرَأة ، المَرأَة (نساء)* woman

صَديق (أَصْدِقاء) friend

مَقالة (ـات) article (newspaper)

كَذّاب (ـون) liar (lying)

رَسّام (ـون) painter, artist

لَحّام (ـون) welder

دَبّابة (ـات) tank (military)

نَجّار (ـون) carpenter

حَمّال (ـون) porter

طَبّاخ (ـون) cook

مُحاسِب (ـون) accountant

مُقاوِل (ـون) contractor

خَبّاز (ـون) baker

كَهرَبائي (ـون) electrician

مُمَرِّضة (ـات) nurse (f)

ضَيْف (ضُيوف) guest

راكِب (رُكّاب) passenger

دَبّاسة (ـات) stapler, stapling machine

ثَلّاجة (ـات) fridge

*Note the different forms of this word with and without the definite article, and its irregular plural (which is from a different root).

Adjectives

خَبير (خُبَراء) experienced, expert

كَثير (ـون) much, many

كامِل complete

قَليل (ـون) little, few

فَقير (فُقَراء) poor

مِصْريّ (ـون) Egyptian

حَزين (حَزانَى) sad

ماهِر (ـون) skilled

مُغادِر (ـون) departing

سَريع (سِراع) quick, fast

Verbs

فَتَّش (II) *examine, search*   قَرَأ   *read*

اِشْتَغَل (VIII) *work*   طَلَب   *request, ask for*

كَسَب   *earn, gain*   أَرْسَل (IV) *send (a person)*

سَأَل   *ask (a question)*   ذَهَب   *go*

Note also the words given within the unit.

Plurals: general principles

As we have already noticed, plurals in Arabic are rather difficult, due to their diverse and unpredictable character. There is no easy way round the problem, and the best way is to learn the plural of each word along with the singular. However, a sketch of the general principles may help you to see some logic in the system.

While English distinguishes only between *one/more than one*, Arabic has a three-way system, distinguishing *one/two/more than two*. The special word form used for *two* of anything is called the *dual* and, although it does not occur all that frequently, you will have to learn to recognise it.

The dual and one type of plural are formed by the addition of special suffixes to nouns and adjectives and are therefore called *external* formations. The other, and more common, type of plural is formed by *changing the internal structure of the word* (and sometimes adding prefixes and/or suffixes of a different nature to those mentioned above). These are therefore called *internal* plurals.

Learn plurals along with their singulars but, if you want to try to follow Arabic logic, have a go at the following:

1   All Arabic noun/adjectives would take an *internal* plural if they could.

2   However, the internal plural patterns available do not cater for very complex words, i.e. those having more than four Arabic letters (in general), so long words have to take the second best option, that is the *external* or suffixed plural.

There are many exceptions to this basic rule, but it is helpful when you need to produce a plural for a new word. The nearer that word is to the simplest three-letter form, the more likely it is to take an internal plural; the more complex its structure, the likelier it is to be driven to the last resort of having a suffix plural (which *one* is explained on pp. 101–2).

Have a look through the plurals in the vocabularies and you will see that this generalisation works. For fun let us take a look at two borrowings from Europe.

1 فِلم *film* (often spelled فيلم in the singular, but the plural is always as given). This is a classic three-letter word like countless original Arabic words (e.g. حِزْب ، قِسْم ، فِكْر), so it immediately takes an internal plural أفلام **'aflaam**.

2 تلفزيون *television*. This is obviously not a genuine Arabic word, as it has far too many letters. So it has to take an external suffix plural تلفزيونات **tilifizyoonaat**. (However, it did make the grade in the end in a shortened form, as the verb تلفز **talfaz** *to televise*)

The internal plural
Note that the most common patterns of the internal plural are listed in Appendix 3, which should be consulted in conjunction with this unit.

As already stated, there is no useful rule governing the formation of a plural from a given singular. The principle of the internal plural is roughly similar to English foot-feet, mouse-mice (English is no more consistent, for example, boot-boots, house-houses). Arabic alters the internal structure of the word by changing the vowelling of the root letters, and also some prefixes and suffixes are used as an integral part of certain plural shapes (e.g. **'a-** on **'aflaam**).

The internal plural is formed from both masculine and feminine words (whether they denote objects or living beings) and the presence of the feminine ending on the singular in no way guarantees that it will be present on the plural:

مَدينة *town*,   plural مُدُن

The opposite also occurs, even, as in this case, on words denoting male human beings:

تِلْميذ *pupil* (m),   plural تَلاميذة

The feminine ending on this latter is part of the plural pattern and has nothing to do with gender or sex.

Adjectives, being as usual regarded as barely distinct from nouns, may also take internal plurals, but *the use of these is restricted to agreement with words denoting male human beings* (see page 103).

Some guidelines on the internal plural

As will be clear from the preceding section, there is little constructive we can say about the internal plural except:

1   Again, learn all plurals along with their singulars.
2   Study Appendix 3, which lists the most common internal plural patterns and gives some of the most frequently occurring correlations with singular shapes. Try to acquire a 'feel' for the shapes.
3   Remember that simple, basic word-shapes will almost certainly have an internal plural form, whereas more complex ones may well have to take an external suffix plural.
4   There are only two singular–plural correlations worth learning, both applying to four-radical words. The majority of four-radical words which have a *short vowel* between C^3 and C^4 take the internal plural pattern $C^1 aC^2 aaC^3 iC^4$, and those which have a *long vowel* in this position take $C^1 aC^2 aaC^3 iiC^4$. (Note that neither of these patterns shows the indefinite accusative marker.) Study the following examples and say them aloud to get the feeling of the patterns.

Short vowel between C^3–C^4			Plural pattern $C^1 aC^2 aaC^3 iC^4$	
مصنع	**maSna:**	*factory*	مصانع	**maSaani:**
مكتب	**maktab**	*desk, office*	مكاتب	**makaatib**
جردل	**jardal**	*bucket*	جرادل	**jaraadil**
ترجمة	**tarjama**	*translation*	تراجم	**taraajim**
درهم	**dirham**	*dirham* (money)	دراهم	**daraahim**

Long vowel between C^3–C^4			Plural pattern $C^1aC^2aaC^3iiC^4$		
مفتاح	miftaaH	*key*	مفاتيح	mafaatiiH	
صندوق	Sunduuq	*box, trunk*	صناديق	Sanaadiiq	
عصفور	:uSfuur	*small bird*	عصافير	:aSaafiir	
مصباح	miSbaaH	*lamp*	مصابيح	maSaabiiH	

The external (suffix) plural
There are two types of external or suffix plural in Arabic, usually referred to as masculine and feminine. We have tried to provide on pp. 98–100 a rough guide as to which sort of nouns you might expect to take an external rather than an internal plural. Having decided or established that a given noun must take an external suffix plural, the following restrictions apply:

Masculine external plural This is formed by adding **-uun** or **-iin**:

	Suffix	Example
Nominative case	ـون -**uun**	مهندسون muhandisuun
Other cases	ـين -**iin**	مهندسين muhandisiin

With one main exception, this type of plural may *only be used on words referring to male human beings.*

Notes:
1 The exception is سنة **sana** *year*, which has the plural سنين/سنون sinuun/siniin and also the alternative سنوات **sanawaat**.
2 Note the slightly hybrid form ابن **ibn** *son*, plural بنين/بنون banuun/baniin, also having the alternative form أبناء **abnaa'**.

3   The nominative case form is used for the *subjects* of normal sentences and the *predicates* of **'inna** sentences (see page 92). The 'other cases' form is used for the *objects* of normal sentences, the *subjects* of **'inna** sentences, also after *all prepositions* and in the *owner* part of possessives. In spoken Arabic the **-iin** suffix is used for all cases.

Summary: You can expect to find the masculine external plural **-uun/-iin** used on fairly complex words denoting *male human beings*.

Feminine external plural   This is formed by adding, for all cases, ـات **-aat**, having first removed the feminine singular ending (ـة) if present.

Suffix	Example	Singular form
ـات aat	مدرّسات **mudarrisaat**	مدرّسة
ـات aat	اجتماعات **ijtimaa:aat**	اجتماع

You will see from the two examples given that this type of plural may be used:

(*a*)   for *females* (e.g. **mudarrisaat** *female teachers*)
(*b*)   for *inanimates* (things, ideas; e.g. **ijtimaa:aat** *meetings*)

Summary: You can expect to find the feminine external plural **-aat** on:

(*a*)   Almost all nouns which denote female human beings and have, in the singular, the feminine ending ـة .
(*b*)   Words of a fairly complex pattern denoting what we call neuters (things, ideas, also sometimes animals which are referred to in English as 'it').

Note the following irregular formations, all basic words for females:

بِنْت   *daughter, girl*, pl. بَنَات

أُمّ   *mother*, pl. أُمَّهَات

أُخْت   *sister*, pl. أَخَوَات

Agreement of adjectives in the plural

We have already learned that the plurals of *things* and *abstracts* are regarded in Arabic as *feminine singulars* (see page 46). A strange fact, but one which we just have to accept and try to think of such plurals as 'she' instead of 'they'. The agreement of adjectives is therefore no problem, as we simply use the feminine singular as in example 1, 'large towns'.

Now, Arabic adjectives (being as usual regarded as being virtually the same as nouns) have equal rights in their choice of a plural form. However, there is a subtle difference, and the following rules apply to all adjectives with the exception of one specific type.

1 For females, the external plural ending **-aat** is used (e.g. example 3 on page 96).

2 For males, either the *masculine external plural* (**-uun/-iin**) or the *internal plural* is used. Which one is used depends again on the shape of the singular of the adjective. If it is complex, for instance, مجتهد **mujtahid** *diligent*, it will take an external plural, but many simple shape adjectives have their own internal plurals. Whichever of these is formed from a particular word must be used *only in agreement with words denoting males*.

It follows from this that adjectives like بعيد *far, distant*, which are not normally applied to human beings, have no plural form of either type, requiring only the feminine singular form to agree with the plural of objects. Of the adjectives given so far, the following have internal plural forms which should now be learned. Adjectives not listed here, but commonly applied to human beings, may be assumed to take the suffix plural **-uun/-iin** when applied to men (e.g. عادلون/عادلين from عادل *just*).

Adjective	Meaning	Male plural form
كسلان	*lazy*	كَسالَى
كبير	*old*	كِبار
صغير	*young*	صِغار
نحيف	*thin*	نِحاف
نظيف	*clean*	نِظاف

Adjective	Meaning	Male plural form
طويل	*tall*	طِوال
قصير	*short*	قِصار
مشهور	*famous*	مَشاهير
شاطر	*clever*	شُطّار
سمين	*fat*	سِمان
جميل	*handsome*	جِمال
مجنون	*mad*	مَجانين
غريب	*strange*	غُرَباء
أجنبي	*foreign*	أَجانِب
عظيم	*great*	عُظَمَاء
ذكي	*intelligent*	أَذْكِياء
جاهل	*ignorant*	جُهّال
جديد	*new*	جُدُد

As adjectives are generally more restricted in their shapes than nouns, there are a few singular–plural correlations worth looking at here, especially $C^1aC^2iiC^3$–$C^1iC^2aaC^3$, as in **kabiir-kibaar** etc.

The agreement of adjectives with plural nouns may be summarised as:

Nouns meaning	Adjective form
Things **Females** **Males**	*Feminine singular*, usually with ـة suffix. *External fem. plural*, suffix ـات. *External masc. plural* ـين/ـون ⎫ depending on *Internal plural* ⎭ shape of singular adjective

Study carefully examples 1–6 on page 96, noting both the form of the plurals used and the noun–adjective agreements.

EXERCISE 9.1

A   Change the following phrases/sentences into the singular.

١	أمور هامّة	٢	الملوك العظماء
٣	كانت المدرّسات الجديدات غائبات		
٤	أخذ الحمّالون الصناديق الثقيلة		
٥	اشتغل الحفّارون في دبي	٦	العمّال مجتهدون
٧	أيّام طويلة	٨	كانت المشروعات فاشلة
٩	خيّاطات ماهرات	١٠	روايات عجيبة
١١	الموّظفون الجدد	١٢	الفروع المركزية الرئيسية

B   Change the following into the plural. (Remember that verbs *preceding* their subject remain singular, and that the **-uun/-iin** plural ending must show the correct case.)

١	مقاول مصرى	٢	النجّار الخبير
٣	مقالة كاملة	٤	محاسب ذكي
٥	رئيس الشركة		
٦	أخذت السكرتيرة الجميلة الدفتر الفارغ		
٧	كتب المدير الاعلان الهامّ	٨	أختي ممرّضة
٩	كلّم المفتّش الراكب المغادر		
١٠	أرسل الوزير الموظّف الى البنك		
١١	ذهب الضيف المصرى الى المدينة الكبيرة		
١٢	سيّارة سريعة ودبّابة ثقيلة	١٣	ليس التمرين صعبا
١٤	وجدت المدرّسة المشغولة الولد الصغير في البيت البعيد		
١٥	الشبّاك مقفول والباب مكسور		

C   Read aloud and translate your answers to A and B.

Plural of the separate personal pronouns
The singular personal pronouns were given on page 39. Now *learn*
the plurals given below. (Remember, for *things*, they = she – هي)

نحن	**naHnu**	*we*
أنتم	**antum**	*you* (m)
أنتنّ	**antunna**	*you* (f)
هُم	**hum**	*they* (m)
هنّ	**hunna**	*they* (f)

Study examples 7–9 on page 96 which employ plural personal
pronouns. In 9, **antum** is prefixed by the question-mark particle **'a-**
(see page 40).

Plural of the demonstratives
When referring to human beings (in the plural) the following forms
are used for *both men and women*. The spelling of both forms is
rather tricky, so pay close attention to it. (For the sign   see page
23.)

هٰؤُلاءِ	**haa'ulaa'i**	these(-people)
أُولٰئِكَ	**uulaa'ika**	those(-people)

Again, because all plurals of objects or abstracts are regarded as
feminine singulars, the singular demonstratives هذه **haadhihi** and
تلك **tilka** are used for 'these' and 'those' respectively. Examples 10
and 11 illustrate the use of the human plural forms.

EXERCISE 9.2

A Apply the appropriate part of هذا *this* to:

٢	المجلّات الاجنبية	١	المرأة الجميلة
٤	الجرائد اليومية	٣	الكهربائيون الماهرون
٦	الترتيبات الجديدة	٥	الضيوف الكثيرون
٨	الامور المعقّدة	٧	القوّاد العظماء
١٠	المصريون الفقراء	٩	الممرّضات الجديدات

B Apply the appropriate part of ذلك *that* to:

٢	الخيّاطون الأجانب	١	العواصم المشهورة
٤	الرجال السمان	٣	الشوارع الطويلة
٦	البنات الصغيرات	٥	المدرّسات الحاضرات
٨	الاصحاب الغائبون	٧	الطائرات الجديدة
١٠	الحكّام الجبابرة	٩	الصحون المكسورة

C Read aloud and translate your answers to A and B.

D In the following, change the pronouns (separate or suffix) and anything else required by the sense into the plural.

٢	مكتبه قريب	١	أنت جاهل
٤	ليس الضيف في بيته	٣	أنا مصرى
٦	هو محاسب مشهور	٥	إنّ الخبّاز صاحبي
٨	أأنت ممرّضة ؟	٧	إنّها ثلّاجة جديدة
١٠	إنّه رسّام مشهور	٩	هي مدرّسة في المدينة

E Read aloud and translate.

108   *Arabic*

Dual nouns and adjectives
The dual must be used when referring to *two* of anything. Although this is not very common in practice, you should at least learn to recognise it. Fortunately, its formation is for the most part regular for both nouns and adjectives. It is an external suffixed formation, parallel to the masculine external plural discussed on page 101.

	Suffix	**Example**
Nominative case	ـان -aan	صاحبان **SaaHibaan**
Other cases	ـين -ayn	صاحبين **SaaHibayn**

Notes:
1 If a word has the feminine ending, this is retained, but changes into an ordinary 't' as it does before all suffixes. Example 13 illustrates this.
2 Agreeing adjectives must take the appropriate masculine or feminine dual ending and also agree with the noun in case. Example 13 again illustrates.
3 In spoken Arabic, the nominative dual form is ignored and the ending -ayn (pronounced as in 'cane') used for all cases. In written Arabic, the use of the cases is exactly as described for the masculine external plural on pp. 101–2.

EXERCISE 9.3

A Put *all* the nouns (and their adjectives) in the following into the dual (remember the ending shows the case).

١ فتّش الموظّف الراكب الغادر   ٢ انّ المقاول حاضر

٣ الدبّاسة على المكتب   ٤ قرأ الكتاب الاجنبي

٥ انّ اللحّام ماهر   ٦ دخل الوزير البيت

٧ السائق في السيّارة الكبيرة   ٨ جريدة يومية حديثة

٩ كلّم المدير العامل الجديد   ١٠ طفل صغير جميل

B Read aloud and translate.

Dual verbs and pronouns

For the sake of completeness, the dual verb suffixes and separate and suffixed pronouns are given here. No exercises on these are provided as they are comparatively rare and also easily recognised in context. Note that there is *no* dual form for the first person (i.e. to translate 'we two') and that the second person ('you two' etc.) does not distinguish between male and female as it does in the singular and the plural. 'They two' (f) is distinguished only in the verb.

	Separate pronoun	Suffix pronoun	Verb past stem suffix*
you two	أنتما antumaa	كما -kumaa	ـتُما -tumaa
they two (m)	هما humaa	هما -humaa	ـا -aa
they two (f)	———	———	ـتا -ataa

*See also Verb Table I

The demonstrative pronouns 'this' and 'that' also have dual forms, but these are also comparatively rare and easily recognisable from context. They will be pointed out as they occur.

Word shape

Schematic	Arabic example	Sound-alike
$C^1aC^2C^2aaC^3$	رسّام	this psalm

Most words describing people and what they do, either by nature or for a living, were originally adjectives in Arabic – presumably qualifying the words 'man' and 'woman'. This word shape is a typical example. Originally an intensive adjective describing someone who does something habitually, repeatedly or excessively, it has gradually acquired almost the status of a noun, describing many trades and occupations. We can still see it in both stages in

the language, for example كذّاب **kadhdhaab** *lying, mendacious* as in
ولد كذّاب *a mendacious boy* and *a liar* as in هذا الولد كذّاب *this boy
is a liar.*
Note again the very grey area which divides adjectives from nouns
in Arabic.

This formation takes the external plural **-uun/-iin**. The feminine
ending ـة can be added to express:

(a)   a female where applicable, eg. خيّاطة *a tailoress* (from خيّاط *a
tailor*)

(b)   a machine, e.g. سيّارة *a going machine, a car* and دبّابة *a crawling
machine, a tank*

Plural of the feminine form is **-aat**.

Unit Ten

Text and translation

They live in a big flat in London.	يسكنون في شقّة كبيرة في لندن ١
The government issues the official statistics at the beginning of the month.	تنشر الحكومة الاحصائيات الرسميّة في أوّل الشهر ٢
He is studying at the University of Cairo.	يدرس في جامعة القاهرة ٣
What do you eat in the morning?	ماذا تأكل في الصباح ؟ ٤
The national troupe will present a programme of folk dance tomorrow.	سوف يقدّم الفريق القومي برنامجا من الرقص الشعبي غدا ٥
I shall go (on) Saturday.	سأذهب يوم السبت ٦
We don't know anything about exports and imports.	لا نعرف شيئا عن الصادرات والواردات ٧
They will never return to their homeland. (*Not they-return to homeland-their ever.*)	لن يرجعوا الى وطنهم أبدا ٨
Did you (f, s) not drink the coffee?	ألم تشربي القهوة ؟ ٩
He is laughing at us.	يضحك علينا ١٠
I shall pay (to) him the money.	سأدفع له الفلوس ١١
He took £2 from me.	أخذ منّي جنيهين ١٢

111

Vocabulary

Nouns

شَقّة (شِقَق) ‏ flat, apartment

إِحْصائِيات ‏ statistics

فَرِيق (أَفْرِقة) ‏ troupe, team

شَيْء (أَشْياء) ‏ thing

وَطَن (أَوْطان) ‏ homeland

قَهْوة ‏ coffee

لُغَة (ـات) ‏ language

سَفِير (سُفَراء) ‏ ambassador

خَبِير (خُبَراء) ‏ expert

بَخِيل (بُخَلاء) ‏ miser

لَنْدَن ‏ London

شَهْر (أَشْهُر ، شُهُور) ‏ month

رَقْص ‏ dance

صادِرات ‏ exports

وارِدات ‏ imports

جُنَيْه (ـات) ‏ pound (£)

اللّٰه ‏ God

أَمِير (أُمَراء) ‏ prince

أَدِيب (أُدَباء) ‏ writer, literary man

عَسْكَرى (عَساكِر) ‏ soldier, policeman

Verbs

نَشَر ‏ (u) publish

قَدَّم ، يُقَدِّم ‏ (II) present

ضَحِك ‏ (a) laugh

سَكَن ‏ (u) dwell, live in

فَهِم ‏ (a) understand

صَرَف ‏ (i) spend (money)

دَرَس ‏ (u) study

عَرَف ‏ (i) know, come to know

دَافَع عَن ، يُدَافِع عن ‏ (III) defend

رَقَص ‏ (u) dance

حَمَل ‏ (i) carry

لَعِب ‏ (a) play

Adjectives*

رَسْمِيّ official	قَوْمِيّ national	آخَر other (f أُخْرَى)
شَعْبِيّ folk	اِنْجِلِيزِىّ (اِنْجِلِيز) English	عَرَبِيّ (عَرَب) Arab,
آخِر last	أَوَّل first (f أُولَى)	Arabic

Other words

غَداً tomorrow†	أَبَداً never†	قَبْل before
بَعْد after	تَحْت under, below	لِـ to, for
عَن from, of, about	لَدَى with (chez)	مَاذَا what? (before verbs)
بِـ with, by means of, in, by etc.	كَثِيراً a lot, much†	

---

*Adjectives take suffixed plural unless indicated otherwise.
†Pronounced ghad**an**, abad**an** and kathiir**an** (see pp. 88–9).

This unit deals with the present tense of the Arabic verb and should be studied in conjunction with Verb Table 1 and Unit 7 which gives all the rules for agreement. Make sure you have mastered Unit 7 thoroughly before proceeding.

Formation of the present tense

Study the present tense column of Table 1 (see page 238), and you will see that this tense is formed by applying *prefixes*, and in some cases *suffixes* as well, to a present stem. (The past tense, remember, was formed by adding suffixes only to a past stem.) With minor exceptions, these same prefixes and suffixes are applied to *all* Arabic verbs, so learn them thoroughly right away. To help you, here is the present tense of 'to write', given in transliteration (without the dual which is fairly rare and easily recognisable). The present stem of this verb is **ktub**, which is given in capitals for clarity. This does *not* indicate any change in the pronunciation of the consonants.

	Singular		**Plural**	
yaKTUB	*he writes, is writing*	**yaKTUBuun**	*they* (m) *write*
taKTUB	*she writes*	**yaKTUBna**	*they* (f) *write*
taKTUB	*you* (m) *write*	**taKTUBuun**	*you* (m) *write*
taKTUBiin	*you* (f) *write*	**taKTUBna**	*you* (f) *write*
aKTUB	*I write*	**naKTUB**	*we write*

Notes:

1 With the exception of the *she*-form, all the third person parts have the prefix **ya-**. The second person (*you*) forms all have **ta-** (reminiscent of the personal pronouns **anta, anti**, etc., which all have a *t* in them). In the singular the suffix **-iin** distinguishes feminine from masculine, and in the plural of both second and third persons, the suffix **-uun** marks masculine and **-na** feminine. The *she-* and *you-* (m sing.) forms are identical, but this does not cause much confusion in practice. In the first person the prefixes **a-** for 'I' and **na-** for 'we' again remind us of the pronouns **anaa** and **naHnu**.

2 In the verbs marked II, III and IV (see Table 2), *all* the prefixes are vowelled *u* instead of *a*, e.g. **yudarris** *he teaches*, etc.

While the present stems of the complex verbs which we have numbered II-X are predictable by rule, those of the simple verbs vary in the *vowel taken by the middle radical* and have to be learned together with their past stems, which also vary. Since only this one variation occurs, it is convenient to give the required vowel (written in English) along with the past stem, thus كَتَب (**u**) means that the middle radical of **katab** will be vowelled **u** in the present stem, i.e. كتب **ktub**. The first radical is *always* vowelless. The vowels for the verbs already given are listed below. Learn them now if you can, but in fact it is not too serious if you get them wrong in speech – or reading. For those who like algebra, the following system usually prevails – but there are always exceptions.

Past Stem	**Vowel on C^2**	$\longrightarrow$	**Vowel on C^2**	**Present Stem**
1 *CaCaC*	*a*	$\longrightarrow$	*u* or *i*	*CCuC* *CCiC*
2 *CaCiC*	*i*	$\longrightarrow$	*a*	*CCaC*
3 *CaCuC*	*u*	$\longrightarrow$	*u*	*CCuC*

The majority of simple verbs are of type 1 in the box above. Type 3 is quite rare. Note that the present stems of derived (II-X) and irregular verbs are given in full in the following list. Rules for these regular formations are given in Table 2 in Appendix 1.

Simple verbs

فتح (a) *open*	دفع (a) *pay*	رفض (i) *refuse*
شرب (a) *drink*	طبخ (u) *cook*	رجع (i) *come back*
دخل (u) *enter*	أكل (u) *eat*	كتب (u) *write*
أخذ (u) *take*	قرأ (a) *read*	طلب (u) *request*
ذهب (a) *go*	كسب (i) *earn*	سأل (a) *ask*

Complex and irregular verbs (past stem followed by he-form of the present)

سافَر ، يُسافِر (III) *travel*	أَجْلَس ، يُجْلِس (IV) *seat*
وَصَل ، يَصِل *arrive*	دَرَّس ، يُدَرِّس (II) *teach*
كَلَّم ، يُكَلِّم (II) *speak to*	اِشْتَغَل ، يَشْتَغِل (VIII) *work*
وَضَع ، يَضَع *put*	كان ، يَكُون *be*
رَتَّب ، يُرَتِّب (II) *arrange*	اِنْتَخَب ، يَنْتَخِب (VIII) *elect*
فَتَّش ، يُفَتِّش (II) *examine*	أَدْخَل ، يُدْخِل (IV) *admit, let in*
صار ، يَصِير *become*	اِجْتَمَع ، يَجْتَمِع (VIII) *hold a meeting*
أَضْرَب ، يُضْرِب (IV) *strike*	أَصْبَح ، يُصْبِح (IV) *become*
وَجَد ، يَجِد *find*	وَظَّف ، يُوَظِّف (II) *appoint*
أَعْلَن ، يُعْلِن (IV) *announce*	أَرْسَل ، يُرْسِل (IV) *send*

Notes:

1   The verb **laysa** *is not* has no present stem since its past tense is used with a present meaning (see page 90).

2 Although no verb for 'is/are' is required in simple equational sentences, **kaan** has a present tense which is used in certain other types of sentence.

3 Verbs with first radical *waaw* (وجد ، وضع) usually drop this completely in the present tense. For this type of verb see Table 4. **kaan/yakuun** and **Saar/yaSiir** suffer from an elided *waaw* and *yaa* respectively in both stems. These are known as Hollow Verbs and are dealt with in Table 5. Start systematically learning these verb types now.

EXERCISE 10.1

A Change the following past tense verbs into the present tense:

٥ فهمَتْ	حملن ٤	ضحكتُ ٣	كتبتم ٢	درسوا ١
١٠ دافعوا	قدّمتم ٩	صرفنا ٨	سكنوا ٧	رقصتِ ٦
١٥ ذهبن	طلبنا ١٤	قرأتِ ١٣	سألَتْ ١٢	فتّشتَ ١١
٢٠ أخذتم	صار ١٩	أصبحوا ١٨	كانَتْ ١٧	اشتغل ١٦
٢٥ دخلتم	اجتمعنا ٢٤	وجد ٢٣	وصلتنّ ٢٢	طبخن ٢١

B Read aloud and translate your answers.

Translation of the present tense
The present tense is really an 'imperfect' tense, i.e. it expresses an action which is imperfect, incomplete, still going on. Thus, **yaktub** comes out in English variously as 'he writes' (habitually or regularly), 'he is writing' (now, and continues to do so), 'does he write', 'yes, he does write', and so on. The same tense with an extra prefix is used for the future (see page 117), and can also be used to translate the past continuous (he was writing') or past habitual ('he used to write'), if the sentence is introduced by **kaan**:

كان يكتب كتابا *he was writing a book*

كان يكتب كتبا كثيرة *he used to write lots of books (many books)*

Compare this usage to the 'he had done ...' construction on pp. 93–4.

As has been said, Arabic has only two tenses, so they have to do a lot of work to cover our multiplicity of English ones. Examples 1–4 on page 111 illustrate some of the different meanings and translations.

The future: 'he will do ...'
As it has so few tenses, Arabic uses the present tense for the future as well. This does not seem so strange if you consider that we usually say 'I am going on holiday in July' rather than 'I shall go ...' In Arabic, however, this use of the future is usually marked by the word **sawfa** placed immediately before the verb, or the shortened form **sa-** which, being a one-letter word, cannot stand alone, and is therefore joined to the verb. Examples 5 and 6 illustrate this.

EXERCISE 10.2

A Translate into Arabic, starting all sentences with the verb and using either **sa-** or **sawfa** (interchangeable) to indicate the future.

1 He is eating the food.
2 The manager will speak to (address) the employees tomorrow.
3 He used to drink coffee.
4 She was living in a big flat in London.
5 They will publish the statistics before Saturday.
6 We understand the Arabic language.
7 The porter was carrying a heavy box.
8 The ambassador travels a lot.
9 The soldiers inspect the suitcases in the airport.
10 The children are playing in the street.
11 We earn the money and spend it.

B Read your answers aloud.

Variations of the present tense
In traditional Arabic grammar, the present (but *not* the past) tense of the verb had various types of ending which changed when the verb was preceded by certain 'governing words'. Most of these variations consist of short final vowels which, of course, are not written anyway, so there is no need to bother with them. However, some parts have altered suffixes which *are* visible in print, so we must be prepared for them, although their use in Arabic is for the most part mechanical, and causes little difficulty. In the majority of

cases they occur after certain easily recognisable words which come before the verb.

In European grammar these variations of the present tense are called 'moods' and individually named *indicative* (the normal unaffected present tense), *subjunctive* and *jussive*. For want of better terminology, we shall use these traditional names, but merely for convenience, as the Arabic versions have little connection with the subjunctives which you may have encountered in European languages. Note again that the occurrence of these variations is, for the most part, purely automatic after certain particles which come before the verb.

Now study the subjunctive column of Table I and note which verb terminations change, and how they change. If you like rules, these changes can be expressed very simply as follows:

Parts of the present tense of the simple verb which have a suffix consisting of a long vowel (*VV*) plus a *nuun* (*N*) drop this *N* to form the subjunctive/jussive. If the result is a verb part ending in **-uu**, an *alif* is written (but not pronounced) after the ending (like all verb parts ending in **-uu** – see page 23):

Present tense (*indicative*) ⟶ *Subjunctive/jussive*
    –*VV N*   ⟶   –*VV*

EXERCISE 10.3 Give the subjunctive/jussive variant of the following verbs in the present tense:

٤ يكونون		٣ تجدون		٢ يرفضون		١ ترجعين	
٨ تذهبين		٧ تسألون		٦ يشتغلون		٥ تدرّسين	
				١٠ تضحكون .		٩ يدافعون	

Negative particles governing the present tense

All these particles mean 'not' in English, and in Arabic are placed directly before the present tense verb. Note that two of them, in addition to negating the verb, change its time signification (although not its grammatical tense). This is a bit tricky, so be careful.

1 *Negating the present tense*, i.e.
    he writes/is writing ⟶ he does not write/is not writing

Use ‏لا‎ (**laa**) with the ordinary (indicative) present tense:

‏يكتب ← لا يكتب‎

Example 7 on page 111, also illustrates this.

2 *Negating the future*, i.e.

He will write ⟶ he will not write

Use ‏لن‎ (**lan**) with the subjunctive and omit the ‏ـس‎ **sa-** or ‏سوف‎ **sawfa**:

‏سوف يكتب/سيكتب ← لن يكتب‎

But note in the plural 'they will not write':

‏لن يكتبوا‎ (**nuun** omitted for subjunctive)

See also example 8 on page 111.

3 *Negating the past*, i.e.

he wrote/has written ⟶ did not write/has not written

Use ‏لم‎ **lam** with the jussive:

‏كتب ← لم يكتب‎ (past tense)

Note again the plural 'they did not write' with **nuun** omitted:

‏لم يكتبوا‎

See also example 9.

Remember that, although the tense here is *present*, the meaning is *past*.

Note that (3) above can also be expressed by using ‏ما‎ **maa** with the *past tense* (see page 82), but this is not so common as the usage given above.

The negation of the verb may be summarised as follows:

Time of action	English	Arabic particle		Verb tense
Present	*does, is doing*	‏لا‎	**laa**	Present
Future	*will/shall do*	‏لن‎	**lan**	Present subjunctive
Past	*did/has done*	‏لم‎	**lam**	Present jussive
		‏ما‎	**maa**	Past

EXERCISE 10.4

A Negate the following sentences, using **lam** with the jussive for past meanings:

١   كانوا هنا أمس

٢   سوف تعلن الجريدة هذه العلاوة غدا

٣   قرأ رئيس الوزراء التقرير الطويل في مكتبه

٤   تدرس أختها اللغة الانجليزية في جامعة لندن

٥   رجعت زوجته الى وطنها

٦   وضعت السكرتيرة الانجليزية التقرير في شنطتها

٧   يكسب كثيرا في وظيفته الجديدة

٨   سأرسل الكهربائي الى المصنع غدا

٩   يشتغل المحاسب في مكتب الاحصائيات

١٠   يصرف البخلاء فلوسهم .

B Read aloud and translate your answers.

Prepositions with the pronoun suffixes

As we have seen (page 47), prepositions are basically words which tell you the *place* or *position* of something in relation to something else, e.g. The book is *on/under/by/beside* the table. However, in both English and Arabic they are also used after certain verbs called *intransitive*, which cannot take a direct object, but require the intervention of a preposition, e.g. you can't 'wait someone', you have to wait *for* him; similarly you sympathise *with* him, insist *on* something, and so on. It is a problem in most languages exactly which preposition to use, as this often cannot be worked out logically. The best way is to learn the preposition with the verb. Remember also that *all* Arabic prepositions govern the *genitive* case, which shows in masculine external plurals, duals and a few special nouns (see pages 101 and 107–8).

When prepositions govern pronouns (to *me*, from *him*, etc.), Arabic uses the suffix pronouns (see page 60) and some variations occur. These mainly affect pronunciation rather than the written word, but should be noted.

1 *First person* ('me', as in 'to me', 'from me') Arabic suffix ي **-ii**

(*a*) As usual, this long-vowel suffix suppresses any short vowel (usually an **-a**) occurring on the end of the preposition, so:

fawqa *above*, plus **-ii** *me*, becomes **fawqii** above me فوقي

ma:a *with*, plus **-ii** *me*, becomes **ma:ii** *with me* معي

(*b*) After preceding long vowels, and the combination **-ay**, the suffix changes to **-ya**, so:

fii *in*, plus *me*, is **fiiya** فيّ

ilay الي *towards*, plus *me*, is **ilayya** الّي (for the form **ilay** الي see Section 3 below).

Note that in **fiiya** in the Arabic script, the first of the two **yaa**'s indicated by the *shadda* sign is used to lengthen the i-vowel. It is probably preferable to write this and other such words in transliteration with two *y*'s: **fiyya**

(*c*) In the two prepositions **min** *from* and **:an** *about, from*, the *n* is doubled before *-ii* is added, so:

min plus **-ii** becomes **minnii** مّني *from me*, and similarly **:an** plus **-ii** becomes **:annii** عّني

2 *Third person* ('him', 'them', as in 'with him', etc.) After prepositions ending in **-i** (like **bi**), **-ii** (like **fii**) or **-ay** (like **ilay**) the third person suffixes which have a short u-vowel (هن ، هم ، ه) change this to an i-vowel. ('Her' **-haa**, which has a long a-vowel, remains unaffected.) Examples:

اليه **ilayhi** *to him* فيهم **fiihim** *in them* (m)

عليهنّ **:alayhinna** *on them* (f)

3 *Changes in the prepositions themselves*
(*a*) The two common prepositions **ilaa**, **:alaa** and the less common **ladaa** (all written with the special final long a-vowel – see page 21) change to **ilay-**, **:alay-** and **laday-** before *all* pronoun suffixes, and this change in turn affects some of these suffixes as described above. Thus:

اليه **ilayhi** *to him* علينا **:alaynaa** *on us* اليك **ilayka** *towards you*

(*b*) The preposition ل **li-**, which is always attached to the following word since it has only one letter (see page 23), changes to **la-**

before *all* pronoun suffixes except **-ii** which, as usual, suppresses any preceding short vowel. Thus:

لنا **lanaa** *to us* لهم **lahum** *to them*, but لي **lii** *to me*

Note that when **li-** is prefixed to words bearing the definite article, the *alif* of the article is omitted. Thus:

للولد **li-l-walad** *to the boy* للمدرسة **li-l-madrasa** *to the school*

If the word begins with the letter *laam*, the *laam* of the article merges with that of the noun/adjective and is written with a *shadda*:

للّغة **li-l-lugha** *to the language* لله **li-llaah** *to God*

Examples 10–12 illustrate some prepositions with pronoun suffixes.

EXERCISE 10.5

A   Combine the following prepositions with the suffix forms of the separate pronouns given, e.g.

من + هي ———← منها

٣ من + أنتم	٢ تحت + نحن	١ في + أنتِ
٦ بعد + هو	٥ الى + أنا	٤ عن + أنا
٩ بـ + هنّ	٨ لدى + نحن	٧ ل + هم
١٢ على + هم	١١ من + أنا	١٠ قبل + أنا

B   Read your answers aloud.

Word shape

Schematic	Arabic example	Sound-alike
$C^1uC^2aC^3aa$'	وزراء	was a rat*

*Cockney/Glasgow pronunciation of final *t* as glottal stop.

This shape is common for the internal plural of nouns of the shape $C^1aC^2iiC^3$, when they refer to male human beings. The nouns in this case are adjectives which have been crystallised into noun form – usually to express the meaning of a person with some particular function or status. It does, however, occur with some uncrystallised adjectives like فقير **faqiir** *poor* and عظم **:aDHiim** *mighty*.

Note that like most words ending in **-aa'** this pattern does not show the indefinite accusative marker.

Examples which have already occurred are:

رئيس/رؤساء *chief, boss* وزير/وزراء *minister*

(Note the different carrier letter for the glottal stop in the plural of **ra'iis**. This is due to the change in the vowelling.) Other examples of this shape are given in the vocabulary of this unit.

Unit Eleven

Units 1–10, heavy going though they may have been, have covered most of the important basic constructions in Arabic. By basic constructions we mean such things as the various noun-adjective phrases, the possessive, the equational sentence, the **'inna**-type sentence, the use of the verb in both tenses and so on. Such constructions are the bricks and mortar of Arabic, being combined together in various ways to produce more complex sentences. Sentence construction in Arabic is surprisingly simple, the key to understanding being the ability to recognise the component parts.

Before proceeding, please make sure that you have mastered the material in Units 1 to 10, and if necessary go back and revise. You can easily look up individual words if you have forgotten them, but you will not be able to understand a complex sentence if you have not mastered the basic structures.

Now that we are able to deal with less contrived, more natural Arabic, the layout of the units has been changed. The new order is:

1   Sample text in mainly unvowelled Arabic.

2   New vocabulary occurring in the text.

3   A literal, word-for-word translation of the text, with notes on difficult constructions. This is to be converted as an exercise into normal idiomatic English, and also the original text should be read aloud in Arabic.

4   Background notes on various aspects of Arab life and society.

5   New grammar and sentence construction introduced by means of an analysis of the text. Mechanical learning of things like verb parts – which there is no easy way to avoid – will be achieved by reference to the tables in the back of the book, which should be committed to memory at the appropriate time. Important new topics are given their own sub-headings within this section.

Text أعياد المسلمين 1

جون كم عيدا عند المسلمين ؟

أحمد الأعياد المهمّة عندنا اثنان

ج وما هما ؟

أ الأوّل هو العيد الصغير واسمه عيد الفطر 5

ج وفي أيّ شهر هو ؟

أ العيد الصغير في أوّل يوم من شهر شوال

ج وما مناسبته ؟

أ مناسبته أنَّ شهر شوال يعقب شهر رمضان وهو شهر الصوم عند المسلمين

ج وما معنى الصوم ؟ 10

أ الصوم معناه أنَّ الناس لا يأكلون ولا يشربون في النهار . هذا معنى الصوم

ج وما هو العيد الآخر ؟

أ هو العيد الكبير أو عيد الأضحى

ج وما مناسبته ؟

أ مناسبته الحجّ وهو يبدأ في آخر يوم من أيّام الحجّ. والحجّ معناه أنَّ الناس 15
يسافرون الى مكّة ويزورون الكعبة

ج وكيف يحتفلون بهذا العيد ؟

أ هم يذبحون فيه ذبائح

ج وما هي الذبيحة ؟

أ الذبيحة هي خروف يذبحونه ويأكلونه في نهاية الحجّ . وهذا عادة عند 20
المسلمين

ج فأعيادكم إثنان فقط اذا ؟

أ لا ، في بعض الأقطار يحتفلون بعيد ثالث

ج وما هو ؟

أ هو مولد النبي في شهر ربيع الأوّل 25

ج نعم ، هذا مثل عيد الميلاد عندنا نحن المسيحيّين .

Vocabulary

Nouns

مُسْلِم (ـون) Muslim   عِيد (أَعْياد) festival, feast day

اِسْم (أَسْماء) name   اِثْنان two (behaves as a dual)

شَوّال Shawwal (month)   فِطْر breaking of a fast

رَمَضان Ramadan (month)   مُناسَبة (ـات) occasion

مَعْنًى (مَعانٍ) meaning (see p. 142 on plural)   صَوْم fast, fasting

نَهار daytime   ناس people

الحَجّ the pilgrimage   الأَضْحَى Sacrifice (festival)

مَكَّة Mecca   عادة (ـات) custom

ذَبيحة (ذَبائِح) slaughter animal for sacrifice   الكَعْبة The Kaaba (shrine)

نِهاية end   خَروف (خِرْفان) sheep

مَوْلِد Mulid (Prophet's birthday)

نَبِي (أَنْبِياء) prophet   قُطْر (أَقْطار) part, area, region

مَسيحِيّ (ـون) Christian   رَبيع الأَوَّل Rabi' al-Awwal (month)

ميلاد birth

عيد الميلاد Festival of *the* birth, i.e. Christmas,   عيد ميلاد birthday

Verbs

بَدَأ (a) to begin   زار ، يَزُور to visit

ذَبَح (a) to slaughter   اِحْتَفَل بِـ ، يَحْتَفِل بِـ (VIII) celebrate something

عَقَب (u) come after, follow

Adjectives

ثالِث *third*   مُهِمّ *important (variant of* هامّ)

Other words

أيّ *which?*   ما *what? (before nouns and pronouns)*

أنَّ *that (conjunction)*   كَيفْ *how?*

فَقَط *only*   إذاً *then, so (pronounce* **idhan***)*

بَعْض *some (of), one (of)*   مِثْل *the like (of), like*

فَـ *so, and*   أوْ *or*

Literal translation

1 **Festivals (of) the-Muslims**
   John How-many festival (are) with the-Muslims?
   Ahmed The-festivals the-important with-us (are) two.
   J And-what (are) they-two?
5 **A** The-first he (is) the-festival the-small and-name-his festival (of) the-fastbreaking.
   J And-in which month (is) he?
   A The-festival the-small (is) in first day of month Shawwal.
   J And-what (is) occasion-his?
   A Occasion-his (is) that month (of) Shawwal he-follows month (of) Ramadan and-he (is) month (of) the-fasting with the-Muslims.
10 **J** And-what (is) meaning (of) the-fasting?
   A The-fasting his-meaning (is) that the-people not they-eat and-not they-drink in the-daytime. This (is) meaning (of) the-fasting.
   J And-what (is) he the-festival the-other?
   A He (is) the-festival the-big or festival (of) the-Sacrifice.
   J And-what (is) occasion-his?
15 **A** Occasion-his (is) the-pilgrimage and-he he-begins in last day of days (of) the-pilgrimage. And-the-pilgrimage meaning-his (is) that the-people they-travel to Mecca and-they-visit the-Kaaba.
   J And-how they-celebrate/with/-this the-festival?
   A They they-slaughter in-him sacrifice(animal)s.

J   And-what she the-sacrifice(animal)?

20 **A**   The-sacrifice(animal) she (a) sheep (which) they-slaughter-him and-they-eat-him in end (of) the-pilgrimage. And-this (is a) custom with the-Muslims.

J   So-festivals-your (are) two only then?

A   No, in some (of) the-regions they-celebrate/with-/(a)-festival third.

J   And-what he?

25 **A**   He (is) birthday (of) the-Prophet in month (of) Rabii: al-Awwal.

J   Yes, this (is) like (the) festival (of) the-Birth with-us we the-Christians.

Background to text

The Muslim festivals
The main two religious festivals celebrated by all Muslims regardless of sect or country of origin are:

:iid al-fiTr (other names: Lesser Bairam, Ramadan Feast; Ar. **:iid ramaDaan**)
Date: 1st of **Shawwal** (see calendar on page 130).

This is usually a holiday of about three days after the fasting month of Ramadan, during which devout Muslims will let nothing (food, drink or smoke) pass their lips between dawn and sunset. On the first day of the feast there are special prayers in the mosque, and the rest of the holiday is traditionally spent feasting with family and friends. Children usually receive gifts of money from their elders, and best clothes are worn.

As you can imagine, total abstention from food and drink during the day causes considerable physical and moral hardship. If you are in a Muslim country during Ramadan, it is polite to show consideration by not eating and drinking in the presence of local people. As frequently most of the night is taken up with making up for the privations of the day, allowance must be made for people not being on their best form.

:iid al-aDHaa (other names: Korban Bairam; Ar. **:iid al-DaHiyya**)
Date: 10th of **Dhu al-Hijja** (see calendar on page 130).

This is the major feast of Islam and again merits a holiday of several days. Even for those not on the Pilgrimage, a large feast is expected, and families who can afford it buy and slaughter a sheep, feast on it with the family, and often give some of the meat to the poor. Again there are special prayers in the mosque and children receive gifts.

Another festival is **mawlid an-nabii** (often pronounced **muulid**) Date: 12th of **Rabii: al-Awwal**

Although not officially prescribed by Islam, this festival is celebrated in varying local forms in many parts of the Arab world.

What to say at festival times

Perhaps the most universal greeting to be exchanged at religious festivals is:

عيدك مبارك **:iidak mubaarak** *May your festival be blessed*

Reply:

الله يبارك فيك **allaah yubaarik fiik** *God bless you*

Another common one, also used on occasions like birthdays, is:

كلّ عام وأنت بخير **kull :aam wa-anta bi-khayr** literally *Every year and (may) you (be) in good (health)* – reminiscent of English 'Many happy returns'. The reply to this is:

وأنت بخير **wa-anta bi-khayr** *And (may) you (be) in-good (health)*

Nowadays the greetings card industry has penetrated the Near and Middle East, so cards are often sent, usually bearing one of the above phrases.

The Islamic calendar

Although not now used much for everyday affairs, the Islamic calendar still governs all religious occasions. The years are reckoned from 16 July 622 AD, the date of the Flight (**hijra**) of the Prophet Muhammad from Mecca to Medina. For this reason, Islamic dates are designated **hijrii** – English abbreviation AH.

The year consists of twelve lunar months adding up to only 354 days, and consequently AH dates are subject to a shift of approximately eleven days forward in comparison to European dates. A good reference is the Muslim year 1400, which ran from 20 November 1979 to 8 November 1980 (leap year).

The European months used in most business transactions and everyday affairs are quite recognisable. Here is a comparative calendar, but remember that because of the shorter Muslim year you cannot say that, for instance, January *equals* **muHarram** – only that both are the first months in their respective calendars.

Arabic abbreviations are ه for هجري **hijrii** and م for ميلادي **miilaadii**, i.e. 'pertaining to the birth' (of Christ):

١٤٠٠ ه 1400 AH   ١٩٨٠ م 1980 AD

الشهر العربي	الشهر الميلادى		الشهر العربي	الشهر الميلادى	
رَجَب	يولْيو	٧	مُحَرَّم	يَناير	١
شَعْبان	أَغُسْطُس	٨	صَفَر	فبراير	٢
رَمَضان	سبْتَمْبر	٩	رَبيع الأَوَّل	مارس	٣
شَوّال	أُكْتوبر	١٠	رَبيع الثاني	أبريل	٤
ذُو القَعْدَة	نُوفِمْبِر	١١	جُمادَى الأُولَى	مايو	٥
ذُو الحِجّة	دِيسِمْبِر	١٢	جُمادَى الآخرة	يونْيو	٦

To complicate matters, there is another set of names for the months of the Christian year, starting with **kaanuun al-thaanii** – Kanun the Second – used in the Eastern Arab world, such as Iraq. Perhaps you had better wait to learn that until you get to Iraq.

Analysis of text and grammar

This section should be studied in conjunction with the Arabic text. Figures refer to line numbers.

1 المسلمين   Suffix masculine plural showing the genitive case because it is the *owner* part of a possessive.

2 كم   For this and other question words, see pp. 132–4. The accusative indefinite marker on **:iid** is required by **kam**.

عند المسلمين   *with the Muslims*, i.e. 'the Muslims have'. See section on 'to have' below. مسلمين is again in the genitive after **:ind**, which is a preposition (see page 102).

3 Note the inanimate plural (**a:yaad**) qualified by *feminine singular* adjective.

4 Note the dual pronoun هما referring to the *two* festivals.

5 Thematic type sentence (see page 136).

7 أوّل يوم – you would probably have expected اليوم الأوّل , which is also possible but less common. شهر شوّال is technically a possessive. **shahr**, being the 'property' word of the possessive, cannot take the definite article.

9 أنَّ is the conjunction 'that' and is used in exactly the same way as **'inna**, i.e. it is followed by a noun or a pronoun suffix (see page 92).

11 معناه   – remember that the final long a-vowel written with a *yaa'* reverts to the normal *alif* if anything – here a pronoun suffix – is added to the word (see page 21). يأكلون and يشربون are plural verbs agreeing fully with their subject الناس because it has preceded them (see page 80).

15-16 آخر يوم is the same construction as used with أوّل in line 7. 'Last day of the days of the Pilgrimage' is a bit picturesque in English, but quite normal in Arabic.

يسافرون and يزورون are plural verbs, because the subject *precedes* the verb.

يزورون – we have already encountered this type of verb, called by the Arabs the 'hollow' verb, because the middle root letter is a *w* (as in this case) or a *y* and tends to disappear, leaving an empty space in the middle. There are three types of this classification, all set out and discussed in Table 5. Learn as much of that as you can now –

at least how to recognise the type, then you can look them up as they occur. We have already had كان of the w-type, and صار which is a y-type. Like all verbs, the hollows occur most frequently in the *he* and *she* forms, and these are both recognisable by the long vowels which occur between the first and third radicals – always **aa** in the past tense, but **uu**, **ii** and more rarely **aa** in the present.

17   The verb يحتفل   *to celebrate*, although transitive in English, always requires the preposition ب before its object in Arabic. With such verbs, it is best to learn the required preposition along with the verb, as the two always occur together.

18   Note the use of **fii** *in* where we would say *on*. Prepositions are always difficult.

20   For the moment, supply the word 'which' between 'sheep' and 'they slaughter it' – i.e. 'A sheep which they slaughter and eat'. Such constructions, called relative clauses, will be explained later.

هذا عادة   you should recognise as a sentence because there is no definite article on **:aada** (and anyway **haadha** is the wrong gender – it refers to the preceding sentence as a whole) – see pp. 53–4.

22 فقط   *only* always follows what it qualifies.

23   يحتفلون   is plural here because no subject has been stated, and therefore must be made clear by the verb (subject is 'they').

26   The نحن here is for emphasis or clarity.

EXERCISE 11.1 Read aloud the Arabic text at the beginning of this Unit, and then translate it into normal, idiomatic English.

Question words

Note that these differ from the question-*mark* words given on page 40 which merely change statements into questions. These marker words are not required when the sentence contains one of the following interrogatives.

What?   There are two words for this: ما used before nouns, separate pronouns and demonstratives, and ماذا before verbs. (Warning: ما is one of the most difficult words in Arabic, having many different usages. We have already seen it – on page 82 – as a negative marker for the past verb, so be careful.) Examples:

ما هو ؟   *What is it (he)?*   ما هذا ؟   *What is this?*

ما اسمه ؟   *What is his (its) name?*

But ماذا أكلوا ؟   *What did they eat ?*

ماذا يحمل ؟   *What is he carrying?*

Note also the appositional construction in the text, using a separate pronoun followed by a noun:

ما هي الذبيحة ؟   *What (is) she, the sacrifice(animal)?*

This is very common. (We would say 'What is *a* sacrifice animal?')

Who?   Only one word, مَنْ, is used before verbs and nouns. It looks very similar to مِنْ *from*, so be careful.

مَن فتح الباب ؟   *Who opened the door?*   مَن هم ؟   *Who are they?*

Also used appositionally, e.g.

مَن هو المدير ؟   *Who is the manager?*

Which? أيّ (feminine أيّة) agrees with the noun in gender.

أيّة بنت ؟   *Which girl?*   أيّ بيت ؟   *Which house?*

The noun after أيّ is singular, indefinite and technically genitive.

How many? كَم Be careful with this one. Its noun is *singular* (!) and in the *indefinite accusative*, so if it is an unsuffixed noun it takes the final *alif* accusative marker (see page 88).

كم سيّارة ؟   *How many cars?*   كم رجلا ؟   *How many men?*

How? كَيفْ is used with nouns and verbs:

كيف الأولاد ؟ *How did you*   كيف سافرت ؟ *How are the*
                travel?   *children?*

Where? أَيْنَ Note also إِلَى أَيْن *Where to?*, and مِن أين *Where from?*

When? مَتَى With verbs:

متي رجعوا ؟ *When did they return?*

Why? لِمَ and لإذا٠are combinations of the preposition لِ *to, for*
and the words given for 'what?' above. When the shorter form ما is
used in such combinations, it is contracted to مَ . Note also the
assimilated form مِـمّا (مِن ما) *From what?*.

EXERCISE 11.2   Interrogatives and interpretation

A   Write down the answers to the following questions on the text
in the form of complete sentences.

١   كيف يحتفل المسلمون بعيد الأضحى ؟

٢   في أيّ شهر عيد الفطر ؟

٣   إلى أين يسافر المسلمون في أيّام الحجّ ؟

٤   ما معنى الصوم ؟   ٥   ما هو العيد الثالث ؟

B   Provide questions which would elicit the following answers.

Example: Answer أذهب الى السينا *I am going to the cinema*
          Question الى أين تذهب ؟ *Where are you going?*

٢ اسمي أحمد		١ يأكلون خبزا	
٤ يسافر في شهر يناير		٣ نفتح الباب بالمفتاح	
٦ هي فاطمة (Fatima, female name)		٥ عندهم بيتان	
٨ شهر شوّال يعقب شهر رمضان		٧ هذا الكتاب من البحرين	
١٠ يشتغل في مصنع السيارات		٩ أقرأ الجريدة في الصباح	

How to say 'to have'

There is no Arabic verb 'to have' and this meaning must be expressed by the use of the prepositions عند *with* (French '*chez*') or لِ *to, for*. Note that the *object* of the English verb – i.e. the thing which you have – becomes the *subject* of the Arabic sentence.

He has a new car ⟶ To him (is) a new car

له سيّارة جديدة

To change the tense, the verb كان must be used:

The boy had a book ⟶ (There) was to the boy (with the boy) a book

كان للولد (عند الولد) كتاب

In the feminine:

We had a fridge ⟶ (There) was to us (with us) a fridge

كانت لنا (عندنا) ثلّاجة

For the future, the *present* tense of the verb 'to be' with the future prefix **sa-** is used:

You will have a guest tomorrow ⟶ (There) will be with you a guest tomorrow.

سيكون عندكم ضيف غدا

The following table shows the process schematically. Note that although *to* – representing the Arabic li- – has been used, in most cases **:ind** *with* would do equally well.

Present	*English*		X	has	Y
	Arabic	To	X	—	Y
Past	*English*		X	had	Y
	Arabic	Was/were to	X	—	Y
Future	*English*		X	will have	Y
	Arabic	Will be to	X	—	Y

'X has Y' (present tense) is negated by the use of the negative verb **laysa** (see page 90), and the other two tenses by applying the relevant negative particles to the verb (see pp. 118–19).

EXERCISE 11.3   'To have'

A   Form sentences of the *X has Y* type from the following constituents, e.g.

The boy, a book ——→ To/with the boy (is) a book ——→

للولد كتاب *The boy has a book*

(Use either **li-** or **:ind** in all cases):

1   The manager, a new secretary (f).   2   The house, two doors.
3   We, a small car.   4   She, beautiful sister.
5   The cupboard, many shelves.
6   The company, a branch in London.   7   He, a new suit.
8   They (m), meat and bread.   9   Ahmed, a small baby.
10   The passenger, a heavy suitcase.

B   Change A 1–5 into the past tense (X had Y)

C   Change A 6-10 into the future (X will have Y).

Thematic sentences

Note the following examples from the text:

الأوّل هو العيد الصغير	*The first is the Lesser Festival*
الصوم معناه أنّ . . .	*Fasting means that* ... (Lit. 'its meaning is that...')
هم يذبحون ذبائح	*They slaughter animals* ...

These illustrate a very common type of Arabic sentence which often sounds strange to the European ear. In each case a *theme* is set at the beginning – always a noun or a pronoun (The first; Fasting; They, in the examples). This theme is what the information contained in the ensuing sentence is really about, although it is not necessarily the grammatical subject of the sentence. The remainder of the sentence then follows, and always contains a *referent* pointing back to the theme, and agreeing with it grammatically. If you examine these predicates carefully, you will find that they are in fact complete Arabic sentences on their own. This is easily demonstrated if you simply chop off the first word (the theme word) of the examples above.

In the first example the referent is the separate pronoun هو , referring to the (masculine singular) theme الأوّل *The first (thing)*. In the second it is the masculine singular suffix pronoun ـه , referring to الصوم, and in the third it is the subject pronoun implicit in the verb يذبحون *they slaughter* (see page 78). A literal translation shows up the construction clearly:

> The first (one), *he* is the Lesser Festival
> The fasting, *his* meaning is ...
> They, *they*-slaughter animals.

Note again how each predicate forms a complete, potentially independent sentence.

In English, of course, such constructions would be considered redundant, but in Arabic they are regarded as good style. Appreciation of the problem, and the application of the literal translation method, will help you to unravel many an apparently complex Arabic sentence.

EXERCISE 11.4

A Change the following into thematic sentences, e.g.

للمدير مكتب كبير ←——— المدير له مكتب كبير

١ عند المسلمين عيد مهم في شهر شوّال

٢ للأمير بيوت في الرياض ولندن ونيو يورك (New York)

٣ للمصريين عيد في شهر أبريل اسمه شم (**Shamm al-Nasim**, an Egyptian
النسيم festival)

٤ للسفير سيارة كبيرة جدًّا   ٥ ليست للحكومة سياسة جيّدة

B Read aloud and translate your answers.

Unit Twelve

١   عصر البترول

شهد العالم الغربي في القرن الماضي ثورة عظيمة هي الثورة الصناعية .
واعتمدت المصانع الجديدة على موارد معدنية أكثرها موجودة في أوربّا
مثل الفحم والحديد .

٥   ولذلك كانت البلاد الغربية مستقلّة الى حدّ ما .
ولكن في سنة ١٨٧٦ اخترع المهندس الالماني المشهور نيكولاس أوتّو آلة من
نوع جديد ، هي آلة الاحتراق الداخلي .
وكان وقود هذه الآلة العجيبة هو البنزين .
والبنزين من منتجات البترول .

١٠   وكما تعرف ، ليس في أوربّا من مصادر البترول الّا قليلا في بحر الشمال .
وأكثر المصادر هي في بلاد الشرق الأوسط كالمملكة العربية السعودية
والعراق وليبيا ودول الخليج العربي كالكويت وقطر والامارات العربية
المتّحدة .
وهكذا بدأت أوربّا تعتمد لحدّ كبير على الاستيراد من العالم الاسلامي .

١٥   وقد ازداد اعتماد البلاد الاوربّية هذا على العرب كثيرا خلال النصف الأوّل
من القرن العشرين .
وارتفع ثمن البترول ارتفاعا كبيرا في السبعينات من هذا القرن وأصبحت
صورة الشيخ زكي يماني صورة مألوفة على شاشة التلفزيون الأوربّي .
وقد خلق عصر البترول هذا علاقات قوية بين أهل الغرب والشعوب
٢٠   العربية .
ومن نتائج هذه العلاقات اهتمام الأوربّيين بلغة العرب وثقافتهم ودينهم
الاسلامي .

Vocabulary

Nouns

عَصْر (عُصور)	age, era		بِترول ، نَفْط	crude oil
عالَم	world		قَرْن (قُرون)	century
ثَوْرة (ـات)	revolution		مَوْرِد (مَوارِد)	resource
أُورُبّا	Europe		فَحْم	coal, charcoal
حَديد	iron		حَدّ (حُدود)	limit, extent; (pl) frontier
بَلَد (بِلاد)	country		آلة (آلات)	engine, machine
نَوْع (أَنْواع)	kind, type		اِحْتِراق	combustion
وَقود	fuel		بَنْزين	petrol
مُنْتَجات	products		مَصْدَر (مَصادِر)	source
بَحْر (بِحار)	sea		الشَرْق الأَوْسَط	the Middle East
الشَمال	North		الجَنوب	South
الشَرْق	East		الغَرْب	West
مَمْلكة (مَمالِك)	kingdom		العِراق	Iraq
لِيبيا	Libya		دَوْلة (دُوَل)	state, nation
خَليج (خُلْجان)	gulf		قَطَر	Qatar
إمارة	Emirate		اِسْتيراد	importation
اِعْتِماد	dependence		عِشْرون	twenty
ثَمَن (أَثْمان)	price		اِرْتِفاع	rise, increase
السَبْعِينات	the Seventies		صُورة (صُوَر)	picture, photograph

شَيْخ (شُيوخ)	sheikh	زَكي يَماني	*Zaki Yamani*
شاشة (ـات)	screen	عَلاقة (ـات)	relationship, connection
أَهْل ...	people of ...	شَعْب (شُعوب)	people
نَتيجة (نَتائِج)	result	اِهْتِمام	interest, concern
ثِقافة (ـات)	culture	دين (أَدْيان)	faith, religion

Verbs

شَهِد (a) witness		اِعْتَمَد عَلَى ، يَعْتَمِد على (VIII) depend on	
اِخْتَرَع ، يَخْتَرِع (VIII) invent		اِزْداد ، يَزْداد (VIII) increase	
اِرْتَفَع ، يَرْتَفِع (VIII) rise, go up		خَلَق (u) create	

Adjectives

غَرْبيّ	western	ماضِي	past (definite form)
صِناعيّ	industrial	مَعْدَنيّ	mineral
أَكْثَر	most	مَوْجود	existing, available
مُسْتَقِلّ	independent	أَلْمَانيّ	German
داخِليّ	internal, interior	سَعُوديّ	Saudi
قَوِيّ (أَقْوِياء)	strong	عَجيب	wonderful
مُتَّحِد	united	إسْلاميّ	Islamic
مَأْلوف	familiar	أُورُبّيّ	European

Other words

الى حدّ ما	*to a certain extent*	لِذٰلِكَ	*because of this, so*
لٰكِنْ ، وَلٰكِن	*but*	كَمَا	*as (Lit. 'like what')*
هٰكَذا	*thus*	خِلال	*during*
بَيْن	*between*		
كَثِيراً	*much, greatly, a lot*	كَـ	*like*

Literal translation

Age (of) the-oil

1 Witnessed the-world the-western in the-century the-past (a) revolution, she the-revolution the-industrial.

And-depended the-factories the-new on resources mineral most-(of)-them existing in Europe like the-coal and the-iron.

5 Because-of-this were the-countries the-western independent' to a-certain-extent.

But in year 1876 invented the-engineer the-German the-famous Nikolaus Otto (a) machine of kind new, she engine (of) the-combustion the-internal. And-was (the) fuel (of) this the-engine the-wonderful he the-petrol. And-the-petrol (is) of the-products (of) the-oil.

10 And-like-what you-know, is-not in Europe of sources (of) the-oil except few in Sea (of) the-North.

And-most (of) the-sources she in countries (of) the-East the-Middle like-the-Kingdom the-Arab the-Saudi and-the-Iraq and-Libya and-states (of) the-Gulf the-Arabian like-the-Kuwait and-Qatar and-the-Emirates the-Arab the-United.

And-thus began Europe she-depends to-extent great on the-importation from-the-world the-Islamic.

15 And/*past marker*/increased dependence (of) the-countries the-European on the-Arabs much during the-half the-first of the-century the-twenty.

And-rose price (of) the-oil rising great in the-seventies of this the-century and became picture (of) the-sheikh Zaki Yamani (a) picture familiar on screen (of) the-television the-European.

And-created age (of) the-oil this relationships strong between people (of) the-West and the-peoples the-Arab.

And-of results (of) these relationships (is) concern (of) the-Europeans with-language (of) the-Arabs and-culture-their and-religion-their the-Islamic.

Background to text

The dependence of the West on Middle Eastern oil, and the business opportunities which stimulate travel between Europe and the Arab countries, need no explanation.

Note that **bitrool** (a more usual pronunciation than official **bitruul**), although obviously derived from English 'petrol', means crude oil, not the refined product. Also given in the vocabulary is **nafT** (cf. naphtha).

The word **shaykh** has many connotations in Arabic – none of them the desert romancer as played by Rudolf Valentino in the early days of the cinema. In most countries it means either a tribal chief or dignitary, or a religious leader or teacher.

Analysis of text and grammar

2 الغربيّ – an adjective formed from the noun الغرب *the West*. See section on page 145 on relative adjectives. الماضي *the past*, although it looks superficially the same, is a completely different sort of word altogether, being derived from the root **m-D-y**. There are quite a number of such words in Arabic, usually characterised by a long a-vowel before the final consonant, and their spelling presents some difficulty. Take the exampleالقاضي/*the judge*. The final *y* of this word is omitted when it is indefinite – قاض (officially pronounced **qaaDin**) – except in the accusative where it reappears along with the usual *alif*-marker, thus: قاضيا (officially **qaaDiyan**). In speech the word is pronounced **qaaDii**, whether with the definite article or not, and the only real difficulty of such words is remembering the presence of the final *y* when looking them up in a dictionary.

هي is used here to separate the two revolution phrases. In English we would use a comma or a hyphen.

3 اعتمد is a so-called Form VIII verb, characterised by the introduction of a -*t*- between the first and second consonants of the root (here **:-m-d**). When composed of all sound letters (i.e. no *w*'s or *y*'s) these, like all derived verbs, present no particular difficulty as they take all the usual prefixes and suffixes to form their tenses – study Table 2. There are quite a few examples of Form VIII verbs in this text – also of its verbal noun. See if you can pick them out.

معدني is an adjective from معدن *metal, mineral* (see page 145).

أكثر is a superlative adjective; see section on page 146.

4 الفحم ، الحديد Note that, when referring to the whole of a class of things, Arabic uses the definite article. We would say 'coal and iron' not 'the coal and the iron'.

5 الى حدّ ما introduces yet another meaning of this ubiquitous word **maa**. Here it means 'a certain'.

6 سنة – ة is pronounced here, because 'year' is regarded in Arabic as the property part of a possessive (see page 61), the owner part being the number.

١٨٧٦ – the Arabic numerals are very difficult, and all but the most pedantic of Arabs would revert to the colloquial form, something like **'alf thamaaniya mi'a sitta wa-sab:iin** (a-thousand eight hundred six and-seventy). Remember the numerals are written *from left to right*. See also Appendix 2.

اخترع is another Form VIII verb. Consult Table 2.

نيكولاس أوتّو– there is no real standard way to spell non-Arabic names. The general tendency is to use lots of long vowels to make clear the pronunciation of the unfamiliar word-shapes.

7 احتراق is another Form VIII verbal noun. Note the shape.

9 من – a very common usage. We would say 'one of'.

10 قليلا – the accusative marker is caused by الّا *except* which requires this case.

11 كالمملكة – prefixed **ka-** meaning 'like, such as'. Technically it requires the genitive case.

12 العراق ، ليبيا – note that some countries have the definite article and some do not. Learn the names as they come.

14 بدأت . . . تعتمد – note this auxiliary verb construction carefully. The auxiliary verb (here بدأت *began*) comes first, and can be in either tense, according to meaning, but the main verb (here تعتمد *depend*) is *always in the present*, regardless of the time-scale.

15 أزداد – this is the Form VIII from a hollow stem, also showing the assimilation of the *-t-* to a *-d-* after the *z* of the root, and is just about as awkward an Arabic verb as you can get. Study Form VIII and the Hollow Verb in the relevant tables.

كثيرا is an indefinite accusative adjective used as an adverb. See page 148.

16 العشرين means literally 'the twenty'. There are no ordinals for the tens in Arabic. See Appendix 2.

17 ارتفاعا كبيرا *a great rising*. Use of the verbal noun after its own verb is very common in Arabic. Without a qualifying adjective it is used for emphasis; with an adjective, as here, it is adverbial (see section on adverbs on page 148). Compare the Biblical 'they rejoiced a great rejoicing' which mirrors the same construction in Hebrew.

19 عصر البترول هذا *this oil age* (age of oil). **haadha** has to follow the possessive phrase because it qualifies the whole thing.

أهل is rather a difficult word to explain. It means 'people' or 'family', but is practically always the first part of a possessive phrase, i.e. the people of something or other, meaning the devotees, followers, those pertaining to, and so on. شعب is the standard word for a people or a populace.

21 ... لغة العرب وثقافتهم – because the possessive in Arabic is expressed by the *juxtaposition* (i.e. placing next to each other) of two nouns, or a noun and a pronoun-suffix, the possession of more than one thing must be rendered as here, 'the language of the Arabs, and their culture, and their ...'. We would say, 'the language, culture, ... etc., of the Arabs'.

EXERCISE 12.1 Read the Arabic text aloud and translate it into idiomatic English.

EXERCISE 12.2 Answer the following questions on the text in complete sentences:

١ متى شهد العالم الغربي ثورة عظيمة ؟

٢ ما هي الموارد المعدنية الموجودة في أوربّا ؟

٣ ماذا اخترع نيكولاس أوتّو ؟ وفي أيّة سنة ؟

٤ هل في أوربّا مصادر كثيرة من البترول ؟

٥ ما هي نتائج العلاقات القوية بين أهل الغرب والشعوب العربية ؟

Forming adjectives from nouns

These so-called relative adjectives are formed from nouns to describe persons or things associated with the noun in some way. English has a variety of suffixes to express such a relationship (England–English; America–American; heaven–heavenly; gold–golden etc.) but Arabic has only one, the ending **-iyy**, usually pronounced simply **-ii**. The doubling sign *shadda* is not consistently marked in Arabic script and printing, however. There are plenty of examples in the text, e.g. غرّبيّ ، معدني etc. See if you can pick out the rest.

Rules
1   The adjective ending is ـيّ (f ـيّة). It takes the suffix plural **-uun/-iin** (m) and **-aat** (f), unless it is applied to a collective word like عرب *Arabs*, in which case the masculine plural simply reverts to the collective form, e.g. المهندسون العرب *the Arab engineers*.
2   Before applying it to a word, it is usual to drop:

   (a)   the definite article, if present, e.g. العراق *Iraq* – عراقيّ *Iraqi*
   (b)   the feminine ending, e.g. صناعة *industry* – صناعيّ *industrial*
   (c)   some other endings, e.g. أمريكا *America* – أمريكيّ *American*

Some words change their internal vowelling before adding the suffix, but these will be noted as they occur, e.g. مدينة *town, city* مَدَنيّ *urban*.

Note that since all Arabic adjectives can be freely used as nouns, adjectives of nationality can also be used to apply to the nationals themselves, e.g.

إنجليزيّ *English* or *Englishman*.

EXERCISE 12.3   Transformation: relative adjectives

Work out the relative adjectives and alter the following sentences as shown in the example:

Muhammad is from Kuwait ⟶ He is a Kuwaiti

محمّد من الكويت ← هو كويتي

١   أحمد من مِصْر (Egypt)   ٢   فاطمة من قطر

٣   جون من أمريكا   ٤   المدرّسون من لُبْنان (Lebanon)

٥   المدرّسات من فَرَنْسا (France)   ٦   الأولاد من الأُرْدُن (Jordan)

٧   المدير من ليبيا   ٨   المهندسون من الكويت

٩   عبد اللّه (Abdullah) من العراق   ١٠   السائق من اليَمَن (Yemen)

Comparative and superlative adjectives

Comparatives in English usually end in -*er* (bigger, longer) and superlatives in -*est* (smallest, shortest). In Arabic the two have identical form, but are distinguishable in the way they are used.

For simple, three-letter adjectives, the comparative/superlative is formed by applying the word-shape '$aC^1C^2aC^3$. This shape does not show the indefinite accusative marker:

كبير   (root k-b-r)   أَكْبَر   *bigger, biggest*

واسع   (root w-s-:)   أَوْسَع   *more spacious, most spacious*

Roots which have identical second and third consonants adopt a slightly different shape, '$aC^1aC^2C^3$:

جديد   (root j-d-d)   أَجَدّ   *newer, newest*

قليل   (root q-l-l)   أَقَلّ   *fewer, fewest*

Roots which have a weak third consonant (*w* or *y*) take the shape 'aC^1C^2aa, with the final long a-vowel written in the form of a *yaa*':

حُلْو   (root H-l-w)   أَحْلَى   *sweeter, sweetest*

ذكي   (root dh-k-y)   أَذْكَى   *more intelligent, most intelligent*

Adjectives of more complex shape cannot generally be fitted into those patterns and use a different construction.

Use of the comparative: 'X is ——er than Y'
The comparative is the same for all numbers and genders, and
'than' is expressed by مِن (**min**):

آسيا أكبر من أوربّا   *Asia is bigger than Europe.*

النساء أذكى من الرجال   *Women are shrewder than men.*

بيته أصغر من بيتي   *His house is smaller than mine (my house).*

Use of the superlative: 'X is the —— est'
There are three ways to express the superlative:

1   By placing the *'aCCaC* form of the adjective directly before the
indefinite singular noun:

هو أطول ولد في المدرسة   *He is the tallest boy in the school.*

هي أجمل بنت في الغرفة   *She is the most beautiful girl
in the room.*

Note again that the adjective does not vary according to
gender. This is probably the most frequently occurring superlative construction.

2   By using the *'aCCaC* form of the adjective as a noun in a
possessive construction with the plural of the qualified noun
(technically, of course, in the genitive):

أكبر البيوت   (lit. 'The biggest of the houses') *The biggest
house*

أصغر المدن   (The smallest of towns) *The smallest town*

3   As a simple defined adjective following its noun in the usual
way:

القائد الأعظم   *The mightiest leader*

When used in this way, a few common adjectives have a form
used for feminine agreement. The shape is $C^1uC^2C^3aa$ (*-aa* again

spelled with a *yaa'*), and the most common adjectives which take it are:

أكبر   كبرى   *biggest*

أصغر   صغرى   *smallest*

أعظم   عظمى   *mightiest*.

When used as a normal adjective like this, the force of the superlative is usually lost, e.g.

بريطانيا العظمى   *Great Britain*

EXERCISE 12.4   Comparative/superlative: translation
Translate the following sentences into English.

١   هذا الباب أعرض من ذلك

٢   القاهرة أكبر مدينة في العالم العربي

٣   كانت سيّارة المدير أجمل السيّارات وأسرعها

٤   الخبز أرخص من اللحم

٥   اللغة العربية أصعب من اللغة الانجليزية واللغة الفرنسية أسهل اللغات

٦   المَغْرِب (Morocco) أقرب البلاد العربية وأبعدها هي اليمن

٧   أكثر البترول موجود في الشرق الأوسط

٨   فستانها من أرخص الفساتين

٩   هذه الرواية من أغرب الروايات الانجليزية

١٠   كانت الشنطة أثقل من الصندوق الصغير

Adverbs

English forms most adverbs from adjectives by the addition of the suffix -*ly* (quick-quickly, slow-slowly). Arabic has no such facility, and commonly employs one of the two following methods.

1   The use of the masculine adjective in the indefinite accusative, e.g.

ذهب سريعا   *he went off quickly*

The accusative ending is usually pronounced in these cases (**sarii:an**). This construction is derived from the Arabic linguistic habit of using verbs with their own verbal noun, noted in line 17 of the text analysis, e.g.

ذهب ذهابا سريعا   *he went a quick going*

The verbal noun is then dropped, leaving behind the agreeing adjective.

2   The use of preposition-noun phrases. The preposition is usually **bi-**, so the English 'with speed' becomes **bi-sur:a** in Arabic:

ذهب بسرعة   *he went off with speed* (quickly)

Unit Thirteen

١ الفتوح الإسلامية

موطن العرب الأصلي هو الجزيرة العربية

وبعد ظهور الاسلام فتحت جنود العرب كثيرا من البلاد المجاورة كسوريا والعراق

٥ وفي افريقيا فتحوا بلاد الساحل الشمالي كلّها من مصر الى المغرب الاقصى

وحكموا اسبانيا مدّة اربع مائة سنة الى أن طردتهم القوات المسيحية في سنة ١٤٩٢

ويبلغ عدد الدول العربية اليوم ثماني عشرة حوالى مائة وثلاثين مليونا

١٠ ويستخدم أهالي تلك البلاد العديدة اللغة العربية في حياتهم اليومية وفي أعمالهم وفي عبادتهم

وسبب انتشار اللغة العربية هذا هو ظهور الاسلام

فالعرب لم يكن لهم شأن عظيم قبله

وذلك أنّ الله أنزل القرآن الكريم على رسوله محمّد باللغة العربية وأمره بأن

١٥ يبشّر قومه بالدين الجديد

وكان ذلك في مكّة التي كان أهلها يعبدون الاصنام

وكان بعض أكابر مكّة يكرهون النبي والرسالة التي جاء بها

ولذلك هاجر الرسول الى المدينة في سنة ٦٢٢

وبعد ثماني سنوات رجع محمّد وأنصاره من المدينة الى مكّة وفتحوها

٢٠ وقد مات النبي في المدينة في سنة ٦٣٢ وواصل خلفاؤه من بعده حركة الفتح

وقد بلغت الجيوش المسلمة في مدّة ثمانين سنة حدود أوربّا

وكان ذلك أساس الامبراطورية الاسلامية التي انحدرت منها البلاد العربية المعاصرة .

Vocabulary

Nouns

فَتْح (فُتوح) conquest

مَوْطِن (مَواطِن) homeland

عَرَب Arabs

جَزيرة (جَزائِر) island; peninsula

ظُهُور appearance

الإسْلام Islam

جُنْدِيّ (جنود) soldier

سورْيا Syria

اِفْريقيا Africa

المَغْرِب الأقْصَى Morocco (Lit. 'the farthest West')

ساحِل (سَواحِل) coast

اِسْبانيا Spain

مُدّة (مُدَد) period, time

مائة (مِئَات)* hundred

قُوّة (ـات) strength: pl. forces

عَدَد (أعْداد) number

ساكِن (سُكّان) inhabitant

ثَلاثون thirty

رِسَالة (رَسَائِل) message; essay

عَمَل (أعْمال) work

عِبَادَة worship

سَبَب (أسْباب) cause, reason

اِنْتِشَار spread, spreading

شأن (شُئُون) matter, affair; importance

القُرآن the Koran

رَسول (رُسُل) messenger; Messenger (of God) – the Prophet

قَوْم (أقْوَام) people

صَنَم (أصْنام) idol

أكَابِر great men, notables

المَدِينة Medina

أنْصَار Helpers (see notes)

خَليفة (خُلَفاء) Caliph

حَرَكة (ـات) movement

جَيْش (جيُوش) army

ثَمَانُون eighty

حُدود border, frontier

*irregular spelling in singular; pronounced **mi'a**

أَساس (أُسُس)‏ basis   مَلْيُون (مَلايِين)‏ million

اِمْبراطُورية empire   حَياة life

Adjectives

كُلّ each, every, all (see notes)   أَصْليّ original

بَعْض some (see notes)   مُجاوِر neighbouring

مُعاصِر contemporary   شَماليّ northern

كَرِيم noble, generous (when applied to the Koran 'holy')   عَدِيد numerous

Verbs

حَكَم (u) rule, govern   فَتَح (a) open; conquer

بَلَغ (u) reach   طَرَد (u) expel

أَنْزَل ، يُنْزِل (IV) send down, reveal   اِسْتَخْدَم ، يَسْتَخْدِم (X) employ

عَبَد (u) worship   أَمَر (u) order, command

واصَل ، يُواصِل (III) continue   مَات ، يَمُوت die

     اِنْحَدَر مِنْ ، يَنْحَدِر مِن (VII) descend from

بَشَّر ، يُبَشِّر (II) preach, propagate   جَاء ، يَجِيء come

كَرِه (a) hate   جَاء بِـ ، يَجِيء بِـ come with, i.e. bring

هَاجَر ، يُهَاجِر (III) migrate

Other words

أَنْ	that (conjunction)	اَلَّذِى	
اَلْيَوْم	today	اَلَّتِي	who, which (see notes)
حَوَالِي	about, approximately	اَلَّذِينَ	

Literal translation

1 **The-conquests the-Islamic**

(The) homeland (of) the-Arabs the-original he (is) the-peninsula the-Arabian. And-after (the) appearance (of) the-Islam conquered (the) soldiers (of) the-Arabs many of the-countries the-neighbouring like-Syria and-Iraq.

5 And-in Africa they-conquered (the) countries (of) the-coast the-northern all-them from Egypt to the-West the-furthest (i.e. Morocco).

And-they-ruled Spain (for the) period (of) four hundred year to that (i.e. until) expelled-them the-forces the-Christian in (the) year 1492. And-reaches (the) number (of) the-nations the-Arab today eight ten (18) and-their-inhabitants (are) about hundred and-thirty million. And-employ (the) people (of) those the-countries the-language the-Arabic in their-life the-daily and-in their-jobs and-in their-worship. And-(the)-reason (of) spread (of) the-language the-Arabic this (i.e. 'this spread of the Arabic language') he (is the) appearance (of) the-Islam. And-the-Arabs not was to-them importance great before-it.

14 And-that (is) that God revealed the-Koran the-Holy upon his-Messenger Muhammad in-the-language the-Arabic and-ordered-him/with/-that he-preach his-people/with/-the-religion the-new.

And-was that in Mecca which was her-people they-worship the-idols ('whose people were worshipping ...').

And-was some (of the) great-men (of) Mecca they-hate the-Prophet and-the-message which he-came with-it ('brought').

And-for-that migrated the-Messenger to Medina in year 622.

And-after eight years returned Muhammad and-his-Helpers from Medina to Mecca and-they-conquered-her.

20 And-/*past marker*/died the-Prophet in Medina in year 632 and-continued his-Caliphs/from/after-him (the) movement (of) the-conquest. And-/*past marker*/reached-the-armies the-Muslim in period (of) eighty year (the) borders (of) Europe.

And-was that (the) basis (of) the-Empire the-Islamic which descended from-it the-countries the-Arab the-contemporary.

Background to text

The role of Islam (accented on the *second* syllable) in the history of the Arabs cannot be overstated. This is for a number of reasons, but perhaps principally because it was from the outset a national *Arab* religion, whose vehicle was the *Arabic* language. The Prophet Muhammad founded the religion on the basis of the Koran, which he claimed was revealed to him direct from God (in Arabic), and is therefore the actual *word of God* – not a creation of man.

As indicated in the text, this religious innovation was not received favourably by some of the powerful families in Muhammad's native Mecca, and he was eventually obliged to flee to Medina where his movement gathered strength, culminating in his conquest of Mecca eight years later. From then on the religious fervour and conquesting zeal of the new Islamic state – for religious and temporal affairs were always inexorably linked in Islam – led the Arabs to colonise a large part of the earth's surface within comparatively few years. The events mentioned in the text ignore the expansion in the East, which was also considerable.

Religion and conquest gave rise to wealth and influence, and these encouraged the arts to flourish. In fact, leaving aside their own considerable original literature, it is to the Arabs that we owe the preservation of much classical thought throughout the Dark Ages in Europe.

States and empires came and went, but the burning spirit of Islam, intermingled with a fierce national pride in being an Arab and speaking Arabic, remains the unifying force to the present day.

The oil-related events of the twentieth century have given the Arabs great wealth and influence, which have made possible material advancement, education, medical and other social benefits. But the Arabs have taken from the West only what they want. Rather than a process of westernisation, we are seeing now in the last decades of the twentieth century a fierce resurgence of Islamic fundamentalism.

A good general sketch of Islamic history is to be found in Bernard Lewis's *The Arabs in History*. There are numerous books on Islam, and Richard Bell's *Introduction to the Qur'an*, revised by W. Montgomery Watt, provides a good starting point for the understanding of this remarkable document. Some of the most important technical terms of Islam are explained below for convenience.

Islam (الاسلام, always with the definite article), the name of the religion.

Muslim (مسلم), an adherent of Islam. Also less accurately spelled Moslem.

The Prophet (النبي) is the name applied to Muhammad, who never made any claim to divinity. Also referred to as

Messenger or Apostle (of God) (الرسول ، رسول الله)

Allah (الله), not a name, but simply a contracted form of the Arabic word الإله, meaning The God.

Hijra, Hegira (الهجرة) Muhammad's flight from Mecca to Medina in 622, the foundation date of the Islamic calendar.

Ansar (الانصار) The Helpers, those who aided Muhammad during his stay in Medina.

Koran (القرآن with the definite article, pronounced **al-qur'aan**) The divine text of Islam. Usually accompanied by the honorific adjective **kariim**, القرآن الكريم *The Holy Koran.*

Caliph (خليفة), literally 'a successor', the usual name for the head of the various Islamic states which evolved after the death of the Prophet.

Analysis of text and grammar

2 موطن is a 'noun of place' formation, alternative to the ordinary noun وطن (see page 55).

أصلي is an adjective formed from the noun أصل *origin*, qualifying موطن, but having to come after the completed possessive construction.

الجزيرة العربية is the common name for the Arabian Peninsula, as the true term for a peninsula شِبْه جزيرة *the semblance of an island, nearly an island* is too clumsy.

5 شَالي is a relative adjective from الشَّال *the North.*

كلّها means 'all of them' – see page 162.

6 مدّة *for the period of.* No preposition is required in Arabic, and the word is technically in the accusative case. This is the rule for many expressions of time and space in Arabic.

Note the irregular spelling of مائة **mi'a** *hundred.* The ة should be pronounced *t* here because Arabic grammar regards 'hundred' and its noun as constituting a possessive phrase ('hundred of years'). For the usage consult the Numbers Table in Appendix 2.

الى أن *until, up to the point that.* Arabic has a single word for 'until' (حتّى), but it is often avoided as it is thought to imply some element of purpose which is not required here. أن is the conjunction 'that', and is followed by a *verb.* If the following word is to be a noun or a pronoun suffix, the form used is أنّ , with doubled *nuun,* and the following construction is exactly as that used after **'inna** (see page 92). وَلكِنَّ *but* behaves in exactly the same way.

8 ثَماني عشرة – see Appendix 2 and the section on page 164.

وسكّانَها introduces a new sentence.

9 مليونا – the numbers 11 to 99 (inclusive) require the indefinite accusative *singular* of the noun, showing, if unsuffixed, the *alif* accusative marker.

10 يستخدم is a Form X verb. Study Table 2 and learn as much as you can about how these work.

أهالي is the plural of أهل , which behaves in the same way as قاضي *judge.* See page 142, note to line 2.

أهل has already occurred (see page 144, note to line 16). The **ahl** of a man are his family or kin, and the word is also used in more traditional areas as a euphemism for wife, as it is considered bad manners to mention a man's womenfolk directly.

12 هذا refers here to انتشار *spreading,* its position in the sentence being caused by the possessive construction.

13 لم يكن لهم شأن عظيم is an idiom, meaning 'they had no great importance'. The usual meaning of شأن is 'matter, affair'.

14 أنزل is a Form IV verb (see Table 2). God is regarded as having 'caused to descend, sent down' (i.e. revealed) the text of the Koran to the Prophet Muhammad.

وأمره بأن – the verb 'to command, order' in Arabic requires the use of the preposition **bi** before the subordinate clause, here introduced by أن *that* ('ordered him that he should preach ... '). See the comments on line 5 above, where *an* is followed by a past tense verb. When, as here, it is followed by a present tense verb, this must be in the *subjunctive mood*. Consult the Verb Tables for the parts of the subjunctive which differ in writing from those of the normal present tense.

15 يبشّر here shows no written difference for the subjunctive. Note the construction after this verb in Arabic – 'his people' is the direct object and الدين is introduced by the preposition **bi**. قوم is another of the many Arabic words for 'people'. It tends to indicate a national or tribal group.

16 التي is a relative pronoun: see page 159. Note the use of **kaan** with the present tense of another verb (يعبدون) to mean 'they were worshipping; used to worship'.

17 بعض – see section on page 162. أكابر – special plural of أكبر when it is used to signify 'great man'. التي is a feminine relative pronoun: see below.

جاء is a hollow verb (see Table 5) whose third radical *hamza* causes some difficulties in spelling. However, it is usually quite easy to recognise. With the preposition **bi**, it means 'to bring' (cf. English 'he came in with a letter' i.e. he brought a letter in).

18 هاجر is a Form III verb. Consult the tables for conjugation.

20 واصل is another Form III verb.

خلفاؤه – such plural forms (see word shape, page 123) with a final *hamza*, when a suffix is added to them, vary the carrier letter of the *hamza* according to the case of the noun – here nominative, which technically has a *-u* ending, hence the *hamza* is written over a *waaw*. This should not cause any difficulty so long as you are aware of the problem.

من بعده – the **min** here is idiomatic and could be omitted without serious damage. مات is a hollow verb – see Table 5.

EXERCISE 13.1   Read the Arabic text aloud and translate it into idiomatic English.

EXERCISE 13.2   Answer the following questions on the text in complete sentences:

١   ما هو موطن العرب الأصلي ؟

٢   من فتح بلاد ساحل افريقيا الشمالي ؟

٣   من طرد العرب من اسبانيا ؟

٤   ما هي اللغة التي يستخدمها سكّان الدول العربية ؟

٥   ماذا كان سبب انتشار هذه اللغة ؟

٦   ماذا كان أهل مكّة يعبدون قبل الاسلام ؟

٧   الى أين هاجر رسول اللّه ، وفي أية سنة ؟

٨   بعد كم سنة رجع محمد الى مكّة ، ومن جاء معه ؟

٩   متى مات النبي ؟

١٠   الى أين وصلت الجيوش المسلمة ؟

Relative clauses

Relative clauses are those which provide supplementary information about their subjects, and in English are usually introduced by *who*, *whom*, *whose*, *which* or *that* (some of which are frequently omitted in speech, e.g. 'The man I met in the pub' is used instead of the more formal 'The man whom I met in the pub'). The subject of a relative clause is the person or thing about which it provides information, and is *not* necessarily the grammatical subject of the sentence. It is called the *antecedent*, and the words like 'who', 'which', etc., are called *relative pronouns*.

For the purposes of Arabic it is necessary to distinguish between *definite antecedents* and *indefinite antecedents*. Here are some English examples:

1 **Definite antecedents**
  The meal which we had last night was delicious. (*The meal* we had . . .)
  Mr Smith who lives next door told me.
  My brother who lives abroad is coming home next week.
  (Revise definites on page 28.)

2 **Indefinite antecedents**
  A play which I always enjoy is 'Hamlet'. (*A play* I always enjoy . . .)
  He is *a character* who never gives in.

Relative pronouns
Arabic does not distinguish between *who* (for people) and *which* (for things) as we do, but the Arabic relative pronouns must agree with their antecedents in *number* and *gender*.

Form	Arabic word	Agrees with
masc. sing.	الّذى **alladhii**	one male; one object of masculine gender
fem. sing.	الّتي **allatii**	one female; one object of feminine gender; plural objects of either gender
masc. plural	الّذين **alladhiina**	plural males only
fem. plural	الّاّتي **allaatii**	plural females only

Note that more rarely you will come across the dual forms اللّذان **alladhaan** (m) and اللّتان **allataan** (f). Both of these are written with an extra *laam* (not pronounced), and like all dual words the **-aan** ending changes to **-ayn** when they agree with words *not* in the nominative case, giving اللّذين **alladhayn** and اللّتين **allatayn** respectively.

To recap, these words are used irrespective of whether the English has 'who', 'that', 'whose', 'which' or any of the other variants and, as illustrated in the next section, are only used when the antecedent is *definite*. If the antecedent is indefinite, they *must* be omitted.

Relative clauses in Arabic

The Arabic relative clause differs from its English counterpart in two important ways:

1 As already stated, if the antecedent is indefinite, the relative pronoun is omitted. This can happen in English, but is optional: e.g. A programme I enjoy is... *or* A programme which I enjoy is .... In Arabic it is a rule. *No* relative pronouns are used with indefinite antecedents.

2 In Arabic the relative clause itself, i.e. that part coming after the relative pronoun if one is used, must satisfy two conditions:

   (*a*) it must constitute a complete and independent sentence on its own, and

   (*b*) it must therefore contain some stated or implied pronoun which refers back to the antecedent. We shall call this the *referent*.

This is best illustrated by examples.

Definite antecedent

English: The newspaper which I read...

Preparing for Arabic:

The newspaper	(note feminine and definite, therefore a relative pronoun is required, so select appropriate one)
Which	(feminine singular relative pronoun required)
I read	(does not contain any referent to newspaper, so supply)
Her	(feminine suffix pronoun because newspaper is a feminine word)
Arabic: الجريدة الّتي قرأتها	(relative pronoun and referent underlined)

Indefinite antecedent

English: A newspaper which I read...

Preparing for Arabic:

A newspaper	(note indefinite, so *no* relative pronoun required)
I read	(no referent, so supply)
Her	(f. suffix pronoun for f. word)
Arabic: جريدة قرأتها	(referent underlined)

For those who have a grammatical turn of mind, what is happening is that in English the form (especially in 'who', 'whom', 'whose') of the relative pronoun tells you what is going on, whereas in Arabic it doesn't, so that must be done by the referent. Study the following examples carefully and you should soon get the hang of it. In practice it is the clauses with indefinite antecedents which will often catch you out as there will be no relative pronoun to herald the fact that a relative clause is to follow.

The official who works in the customs...
⟶ The official/who/*he*-works in the customs...

⟶   الموظّف الّذى يشتغل في الجمارك

(The referent here is the prefix of the verb which, remember, means not just 'works', but 'he-works')

An official who works in the customs...
⟶ An official/*he*-works in the customs...

حـ   ⟶   موظّف يشتغل في الجمارك

(Exactly as above, but relative pronoun omitted with indefinite antecedent.)

The Muslims, whose home was the Arabian Peninsula
⟶ The Muslims/who/*their* home was the Arabian Peninsula

⟶   المسلمون الّذين كان موطنهم الجزيرة العربية

(The referent is the **-hum** suffix, referring back to 'The Muslims')

The man in whose house I live...
⟶ The man/who/I live in *his* house

⟶   الرجل الّذى أسكن في بيته

A house in which I live...
⟶ A house/I live in *it*

⟶   بيت أسكن فيه

The manager, whose name is Yousif
⟶ The manager/who/*his* name (is) Yousif

⟶   المدير الّذى اسمه يوسف

Study also the examples in the text.

EXERCISE 13.3   Supply the appropriate relative pronoun (if any) in the following sentences:

١   المصنع ـــــ أشتغل فيه كبير   ٢   جاء رجل ـــــ لم أعرفه

٣   هذه هي الجريدة ـــــ قرأناها أمس

٤   كلّم المدير الموظّفات ـــــ وصلن اليوم

٥   جاء سليم بطعام ـــــ أكلناه

٦   يبلغ عدد الدول ـــــ انحدرت من الامبراطورية الاسلامية ثماني عشرة

٧   كان محمد ـــــ مات في المدينة رسول الله

٨   الطائرة ـــــ وصلت في الصباح جاءت من لندن

٩   هو رجل ـــــ لا يضحك كثيرا

١٠   أرسلوا مدرّسة ـــــ لا تعرف اللغة العربية

EXERCISE 13.4   Read aloud and translate your answers.

Some, all, each and every

These are expressed in Arabic by two words which are actually nouns:

بَعْض   *a part* (*of something*)

كُلّ   *the whole* (*of something*)

بعض usually forms the first part of a possessive construction, the second part being a plural definite noun in the genitive, e.g.

بعض الكتب   *some of the books*

بعض المسلمين   *some of the Muslims*   (plural suffix **-iin** showing genitive case)

In certain contexts it may be translated 'one of' instead of 'some of' according to the sense, and it is occasionally used with singular nouns.

كُلّ has several different usages which must be studied carefully.

(*a*) with a definite plural noun, again technically in the genitive. In this case it means *all*.

كلّ المسلمين (the) totality (of) the-Muslims
all Muslims, all of the Muslims

This construction is frequently inverted according to the 'thematic' principle (see page 136), giving for the above:

المسلمون كلّهم the-Muslims (the) totality-(of)-them

(*b*) with a *definite* singular noun (genitive), meaning 'all, the whole'

كلّ اليوم '(the) whole (of) the-day' *All day, the whole day*,
or thematic

اليوم كلّه 'the-day (the) whole-(of)-it', with the same meaning.

(*c*) with an *indefinite* singular noun (genitive), in which case it means 'each, every'.

كلّ يوم *each day, every day*

كلّ رجل *each man, every man*

Be careful not to confuse (*b*) and (*c*).

EXERCISE 13.5 Read aloud and translate the following sentences:

١   التاجر يسافر الى وطنه كلّ سنة

٢   اجتمع المدرّسون كلّهم في مكتب المدير

٣   نشرت بعض الجرائد هذا الاعلان الهامّ أمس

٤   كلّ تلميذ له قلم وورقة

٥   دفعت الشركة الفلوس كلّها للعمّال

٦   كان بعض الأولاد يلعبون في الشارع

٧   كان الضيوف كلّهم يأكلون ويشربون كثيرا

٨   لكلّ باب مفتاحه

٩   ليست مصادر البترول كلّها في الشرق الأوسط

١٠ بعض الشبابيك مفتوحة وبعضها مقفولة

The numerals 11 to 99

Revise the numbers 1 to 10 (see page 33).

As already stated, the use of the numbers in Arabic is exceedingly difficult and is dealt with in Appendix 2. However, so that you can read numbers aloud and ask prices and things, here are some more, again in a colloquial form.

The teens

١١	**iHda:shar** احدى عشر		١٦	**sitta:shar** ستّة عشر
١٢	**ithna:shar** اثنا عشر		١٧	**saba:ta:shar** سبعة عشر
١٣	**thalathta:shar** ثلاثة عشر		١٨	**thamanta:shar** ثمانية عشر
١٤	**arba:ta:shar** اربعة عشر		١٩	**tisa:ta:shar** تسعة عشر
١٥	**khamasta:shar** خمسة عشر			

Note that the common element (equivalent to our -teen) is **a:shar**, which is a slightly altered form of the written **:ashar**.

The tens

In written Arabic these also have a nominative case form ending in **-uun**, but they are universally pronounced with the accusative/genitive ending **-iin** in everyday speech. They are easy to remember as – with the exception of twenty – they closely resemble the equivalent unit numbers with the addition of **-iin**.

٢٠	**:ishriin** عشرين		٦٠	**sittiin** ستّين
٣٠	**thalathiin** ثلاثين		٧٠	**sab:iin** سبعين
٤٠	**arba:iin** أربعين		٨٠	**thamaniin** ثمانين
٥٠	**khamsiin** خمسين		٩٠	**tis:iin** تسعين

Tens with units

The units are placed before the tens, thus:

> 23 **thalaatha wa:-ishriin** *three and-twenty* ثلاثة وعشرين

> 65 **khamsa wa-sittiin** *five and-sixty* خمسة وستّين

Agreement with nouns

In writing, the numbers must agree with their nouns in gender (see Appendix 2). Also note that with the numbers 11 to 99 inclusive, the noun is in the accusative *singular*. Unsuffixed nouns, therefore, show the *alif* accusative marker (pronounced **-an** in formal speech only).

14 books   أربعة عشر كتابا   **arba:ata:shar kitaaban**

Note that in Arabic, the noun is plural *only* after the numerals 3 to 10 inclusive, thus:

5 books   خمسة كتب   **khamsa kutub**

Hundreds, thousands and millions

١٠٠	مائة	**mi'a**
٢٠٠	مائتان	**mi'ataan** dual form, inflecting **-aan/-ayn**
٣٠٠	ثلاث مائة	**thalaath mi'a** ... and so on, using

the *feminine* form of the unit numeral (see Appendix 2) and, strangely, the *singular* of **mi'a** (although we also say three hundred, not hundreds).

١٠٠٠	ألف	**alf**
٢٠٠٠	ألفان	**alfaan** dual form inflecting as above.
٣٠٠٠	ثلاثة آلاف	**thalaathat aalaaf** ... and so on, using the *masculine* form of the units and pronouncing the 't' of the ending because it comes between two vowels.

After hundreds, thousands and millions (given above in vocabulary) the noun is in the *indefinite singular*, technically genitive as the Arabs regard this as a possessive construction 'a hundred of book'. Hence the ending of **mi'a** must be pronounced **t** (see p. 61).

EXERCISE 13.6   Do the following simple calculations (aloud) in Arabic, using the colloquial forms of the numbers. Here are the technical terms:

plus زَائِد   *minus* نَاقِص   *multiplied by* في   *divided by* عَلَى   *equals* يُساوى

٤ ١٩	٣ ١٩٢ =	٢ ١٤	١ ٦٤
٤ ×	٣	٨ −	٢٣ +
=		=	=

٨ ٧٢ =	٧ ٥٦	٦ ٤٤٧٩	٥ ٤٥٦٢
٦	٤ ×	٢١٥٥ −	١٦١٤ +
	=	=	=

٩   ٢١ − ٦٩ + ٣٢ =   ١٠   (٢ + ٥) × ٧ =

Unit Fourteen

التركيب الاجتماعى عند العرب ١

من الطبيعي أنّ تركيب المجتمع العربي يختلف من بلد الى بلد
ولكنّه مع ذلك لم يبعد كثيرا عن نظامه الأصلي الذى نقرأ عنه في كتب
التاريخ

ويصحّ هذا حتى في البلدان الأكثر تقدّما من ناحية التعليم والسياسة والثروة ٥
المادية

وكانت القبيلة أساس المجتمع العربي في أوّل تاريخه وما زالت تلعب دورا
مهمًّا الى الآن

ومن الصعب ان نحدّد بالضبط ما هي القبيلة وممّا تتكوّن

فهناك قبائل كبيرة ذات شأن عظيم وفي نفس الوقت قبائل صغيرة ليست لها ١٠
أهمّية الّا في المناطق الخاصّة بها

ورئيس القبيلة هو شيخها وقد أصبح شيوخ بعض هذه القبائل العظيمة
حكّاما لدول حديثة

وعادة العرب في اسمائهم أن يحمل الرجل اسم أبيه واسم جدّه

وفي آخر اسمه نجد نسبته أى اسم قبيلته ١٥

ومثل ذلك «حسن بن علي بن سالم التيمي» قد يكون اسما لرجل اسم أبيه
علي واسم جدّه سالم وقبيلته تميم

والقبيلة تنقسم الى عائلات وتكون العائلة تحت رئاسة أكبر رجالها في السنّ

وأمّا النساء فوقفهنّ في العائلة كما هو في القبيلة ضعيف جدّا فحقوقهنّ لا
تساوى حقوق الرجال ٢٠

وعلى أعضاء العائلة أن يشاوروا ربّ الأسرة في كلّ أمر هامّ مثل الزواج
والطلاق وبيع الأراضي وشرائها مثلا

ومن الممكن أن يشاور ربّ الأسرة شيخ القبيلة اذاكان هو نفسه غير قادر

167

على حلّ أمر ما

25   ومن أجل ذلك فكلّ حاكمّ أو شيخ قبيلة يعقد مجلسا يوميا يستقبل فيه
أبناء قبيلته ليسمع طلباتهم وشكاياتهم .

Vocabulary

Nouns

تَرْكِيب structure, composition	مُجْتَمَع (ـات) society
نِظَام (أَنْظِمة ، نُظُم) system	تاريخ history; date
تَقَدُّم progress	بُلدَان countries (alternative form of بِلاَد)
سِياسة politics	
قَبِيلة (قَبائِل) tribe	ثَرْوَة wealth
نَفْس (أَنْفُس ، نُفُوس) self; same	دَوْر (أَدْوار) role
أَهَمِّية importance	ذَات (ذَوات) possessor of (f. — see page 176)
عَادة (ـات) custom, habit	مِنْطَقة (مَناطِق) region, area
جَدّ (أَجْداد ، جُدود) grandfather	أَب (آباء) father
حَسَن Hassan	نِسْبة (نِسَب) nisba (see literal translation)
اِبْن (أَبْناء) son	مَثَل (أَمْثال) example; proverb
سَالِم Salem	
رِئاسَة leadership	عَلِي Ali
سِنّ age	عَائِلة (ـات) family
حَقّ (حُقوق) right	أُسْرة (ـات ، أُسَر) family

مَوْقِف (مَوَاقِف) position; status

رَبّ (أَرْباب) lord

عُضْو (أَعْضاء) member; limb

طَلاق divorce

زَواج marriage

شِراء buying

حَلّ (حُلُول) solution

مَجْلِس (مَجالِس) council, assembly

بَيْع selling

شِكاية (ـات) complaint

طَلَب (ـات) demand, request, application

Adjectives

طَبيعيّ natural

اِجْتِماعيّ social

تَميمي Tamimi; of the Tamim tribe

مادّيَ material

خاصّ بِـ belonging to, pertaining to

خاصّ special, private

ضَعيف (ضِعاف ، ضُعَفَاء) weak

مُمْكِن possible

قادِر (ـون) able; capable

Verbs

بَعُد عَنْ (u) be far from

اِخْتَلَف ، يَخْتَلِف (VIII) differ, be different

زال ، يَزَال cease

صَحّ ، يَصِحّ be right, valid

تَكَوَّن مِنْ ، يَتَكَوَّن مِنْ (V) consist of

حَدَّد ، يُحَدِّد (II) define

اِنْقَسَم ، يَنْقَسِم (VII) be divided

وَجَد ، يَجِد find

شاوَر ، يُشاوِر (III) consult, ask for advice

ساوَى ، يُساوِى (III) equal

سَمِع (a) hear

اِسْتَقْبَل ، يَسْتَقْبِل (X) receive (visitors, etc.)

عَقَد (i) hold (meetings, etc.)

Other words

مَعَ ذٰلِك	despite this	حَتَّى	until, even
مِنْ نَاحِيَة	as regards, from the point of view of	اَلآن	now
بِالضَّبْط	exactly	أَمَّا	as for
كَمَا	like, just as	جِدًّا	very
مَثَلاً	for example	إِذَا	if
مِنْ أَجْل	because of, for the purpose of	أَىْ	that is, i.e.
غَيْر	not, other than		

Literal translation

1 **The-structure the-social with the-Arabs**
   (It is) of the-natural that (the) structure (of) the-society the-Arab he-differs from country to country.
   But-he with that not he-is-far much from his-system the-original which we-read about-it in books (of) the-history.
5 And-he-is-right this even in the-countries the-most (in respect of) progress from (the) direction (of) the-education and-the-politics and-the-wealth the-material.
   And-was the-tribe (the) basis (of) the-society the-Arab in (the) first (of) its-history and-not she-ceased she-plays (a) role important to now. And-(it is)-of-the-difficult that we-define with-the-exactitude what (is) she-the-tribe and-of-what she-consists.
10 And-there (are) tribes big possessors (of) importance great and in (the) self (of) the-time tribes small is-not to-them importance except in the-regions the-pertaining to-them.
   And-head (of) the-tribe he (is) her-sheikh and-/past marker/became (the) sheikhs (of) some (of) these the-tribes the-great rulers to-states modern.
   And-(the)-custom (of) the-Arabs in their-names (is) that carries the-man (the) name (of) his-father and-(the)-name (of) his-grandfather.
15 And-in (the) last (of) his-name we-find his-*nisba*, that-is (the) name (of) his-tribe.
   And-(an)-example (of) that 'Hassan bin Ali bin Salem al-Tamimi'/*doubt marker*/ he-is (a) name to-(a)-man (who) name (of) his-father (is) Ali and-

name (of) his-grandfather (is) Salem and-his-tribe (is) Tamim. And-the-tribe she-divides to families and would-be the-family under (the) headship (of the) biggest (of) her-men in the-age.

19 And-as-for the-women so-their-status in the-family like-what he (is) in the-tribe (is) weak very and-their-rights not they-equal (the) rights (of) the-men.

And-(it is incumbent)-upon (the) members (of) the-family that they-consult (the) lord (of) the-family in every matter important like the-marriage and-the-divorce and (the) selling (of) the-lands and-their-buying for-instance.

And-(it is)-of the-possible that consults (the) lord (of) the-family (the) sheikh (of) the-tribe if was he his-self not capable of solving (an) affair any.

25 And-for (the) purpose (of) that so-every ruler or sheikh (of) tribe he-holds (a) council daily (which) he-receives in-it (the) sons (of) his-tribe (in order) to-he-hears their-requests and-their-complaints.

Background to text

Note: The text was written mainly thinking of the Arabian Peninsula where the tribal system is still quite strong. Although it is much diluted in more Westernised societies such as Egypt and Iraq, it is by no means dead, especially in rural areas.

As we have seen in previous units, the spread of Arab influence in the world started with the rise of Islam, and Islam was born in a strictly tribal society and tailored to its needs. When the Arabs conquered and settled in other countries, they naturally took with them their tribal habits, now endorsed by their own religion.

The sheikh of a tribe was, as far as we know, never elected in the democratic sense, rather certain families established themselves by fair means or foul as leaders and handed down their authority to their sons, forming dynasties which might last for hundreds of years. The powers of these sheikhs are temporal and strictly speaking have nothing to do with religion, although some great families have allied themselves to religious causes. At present, practically the whole of the Arabian Peninsula except the Yemen is ruled by tribal sheikhs or heads of great families who now find themselves governing oil-rich states. The most prominent of these is the Kingdom of Saudi Arabia which is ruled by the great Al Saud family which originated in central Arabia (Nejd) and was aided to power by its endorsement of the Wahhabi movement, a kind of Islamic puritanism whose effect is still very much felt in the Kingdom.

Undemocratic though it may seem to us, this tribal system works

well enough within its own society, a key feature being the accessi-
bility of the sheikh to *all* his people. In theory at least, any subject,
regardless of social standing, has the right to approach his overlord
in person in his **majlis** and state his case or request.

Most countries now have legal systems based on the Islamic Law
(the sharia), and usually supplemented by some other code of law
imported from the West. But traditional tribal law always runs as a
strong undercurrent to the two.

The Arab family is a very close-knit unit and is run as a male
hierarchy; the eldest man acting as family overlord and advisor. As
stated in the text, he is treated with respect and consulted on all
important family issues. In the case of the premature death of a
family head, these duties may devolve on quite young men.

Women, unfortunately, are not highly rated either in Islamic law
or the tribal code. Their inheritance, for instance, is officially half
that of a man's, and in many countries they still suffer from severe
social restrictions. Marriage is usually a family arrangement, a
dowry being paid for the bride.

In the more traditional countries it is considered impolite for an
outsider – be he Arab or European – to enquire after, or even
mention, the female members of a man's family. So leave the
subject alone. European women are regarded as a sort of third sex,
and will have few problems in the more Westernised countries, but
again discretion is advised, especially in rural areas. In the more
traditional countries, they may find themselves subject to some of
the strictures applied to the local women.

Analysis of text and grammar

1 اجتماعي comes from a slightly different derivative from that of
the noun مجتمع *society* in line 2.

2 من الطبيعي – the **min** here is idiomatic – and very common (cf. 'of
the essence', 'of necessity').

3 كثيرا is adverbial, showing the indefinite accusative marker,
which should be pronounced **-an**.

5 يصحّ is a so-called 'doubled' verb, because its second and third
radicals are identical. These verbs are quite tricky, and you have to
learn when to write these radicals together with *shadda* (the
doubling sign) and when to write them separately. The full conjugation of such verbs is set out in Table 3, so start to get
acquainted with them now.

حتّى means 'until', but is very often used in the sense of 'even'.

تقدّما is a literary use of the indefinite accusative, related to the adverbial use mentioned above. It is known as 'the accusative of respect', i.e. it provides the information 'in respect of what'. Here, 'most in respect of (as regards) progress'. As in adverbs, the accusative marker ending should be pronounced **-an**.

من ناحية **naaHiya** is a noun meaning 'direction' and its use here is related to the English 'from the point of view of'. Thus technically it stands in a possessive construction with the next word, and the *t* of the feminine ending should therefore be pronounced.

7 ما زالت – see section on page 178.

9 من الصعب– cf. من الطبيعي (line 2).

ممّا *mimmaa* is a contracted form for **min + maa** (cf. the further contracted interrogative forms given on page 134.

تكوّن is a Form V verb.

10 ذات is the feminine form of ذو (see section on page 176). نفس is a feminine noun meaning 'soul', and is very commonly used to express 'the same'. It is usually used as the first term in a possessive construction.

14 اسمائهم **ism** is technically the forename, or what we call the Christian name. The method of naming described here is the traditional one, but it still applies in varying degrees in many Arab countries.

أبيه – see section on page 175.

15 نجد *we find*. This verb has *waaw* as its first radical and the type is given in Table 4. The main feature of such verbs is that they lose their first radical in the present tense.

نسبة is the relative adjective (see page 145) formed from the name of a man's tribe, family or place of origin, and the nearest Arab equivalent of our surname.

16 مثل is close to, but not to be confused with, the differently vowelled **mithl** *like*.

بن is a contracted form of ابن used only in names between two other elements (i.e. not at the beginning of a name like Ibn Khaldun), and is pronounced **ibn** or **bin** depending on where you are.

قد يكون– first revise the use of **qad** with the past tense (see page 82). When this particle is used, as here, with the present tense, it imparts a flavour of doubt or hypothesis to the verb. Translate it here as 'might be', 'would be', 'could be'. Note that two distinct names سالم and سليم exist – not always differentiated in English spelling. The same applies to راشد and رشيد .

18 تنقسم is a Form VII verb (see Table 2). تكون – even without the use of **qad** (see above), the present tense of **kaan** often has a sense of doubt or supposition. The nearest English translation here is 'will be'.

19 أمّا *as for* is a common introductory particle to a thematic type sentence whose predicate is *always* introduced by **fa-** (here كما هو literally means 'like-what he (is)'.جدّا (فوقهنّ), pronounced **jiddan**, is another adverb with the accusative marker.

20 تساوى is a Form III verb with final radical *y*. The so-called 'third weak' verbs – i.e. those having *waaw* or *yaa* as their final radicals – are the most difficult of all. Consult Tables 6–9 and start learning those immediately.

21 على – this preposition quite often has the meaning 'incumbent upon'.

يشاوروا is a subjunctive Form III verb after **an**, showing the omission of the final **nuun** (see section on page 177).

22 مثلا is another accusative marker adverb, prounced **mathalan**.

23 من الممكن – see remarks on line 2 above.

اذا كان – conditional clauses (i.e. those beginning in English with 'if') nearly always go in the *past tense* in Arabic, no matter what the English tense, hence here the past verb **kaan**. To take an extreme example, English 'If I see him tonight I shall tell him' would be rendered in Arabic as 'If I *saw* him tonight, I *told* him'. When translating from Arabic, simply use the tense required by English. (See page 217 for a fuller treatment of the conditional.)

غير is actually a noun meaning 'something other than'; **ghayr** is very frequently used to negate adjectives, much like our English prefix **un-**, e.g. here 'other than able, not able, unable'.

24 على is required in Arabic after **qaadir**.

أمر ما – this use of the ubiquitous **maa** after an indefinite noun means 'a certain, any'.

25 فكل – the **fa-** is idiomatic. شيخ قبيلة is an indefinite possessive 'a sheikh of a tribe'. يستقبل is a Form X verb.

ليسمع *in order that he hear*, *to hear* (see section on page 177).

EXERCISE 14.1 Read the Arabic text aloud and translate it into idiomatic English.

Irregular nouns

The nouns أب *father* and أخ *brother* are quite regular when they appear independently. However, when they appear as the first element of a possessive construction (as they frequently do) they have the odd feature of showing their case-endings by means of a long vowel, which of course affects the way they are written.

The Arabic case endings, originally shown by means of vowel signs and now omitted altogether, are: nominative -*u*, accusative -*a* and genitive -*i*. In the case of the nouns mentioned above, these short vowels are lengthened in the usual way, by the addition of the letters *waaw*, *alif* and *yaa'* respectively. Remember, this only happens when the word is the first part of a possessive, the owner part being either another noun or a pronoun suffix. Study the following table:

	Ali's father	*Her brother*
Nominative	أبو علي abuu :alii	أخوها akhuu-haa
Accusative	أبا علي abaa :alii	أخاها akhaa-haa
Genitive	أبي علي abii :alii	أخيها akhii-haa

Notes:

1   As usual, the pronominal suffix -*ii* *my*, being a vowel itself, suppresses all vowels before it, giving أبي **abii** *my father* and أخي **akhii** *my brother* for all three cases.

2   **Abuu** occurs frequently in personal and place names (such as أبو ظبي   *Abu Dhabi*) and there is a reluctance in modern Arabic to change the form according to case. Thus, in a newspaper, you will more often find في أبو ظبي *in Abu Dhabi* than the technically correct في أبي ظبي In spoken Arabic, only the nominative form is used.

Related to these is the word ذو , which *always* occurs as the first element of a possessive – in fact meaning 'the owner, possessor (of)'. Study the example ذو شأن 'possessor of importance', i.e. *important* (of people or places) in the three cases:

Nominative	ذو شأن	**dhuu sha'n**
Accusative	ذا شأن	**dhaa sha'n**
Genitive	ذى شأن	**dhii sha'n**

Note, for example, رجل ذو شأن *a man of importance, an important man*. This word has a feminine ذات **dhaat** which behaves regularly, قبيلة ذات شأن *a tribe of importance*, plural ذوات **dhawaat** (also regular). The plural of the masculine ذو **dhuu** is ذوو **dhawuu** in the nominative and ذوى **dhawii** for the other two cases.

EXERCISE 14.2   The genealogy of Muhammad X. See if you can work out the following.

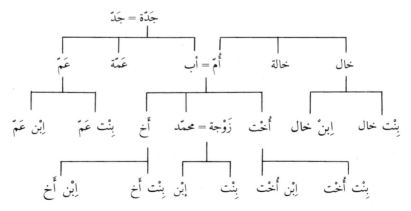

Now try and translate the following relationships to Muhammad:

١ أمّه زوجة أبيه   ٢ خاله أخو أمّه

٣ جدّته أمّ أبيه أو أمّ أمّه   ٤ أبوه جدّ ابنه وجدّ بنته

٥ بنت عمّه أخت ابن عمّه   ٦ جدّه زوج جدّته

٧ عمّه أخو أبيه   ٨ زوجته أمّ ابنه

٩ أخوه ابن أبيه   ١٠ ابن أخيه أخو بنت أخيه

Conjunctions followed by verbs

Arabic has ten common conjunctions ('words which join clauses')
which are followed immediately by a verb in the *present tense
subjunctive*. (For the parts of the subjunctive which differ from the
indicative, consult the Verb Tables.) Of these, one means simply
'that' and the rest all mean 'in order that', 'so that' or its negative
'in order that not', 'so that not', 'lest'. All this latter set introduce
clauses of purpose which answer the question 'For what purpose is
the action of the main verb taking place (or has taken place)?'. In
English we frequently use an infinitive, '*to* do something', but this is
not possible in Arabic. The following example shows the process:

English: I am going out to buy a newspaper.
Arabic: I go out so that I (may) buy a newspaper.

Note that both verbs are in the I (first person) form.
   The Arabic conjunctions are:

أن **an** *that*

ألّا **allaa** (assimilated form of **an laa**) *that not*

لـ **li**			**Negatives**
كي **kay**		كيلا **kaylaa**	
لكي **likay**	so that, in order that	لكيلا **likaylaa**	so that not, lest
لأن **li'an**		لئلّا **li'allaa**	
حتّى **Hattaa**			

Notes:

1 أن **an** may, according to the sense required, be followed by a
past tense verb, which of course has no subjunctive form.

2 حتّى **Hattaa**, which really means 'until', can be followed by an
indicative or a past tense verb if no meaning of purpose is intended.

EXERCISE 14.3   Translate into English:

١   أمره بأن يذهب الى المدينة ليشاور الخبراء في المصنع

٢   سافر الى البحرين لكي يكلّم وزير التعليم

٣   وصل أخي سليم الى مكّة أمس كي يحتفل بالعيد

٤   طلبنا منهم أن يدفعوا اليوم ولكنّهم رفضوا

٥   كانت تتكلّم اللغة العربية كيلا يفهم ابنها الصغير

٦   جاء العمّال الى العاصمة ليستقبلوا رئيسهم

٧   رفضت المطبعة أن تنشر المجلّة الجديدة

٨   على الجيش أن يدافع عن الوطن

٩   من الصعب أن نحدّد ما هي الاشتراكية بالضبط

١٠   أذهب الى المكتبة كلّ يوم لأقرأ الجرائد

'Still' and 'almost'

A number of such ideas which are expressed in English by means of
adverbs are expressed in Arabic by the use of auxiliary verbs. Those
perhaps most 'foreign' to the English mind are *still* and *almost*.

Still
This is expressed by the negated verb **zaal** (present tense **yazaal** –
see Hollow Verb Table 5), which means 'to cease'.

English: The tribe still plays an important role
Arabic: Not she-ceased the-tribe she-plays role important.

ما زالت القبيلة تلعب دورا مهمًّا

Note that both verbs are in the she-form ('tribe' being a feminine
noun), and that the subject, if stated, comes between the two verbs.
The main verb is always in the *present tense*. Instead of using the
negative word **maa**, **lam** is frequently used, and of course puts the
verb **zaal** in the jussive. (Revise pp. 118–19 on the negatives, also
the jussive form of the hollow verbs, Table 5.)

لم تزل القبيلة تلعب دورا مهمًّا

Instead of a verb, the main clause can be a noun sentence. In this case, the predicate goes in the accusative indefinite, just as it does after **kaan** and the verbs 'to become' (see pp. 89–91).

English: He is still ill.
Arabic: Not he-ceased ill.

$$ \text{لم يزل مريضا} \quad or \quad \text{ما زال مريضا} $$

(cf. the same construction كان مريضا *He was ill*)

Almost
This is expressed by the verb **kaad** (present tense **yakaad**), which means 'to be on the point of (doing something)'. This is always followed by a verb in the present tense.

English: We almost reached the frontier.
Arabic: We-were-on-the-point-of we-reach the-frontier

$$ \text{كدنا نبلغ الحدود} $$

EXERCISE 14.4 Translate into English:

١ ما زلت أدرس تاريخ الجزيرة العربية

٢ كادت الشركة توظّفها سكرتيرة للمدير

٣ لم يزل التجّار يقدّمون طلبات وشكايات

٤ ما زالت البنت الصغيرة تسأل عن أبيها

٥ لم يزل المهندسون المصريون يكسبون كثيرا في دول الخليج

٦ كاد البرنامج التلفزيوني يبدأ

Unit Fifteen

Text

١ في المطار

المسافر (لسائق التاكسي) خُذْني إلى المطار من فضلك

السائق نعم يا سيدي . سيادتك ستسافر إلى أين إن شاء الله ؟

المسافر إلى الخرطوم

٥ السائق زين . الطائرة ستقوم الساعة كم ؟

المسافر الساعة عشرة ونصف

السائق جميل جدّاً . عندنا وقت كاف . (في المطار) وصلنا . أين تريد أن أقف ؟

المسافر قِفْ هناك عند الباب الرئيسي

السائق (يأخذ الحقائب من السيّارة ويعطيها للحمّال) خُذ الشنط يا حمّال

١٠ المسافر كم الأجرة ؟

السائق خمسة دنانير من فضلك

المسافر (يعطيه الفلوس) تَفَضَّل الفلوس

السائق شكرا . مع السلامة

المسافر (لضابط الشرطة) من فضلك أين مكتب الخطوط الجوية الوطنية ؟

١٥ الضابط إذْهَب إلى آخر هذه القاعة الكبيرة ولِفّ على يمينك . بعد ذلك أُدْخُل أوّل باب على اليسار وستجد المكتب أمامك

المسافر شكراً جزيلاً (ينصرف والحمّال يتبعه حاملاً الحقائب) . يصلان إلى مكتب شركة الطيران) صباح الخير

موظّف الشركة صباح النور (يتعرّف على المسافر) آه مرحبا يا ميستر سميث . كيف حالك ؟

المسافر الحمد لله بخير . أنا حجزت في طائرة الخرطوم للساعة عشرة ونصف ، درجة أولى

الموظّف نعم صحيح . هذه رحلة رقم ٢٥٧ . هات التذكرة من فضلك

20 **المسافر** تفضّل

الموظّف يا حمّال ، ضَع الشنط على الميزان . أشكرك . (للمسافر) تفضّل بطاقة الركوب . إذهَب من فضلك من هنا إلى الجمارك لتفتيش الحقائب وجواز السفر . وستركب الطائرة من بوّابة رقم ثمانية . رحلة طيّبة .

المسافر شكرا (يتّجه نحو الجمارك)

الموظّف لحظة يا سيدي

المسافر نعم

25 **الموظّف** للأسف جاءنا الخبر الآن أنّ رحلة سيادتك ستتأخّر ثلث ساعة . أنا متأسّف

المسافر لا يهمّ (يصل عند ضابط الجوازات)

ضابط الجوازات الجواز من فضلك (يأخذ الجواز من المسافر ويطّلع عليه ، ثمّ يردّه إليه) شكرا . اِذهَب من فضلك إلى ضابط الجمارك هناك

ضابط الجمارك هل مع حضرتك ممنوعات ؟

المسافر لا ، لا شيء

30 **ضابط الجمارك** من فضلك اِفْتح هذه الشنطة الكبيرة للتفتيش (المسافر يفتح الحقيبة والضابط يفتّش ما فيها) شكرا

تنبيه من إذاعة المطار نرجو من المسافرين على الرحلة رقم ٢٥٧ المتّجهة إلى الخرطوم أن يتّجهوا إلى بوابة رقم ثمانية فورا للركوب . شكرا

Vocabulary

Nouns

تاكْسي (ـات) ⎱ *taxi*
سَيّارة أُجْرة (سيارات أجرة) ⎰

الخَرْطوم *Khartoum*

حَقيبة (حَقائب) *suitcase, bag*

دينار (دَنانير) *dinar (currency)*

شُرْطة ⎱ *police*
بوليس ⎰

جَوّ *air, weather*

طَيَران *aviation, flying*

رِحْلة (ـات) *journey*

رَقْم (أَرْقام) *number, numeral*

تَذْكَرة (تَذاكِر) *ticket*

بِطاقة (ـات ، بَطائق) *card (e.g. identity, etc.)*

تَفْتيش *inspection*

سَفَر *travelling*

بَوّابة (ـات) *gate, gateway*

أَسَف *sorrow*

مَمْنوعات *prohibited items*

إذاعة *broadcasting*

سَيِّد (سادة) *gentleman*

سَيِّدة (ـات) *lady*

أُجْرة *fee, hire, rent*

ضَابِط (ضُبّاط) *officer*

خَطّ (خُطوط) *line*

قاعة (ـات) *hall, large room*

حال (أَحْوال) *condition, state*

خَيْر *well-being; also used adjectivally 'better, best'*

دَرَجة (ـات) *class, degree, step*

ميزان (مَوازين) *balance, scale, weighing machine*

رُكوب *mounting, boarding*

جَواز (ـات) *pass, permit*

جَواز السَفَر *passport*

لَحْظة (ـات) *moment*

خَبَر (أَخْبار) *news, information*

تَنْبيه *announcement, alert*

نُور (أَنْوار) *light*

حَمْد *praise*

Adjectives

زَيْن good, beautiful

كَاف enough (definite form كافي)

وَطَنيّ national

جَزيل abundant, many (usually used with 'thanks')

يَسار (يُسْرَى) left

يَمين (يُمْنَى .f) right

صَحيح correct, right

طَيِّب good, well

مُتَأَسِّف sorry

مَمْنوع forbidden, prohibited

مُتَّجِه الى/نَحْو heading for, having as a destination

جَوّيّ air (adj), pertaining to air

Verbs

شاء ، يَشاء wish

أراد ، يُريد (IV) want, wish for, desire

وَقَف ، يَقِف stop, stand

أَعْطَى ، يُعْطي (IV) give

لَفّ ، يَلِفّ turn, wrap round

اِنْصَرَف ، يَنْصَرِف إلى (VII) go away, go off to

تَبِع (a) follow

تَعَرَّف على ، يَتَعَرَّف على (V) recognise

حَجَز (u) book, reserve

شكَر (u) thank

رَكِب (a) ride, mount, board

تَأَخَّر ، يَتَأَخَّر (V) be late

أَهَمّ ، يُهِمّ (IV) be important

اِتَّجَه يَتَّجِه الى/نحو (VIII) go in the direction of, head for

اِطَّلَع ، يَطَّلِع على (VIII) look at, examine

رَدّ ، يَرُدّ give back, return

فَتَّش ، يُفَتِّش (II) inspect, examine

رَجَا ، يَرْجُو ask, request, wish for (see notes)

قَام ، يَقُوم rise, stand up; of passenger vehicles 'leave, depart'

Other words (phrases and greetings are discussed in the notes)

مِن فَضْلَك   *please*

إِنْ   *if*

شُكْراً   *thanks*

مَعَ السَّلامة   *good bye*

آه   *ah!*

صَباح الخَيْر   *good morning*

مَرْحَباً   *hello (Lit. 'welcome')*

هَات   *bring! give! (imperative)*

نَحْو   *towards, in the direction of*

الحَمْدُ لِلّه   *Praise be to God!*

يا   *particle used when addressing someone*

سِيادَتَك
حَضْرَتَك   } *polite forms of address, 'sir'*

تَفَضَّل   *please, if you please*

أَمام   *in front of, before*

وَراء   *behind*

صَباح النُّور   *good morning (reply)*

كَيْف حالَك ؟   *how are you?*

هُنا   *here*

لِلأَسَف   *unfortunately*

Literal translation

Note: Greetings, terms of address and polite phrases have not always been translated literally as this serves only to confuse the issue. They are discussed on pp. 188–90.

1 **In the-Airport**

the-Traveller   (to-driver (of) the-taxi) Take-me to the-airport please.

the-Driver   Yes /0/ sir, Sir/*future marker*/-you-travel to where, if wished God ('If God wills')?

the-Traveller   To Khartoum.

5 **the-Driver**   Good. The-plane /*future marker*/ she-leaves the-hour how-many?

the-Traveller   The-hour ten and-half.

the-Driver   Fine very. With-us time sufficient. (in the-airport) We-(have)-arrived. Where you-want that I-stop?

the-Traveller   Stop there at-the-gate the-main.

the-Driver   (he-takes the-bags from the-car and-he-gives-them to-the-porter) Take the-cases /0/ porter.

10 **the-Traveller**   How-much the-fee?

the-Driver   Five dinars please.

the-Traveller   (he-gives-him the-money) If you please, the-money.

the-Driver   Thanks. Good bye.

the-Traveller   (to-officer (of) the-police) Please, where (is) office (of) the-lines the-air the-national?

15 **the-Officer**   Go to (the) last (of) this the-hall the-big and-turn to your-right. After that enter first door on the-left and- /*future marker*/ -you-find the-office before-you.

the-Traveller   Thanks many. (He-goes-off and-the-porter he-follows-him carrying the-bags. They-two-arrive at (the) office (of) company (of) the-aviation) Good morning.

Official (of) the-Company   Good morning. (He-recognises /on/ the-traveller) Ah hello /0/ Mr Smith. How (is) your-condition?

the-Traveller   The-praise (be) to-God, in-well-being. I I-booked in (the) plane (of) Khartoum for-the-hour ten and-half, class first.

the-Official   Yes correct. This (is) journey number 257. Give the-ticket please.

20 **the-Traveller**   (Here you are) if you please.

the-Official   /0/ porter, put the-cases on the-scale. I-thank-you. (to-the-traveller) If you please (the) card (of) the-boarding. Go please from here to the-customs for-examination (of) the-bags and permit (of) the-travelling (passport). And-/*future marker*/-you-board the-plane from gate number eight. Journey good.

the-Traveller   Thanks. (he-heads towards the-customs)

the-Official   Moment /0/ sir!

the-Traveller   Yes?

25 **the-Official**   To-the- sorrow he-came-(to)-us the-news now that (the) journey (of) sir /*future marker*/ she-is-delayed third (of an) hour.

the-Traveller   Thanks. Not it-is-important. (he-arrives at (the) officer (of) the-passports)

Officer (of) the-Passes   The-pass please. (he-takes the-pass from the-traveller and-he-looks at-it then he-returns-it to-him) Thanks. Go please to (the) officer (of) the-customs there.

Officer (of) the-Customs   /*question marker*/ With-sir forbidden (articles)?

the-Traveller   No not (a) thing.

30 **Officer (of) the-Customs**   Please open this the-case the-big for-the-examination. (the-traveller he-opens the-bag and-the-officer he-examines what (is) in-it) Thanks.

Announcement from (the) public-address (of) the-Airport   We-request from the-travellers on the-journey number 257 the-going to Khartoum that they-go to gate number eight immediately for-the-boarding. Thanks.

Background to text

The background this time is linguistic. The Arabic you are learning in this book is the literary language – the only one which is normally written down – without the traditional grammatical endings which are used in formal situations. Even this, however, sounds stilted in modern dialogue such as the text. This has been felt by many Arab playwrights and one solution has been to use mainly literary words, but couched in the structures of colloquial speech. This has been done in the text to make it sound more realistic. The effect is mainly on the word order, and some features have been pointed out in the analysis. Times and greetings have been given in pure colloquial, and the greetings in the vocabulary have been given in colloquial form. For instance, to give the phrase 'please' its full inflected form **min faDlika** would be absurd, and the compromise form usually used in this book, that of omitting the last vowel, would give **min faDlik** which an Arab would take as being addressed to a woman!

Arabic is a very polite language with a host of specific greetings and formal replies which vary from place to place. The list given in this unit can therefore only hope to cover the most common and universal of these.

Analysis of text and grammar

2 تاكسي is the Arabic version of this almost universal word. The more formal سيّارة أجرة *car of hire* is also given in the vocabulary.

خذ – for this and all imperatives, see pp. 191–4. The same applies to من فضلك and all polite phrases, greetings and terms of address. **3** يا is a vocative particle, almost always used when addressing someone directly. See also page 196.

6 الساعة عشرة ونصف – all times are given in the colloquial form (see page 56). The correct formal Arabic is الساعة العاشرة والنصف 'the-hour the-tenth and-the-half'. For the ordinal numbers, see Appendix 2.

7-8 تريد أن أقف – note the construction 'you wish that I stop', i.e. you wish me to stop. أراد is a Form IV hollow verb, see Table 5.

9 قف is the imperative form of وقف Verbs having *waaw* as their first radical lose it in the present tense, and hence in the imperative (see Table 4 and pp. 191–6).

حقائب, singular حقيبة, is again a more 'formal' word than شنطة. This is a matter of style.

يعطيها is a Form IV verb with third radical **yaa** (see Table 9). This verb can either take the preposition **li** *to*, or can take two objects (see comments to line 12).

12 يعطيه الفلوس *gives him the money*. The construction parallels the English usage, although in grammar the 'him' (for 'to him') is described as the *indirect* object of the verb. Arabic simply says that the verb has two objects.

14 شرطة exists side by side with the more familiar sounding بوليس.

15 أوّل باب *the first door*. Note carefully this rather odd construction, where **awwal** is used like a superlative (see page 147). This is very common, and better style than the possible الباب الأوّل.

اليسار *the left*. Note that الشمال is also used for both left and North (possibly as this is to your left when you are facing East to Mecca).

16 حاملا shows the adverbial use of the indefinite accusative of the active participle. The Arabs call this usage 'circumstantial', the carrying being the circumstance which prevailed while the porter was following.

يصلان is a full dual form verb, used because the two subjects have already been mentioned (the passenger and the porter).

مكتب شركة الطيران is a double possessive phrase (the office of the company of the aviation), so شركة cannot take the definite article.

18 طائرة الخرطوم للساعة ..... – the Arabic says 'the plane of Khartoum to (i.e. belonging to, of) the hour ...'

19 رحلة , literally 'journey', but here, of course 'flight'.

21 بطاقة الركوب **biTaaqa** is the common word for cards which identify one in some way, here as a passenger entitled to board the plane. ركوب is from the verb ركب which carries both the meanings 'to ride, be riding' and 'to get in or mount'.

22 يتّجه is a Form VIII verb from the root وجه , meaning 'face, direction' (see Table 2). The active participle occurs in line 31.

25 تتأخّر and متأسّف are both parts of Form V verbs from roots with first radical *hamza* (see Table 2). ثلث means 'third' (of an hour, i.e. 20 minutes) – see page 56.

26 يهمّ is a Form IV verb having second and third radicals the same (see Table 3).

27 اطّلع is a Form VIII verb, assimilated (see Table 2 and notes).

ردّ is a Form I Verb with second and third radicals the same (Table 3).

29 لا شيء *no thing*. This **laa** used before nouns denies the existence of the whole class of things, e.g. لا إله الّا اللّه 'There is no (other) god except Allah (The God)', the Muslim confession of monotheism.

31 نرجو من is the formal and written way to express 'please' in Arabic, something like 'we respectfully request...'. In spoken Arabic, of course, **min faDlak** is used. On posted notices, the verbal noun رجاء **rajaa'** is often used instead of the verb, e.g. الرجاء عَدَم التدخين 'Please lack (of) smoking', an alternative to the more brusque ممنوع التدخين 'Forbidden smoking', *No Smoking*. For رجا see Table 6.

فورا is an adverbial accusative, 'instantly, immediately'.

EXERCISE 15.1 Read the Arabic text aloud and translate it into idiomatic English.

Greetings, polite phrases and forms of address

Note: As above, these are given in the spoken form. Since many Arabic dialects have lost the distinction between the masculine and feminine forms of 'you' *in the plural*, phrases are given in the *masculine singular*, followed – if applicable – in brackets by the *feminine singular* and *masculine* (i.e. common gender) *plural* in that order. If no such information is given, it means that the phrase need not normally be changed according to the number of the person(s) addressed.

Hello and goodbye A normal, casual greeting is مرحباً **marHaban**, or, without the accusative ending **-an**, simply مرحب **marHab**. Equally common is أهلاً **ahlan**, or the fuller form أهلاً وسهلاً **ahlan wa-sahlan**. The reply to give to these is simply to repeat the phrase used by the speaker, or a variation upon it by the use of the alternative phrase. The whole exchange is usually repeated at least twice.

When someone *leaves you* (important), you can say مع السلامة

ma: as-salaama, and he will reply الله يسلّمك **allah yisallimak**; (f. **-ik**, plural **-kum**). Rough meanings are '(May you go) in safety', reply 'God give you safety'. The slightly more formal السلامُ عليكم **as-salaamu :alaykum** (endings not usually altered) can be used for both hello and goodbye, but only by the person entering upon or leaving an established person or group (e.g. a man in his own house or office, a group of people already sitting together). The reply is وعليكم السلام **wa-:alaykum as-salaam**. The phrases mean 'Peace be upon you' and 'And upon you be peace'. Some people disapprove of their use by Christian Europeans.

How are you? This is expressed by various combinations such as:

كيفك ؟	**kayf-ak; -ik, -kum**	*How (are) you?*
كيف حالك ؟	**kayf Haal-ak; -ik, -kum**	*How (is) your-condition?*
كيف الحال ؟	**kayf al-Haal**	*How (is) the-condition?*

There are, however, many dialect variants of this, too numerous to give here. The above will be universally understood, and you can soon pick up the local versions.

The reply is *always* الحمد لله **al-Hamdu li-llaah** *Praise (be) to God!* with the optional بخير **bi-khayr** *Well* placed before or after it. The u-vowels on al-Hamd*u* and as-salaam*u* in the previous section are remnants of the Classical Arabic case system preserved in these stock phrases.

Please and thank you 'Please', when making a request, is almost universally من فضلك **min faDl-ak; -ik, -kum** *From your-kindness*, and 'Thank you' is شكراً **shukran** *Thanks*, or the slightly more formal أشكرك **ashkurak; -ik, -kum** *I thank you.*

In English we do not usually reply to a 'Thank you' – although phrases like 'Don't mention it' exist – but in Arabic it is polite to reply عفواً **:afwan**, i.e. 'exemption' (presumably from any further duty of thanking).

How to address people
Note: See also page 196 on the use of the vocative particle *yaa*.

This is again a very complex subject, showing wide variation from country to country. For instance **sayyid**, used in the more Westernised countries as a simple equivalent of English 'Mr.', originally meant a direct descendant of the Prophet Muhammad. In some countries it retains this (or related) meanings and should therefore be used only in addressing those deserving of the title. We can therefore attempt only a general sketch, omitting, of course, people who have genuine titles like Doctor, Minister, etc. سيادتك pronounced **sayadt-ak, -ik** and حضرتك **HaDrit-ak, -ik** are fairly respectful, and used for managerial, professional people, usually around middle age or over.

سيّد **sayyid** is a general term of address (see above), more often written than spoken, except in the phrase يا سيدى pronounced **yaa siidii**. The female سيّدة **sayyida** is even less used in speech, often replaced by French *madame*.

For younger men of the educated classes, use أستاذ **ustaadh**, which originally meant 'teacher', and again still retains this meaning in many countries. Its feminine form أستاذة **ustaadha** is also sometimes used, and the term for 'Miss' is آنسة **aanisa**.

TfaDDal-ing and Inshalla-ing

Every expatriate working in an Arab country knows these two terms. The first, تفضّل **tfaDDal** (to females **tfaDDalii**, to a group **tfaDDaluu**), means something like 'If you please'. It is used very frequently, perhaps most commonly in the following situations:
1. When giving or offering something to someone (e.g. food, a drink, payment, etc.)
2. When asking someone to precede you, e.g. through a doorway. (This is sometimes fiercely competitive, with **tfaDDals** flying in all directions.)
3. When inviting someone into a room, or to take a seat.

Remember the ending is changed according to the sex and number of the person(s) you are addressing. The ending for a group of women (in the countries where it is still preserved) is **-an** (**tfaDDalan**). Otherwise the masculine is used for both genders.

The second term إن شاء الله (correctly pronounced **in shaa' allaah** with a glottal stop at the end of **shaa'**, but often corrupted by foreigners to a sort of one word **inshalla**) means 'If God wills' or 'God willing'. The Arabs frequently apply this to any utterance relating to the future, this being completely in the hands of God.

Giving orders

The mood of the verb used in issuing direct orders or commands is called the *imperative*. Bear in mind that, when you use an imperative verb, you will be talking to one or more people, male and/or female. The imperative is formed from the *jussive* of the verb, so have a look at the jussives in the verb tables. These are often the same as the subjunctives in written form, but not always, so make sure you have got the right one.

Bearing all the above in mind, the imperative of any verb can be worked out by applying some simple rules. Note that the following rules omit reference to the dual imperative, used in writing – but not speech – when addressing two people. This is done to save clutter, but if you need a dual imperative, work it out in the same way from the dual part of the jussive.

Step One Work out whom you are addressing (one man, one woman, several men, several women). For a mixed group use the masculine plural form (also addressing women in many dialects of spoken Arabic which have lost the feminine plural ending).

Step Two Select the appropriate part of the *jussive* verb (which may or may not look the same as the subjunctive form: check this). This will always begin with the prefix **ta-** or **tu-**, the 'you' forms.

Step Three Remove the entire *prefix* (but leave any suffixes present alone), and in many cases the result will be the required imperative form. There are two main groups which require further treatment.

1 Imperatives derived according to the above rules from Form IV verbs.
2 Verbs where the word resulting from the application of steps one to three above *begins with an unvowelled letter*, a serious error in Arabic!

In both these cases, a further step must be taken:

Step Four Write an *alif* in front of the word resulting from steps one to three. This *alif*, of course, must have a vowel and the rules for *which* vowel are given below. With the exception of Form IV verbs, this vowel is not all that important, and is in practice frequently elided, so if you want to take a short cut, apply an i-vowel and the result will be understandable in most cases. The table overleaf gives some examples, which are followed by the rules.

Formation of the Arabic imperative

Verb	Person(s) addressed	Jussive you-form	Prefix deleted
وقف *stop*	one male	تَقِف	قِف
ذهب *go*	one male	تَذْهَب	ذْهَب
كتب *write*	one female	تَكْتُبِي	كْتُبِي
انصرف *go away*	pl. males	تَنْصَرِفُوا	نْصَرِفُوا
قدّم *present*	pl. females	تُقَدِّمْنَ	قَدِّمْنَ
قام *stand up*	one male	تَقُم	قُم
اشتغل *work*	pl. males	تَشْتَغِلُوا	شْتَغِلُوا
وضع *put*	one female	تَضَعِي	ضَعِي
فتح *open*	one male	تَفْتَح	فْتَح
لفّ *turn*	one male	تَلِفّ	لِفّ
أرسل *send*	pl. males	تُرْسِلُوا	رْسِلُوا

Step *4* action required	*Alif* and vowel applied	Check
—	—	Truncated jussive form does not begin with un-vowelled letter.
√	اِذْهَب	*Alif* applied, vowelled *i* since second radical takes *a*.
√	اُكْتُبِي	*Alif* applied, takes u-vowel because second radical has *u*.
√	اِنْصَرِفُوا	Derived from Form VII verb, so *alif* takes *i*.
—	—	Truncated jussive form stands
—	—	Truncated jussive form stands.
√	اِشْتَغِلُوا	Derived from Form VIII verb, so *alif* takes *i*.
—	—	Truncated jussive form stands.
√	اِفْتَح	*Alif* required, takes i-vowel because middle radical takes *a*.
—	—	Truncated jussive form stands.
√	أَرْسِلُوا	Derived from Form IV verb, so must always take a-vowel with *hamza*.

A   All Form IV Verbs   The *alif* (which, incidentally, is necessary whether or not the result of Step Three begins with an unvowelled letter) takes an a-vowel, written with *hamza* (preferably) and never elided.

B   Illicit Results of Step Three (beginning with an unvowelled letter). These will be derived from original verbs of one of two groups, either

1 A verb of one of the Forms VII, VIII, IX (unlikely) or X. In this case the vowel for your *alif* is an i-vowel, and can be elided.

2 A Form I verb, in which case you must check the characteristic vowel of the present tense, i.e. the one which goes on the *middle* radical. If this is a u-vowel, your *alif* also takes a u-vowel. If it is anything else (*a* or *i*), the *alif* takes an *i*. Both of these can also be elided after preceding words ending in a vowel.

The table gives some examples to help you.

Irregular imperatives

A few common imperatives either do not follow the rules given in the previous section, or do not apparently relate to their verbs at all.

خذ **khudh**, خذى **khudhii**, خذوا **khudhuu**, خذن **khudhna**,

from أخذ *take!*

كل **kul**, كلي **kulii**, كلوا **kuluu**, كلن **kulna**

from أكل *eat!*

In these the initial *hamza* of the root has been lost. There are two verbs 'to come' in Arabic, أتى **ataa** and جاء **jaa'**, but the imperative usually used relates to neither root. This is

تعال **ta:aala** (f) تعالي **ta:aalii** (pl) تعالوا **ta:aaluu** *come!*

There is also the irregular (but common)

هات **haat**, (f) هاتي **haati** short final vowel, (pl) هاتوا **haatuu** meaning 'give!', 'bring!"

EXERCISE 15.2 Give the imperative forms of the following verbs in the masculine singular, feminine singular and masculine plural forms:

تبع — فتّش — أكل — شرب — رقص — قام — ضحك — قدّم —
سمع — كان — ردّ — أعطى — طلب — وقف — جاء — استقبل —
دفع — احتفل — لفّ — اشتغل — زار — أرسل — علّم — بدأ

Negative commands – 'Don't ... !'

These are simply expressed by the negative word لا plus the appropriate part of the jussive verb (according to the person(s) addressed).

لا تذهب *Don't go* (to a man)

لا تشتغلي *Don't work* (to a woman)

لا تقوموا *Don't stand up* (to men)

لا ترسلن *Don't send* (to women)

EXERCISE 15.3 Translate the following sentences:

١ ادخل المطار من الباب الكبير ولفّ على يسارك عند مكتب الجمارك

٢ رتّبوا هذه الكتب على الرفّ من فضلكم

٣ اسألي الأستاذ عبد الله عن تاريخ العرب

٤ يا أحمد خذ هذه الشنطة الثقيلة وضعها في السيّارة

٥ تفضّلوا اجلسوا . كلوا واشربوا .

٦ اطلب من التاجر أن يردّ اليك الفلوس فورا

٧ لا تقف هنا ، اذهب الى آخر الشارع وقف عند المصنع

٨ لا تكلّموني بالانجليزيّة . لا أفهم الّا العربية

٩ اكتبي اسمك هنا وقدّمي الورقة للسكرتيرة

١٠ يا سيدى أعطني الجواز من فضلك كي أطّلع عليه

Vocative particles

In Arabic, when addressing someone directly (even in spoken Arabic) it is customary to use the vocative particle يا *yaa*. We have traces of this sort of thing in archaic and poetic English ('*O great king...*'), and perhaps the 'oh' in expletives such as 'Oh Lord' is more of a vocative than an interjection. In Arabic we have it before names and ordinary nouns:

يا محمّد   *Muhammad!*   يا ولد   *boy!*

In more formal Arabic, there is the compound expression يا أيّها **yaa ayyuhaa** for males and يا أيّتها **yaa ayyatuhaa** for females, which is followed by words having the definite article. The *yaa* can sometimes be omitted:

أيّها السيّدات والسادة   *Ladies and gentlemen...*

يا أيّها المواطنون   *Fellow countrymen!*

EXERCISE 15.4   Translate into Arabic:
1   Don't play in the street, boy.
2   Return the passport to him at once, please. (m, s)
3   Don't laugh (m, pl), this is an important matter.
4   Don't be late, Fatima, the plane leaves at 4.30.
5   Open the book (m, s) and read what is in it.

EXERCISE 15.5   See what you can make of the following short piece from a newspaper. New words are given.

prices   transportation   organise

شركة مصر للطيران تُنَظِّم رحلات خاصّة لنَقْل المصريين من امريكا وكندا بأسْعَار

each of   organisation   decide   tourist (adj)

سياحيّة . قَرَّرَت شركة مصر للطيران تَنْظِيم رحلات طيران خاصة إلى كل من

summer   season

أمريكا وكندا بأسعار سياحية ، وذلك لنقل المصريين خلال مَوْسِم الصَيْف

services   fixing   also

وقرّرت أيْضاً تثْبِيت أسعار تذاكر الطيران والخَدَمات السياحية في مصر .

Unit Sixteen

الأدب العربي

Text

١   يبتدىء الادب العربي في عصر الجاهلية أى قبل مجيء الاسلام

٢   وكان للقبائل حينئذ شعراء يفتخرون بها ويتنافسون في أشعارهم

٣   وقد جُمِعَت أحسن قصائد شعراء الجاهلية في ديوان يُسَمَّى المعلّقات السبع التي لم يزل الناس يقرأونها ويدرسونها الى الآن

٤   وقد ازدهرت الآداب والفنون في عهد العبّاسيين الذين دامت خلافتهم من سنة ٧٥٠ الى سنة ١٢٥٨

٥   وقد كُتِبَت آلاف من الكتب في التاريخ والعلوم الدينية والشعر والنثر الفنّي

٦   ولسوء الحظ لا نعرف الكثير عن هذا التراث الغني في بلاد الغرب لعدم وجود ترجمات له باللغات الأجنبية

٧   وعلى العموم فانّ أهل الغرب يجهلون الأدب العربي جهلا تامّا باستثناء كتاب ألف ليلة وليلة وهو مجموعة من القصص والخرافات الشرقية

٨   وأمّا الأدباء والنقّاد العرب فلا تُعْتَبَر هذه المجموعة كتابا ذا قيمة عندهم بالرغم من أنّه قد ألهم عددا كبيرا من الأعمال الأدبية والفنّية في الغرب

٩   وقد وصل هذا التأثير حتّى الى الثقافة الشعبية ومن أمثلة ذلك مسرحية الأطفال المعروفة (علاء الدين والمصباح السحرى) التي شاهدناها جميعا ونحن صغار

١٠   وقد وصلت هذه القصّة الصينية الأصل الينا عن طريق ألف ليلة وليلة

١١   ولم يتوقّف التأليف والتصنيف عند العرب خلال عصور الظلام في أوربّا

١٢   وأسهم الأدباء العرب بأعمالهم في العلوم والفلسفة والرياضيات والكيمياء وعلم الفلك التي تُرْجِم بعضها من اليونانية ولو لا ذلك لفُقِدَت هذه الكتب النفيسة

١٣   وبعد القرن الرابع عشر تقريبا أخذ الأدب العربي ينحطّ انحطاطا تدريجيا حتى نهضته في القرن العشرين

197

Vocabulary

Nouns

أَدَب (آداب)   *literature*

مَجِيء   *coming*

شِعْر (أَشْعار)   *poetry, piece of poetry*

دِيوان (دَواوين)   *anthology, diwan: also chancellery*

فَنّ (فُنون)   *art, craft*

عَبّاسيّ (ـون)   *Abbasid*

عِلْم (عُلوم)   *science, knowledge*

سُوء (أَسْواء)   *evil, badness*

تُراث   *heritage*

وُجود   *existence*

جَهْل   *ignorance*

لَيْلَة (لَيال، اللَيالي .def)   *night*

قِصّة (قِصَص)   *story, short story*

ناقِد (نُقّاد)   *critic*

عَمَل (أَعْمال)   *work*

مِثال (أَمْثِلَة)   *example*

عَلاء الدين   *Aladdin*

أَصْل (أُصول)   *origin*

الجاهِلِية   *'The Ignorance' (referring to the period before Islam)*

شاعِر (شُعَراء)   *poet*

قَصيدة (قَصائِد)   *poem, ode*

مُعَلَّقَة (ـات)   *moallaqa (see notes)*

عَهْد (عُهود)   *age, period*

خِلافة (ـات)   *caliphate*

نَثْر   *prose*

حَظّ   *luck, fortune*

عَدَم   *lack of something, non-existence*

عُموم   *generality*

اِسْتِثْناء (ات)   *exception*

مَجْموعة (ـات)   *collection*

خُرافة (ـات)   *fable, tale*

قِيمة   *value*

تَأْثير   *influence*

مَسْرَحِية (ـات)   *play, theatrical piece*

مِصْباح (مَصابيح)   *lamp*

تَأْلِيف authorship, act of writing   طَريق (طُرُق) way (sometimes f)

ظَلام darkness   تَصْنِيف composition

الرياضِيات mathematics   فَلْسَفة philosophy

عِلمْ الفَلَك astronomy   الكِيمْياء chemistry

نَهْضة (ـات) renaissance   اِنْحِطاط decline

Adjectives

حَسَن good, handsome   أَحْسَن better, best

دِينيّ religious   فَنِّي artistic

غَنِيّ (أَغْنِياء) rich   تامّ complete

شَرْقِيّ eastern, oriental   أَدَبِيّ literary

مَعْروف known, well-known   سِحْرىّ magic

صِينيّ Chinese   يونانيّ Greek

نَفِيس precious   تَدْريجيّ gradual

Verbs

اِبْتَدَأ ، يَبْتَدِىء (VIII) begin   اِفْتُخَر ، يَفْتُخِر بِـ (VIII) glory in, boast about

تَنافَس ، يَتَنافَس (VI) compete   جَمَع (a) collect, gather

سَمَّى ، يُسَمِّي (II) call, name   اِزْدَهَر ، يَزْدَهِر (VIII) flourish

دام ، يَدوم last   جَهِل (a) be ignorant of, not know

اِعْتَبَر ، يَعْتَبِر (VIII) consider, think   أَلْهَمَ ، يُلْهِم (IV) inspire

تَوَقَّف ، يَتَوَقَّف (V) pause, stop

تَرْجَمَ ، يُتَرْجِم   *translate*

أَسْهَمَ ، يُسْهِم   (IV) *contribute, take a share in*

اِنْحَطَّ ، يَنْحَطّ   (VII) *decline*

فَقَدَ   (i) *lose*

Other words

حِينَئِذٍ   *then, at that time*

لِسُوءِ الحَظّ   *unfortunately*

عَلى العُموم   *in general*

بِاسْتِثْناء   *with the exception of*

بِالرَغْم من   *in spite of*

جَمِيعاً   *all, wholly*

لَوْ   *if*

تَقْرِيباً   *approximately*

Literal translation

The-Literature the-Arabic

1 Begins the-literature the-Arabic in (the) age (of) the-Ignorance that-is before (the) coming (of) the-Islam.

2 And-was to-the-tribes then poets (who) they-boasted about-them and-they-competed in their-poems.

3 And-/*past marker*/ were-collected (the) best (of the) odes (of the) poets (of) the-Ignorance in (an) anthology (which) is-called the-Mu'allaqat the-Seven which not ceased the-people they-read-them and-they-study-them to now.

4 And-/*past marker*/ flourished the-literatures and-the-arts in (the) age (of) the-Abbasids who lasted their-caliphate from year 750 until year 1258

5 And-/*past marker*/ were written thousands of-the-books on the-history and-the-sciences the-religious and-the-poetry and-the-prose the-artistic.

6 And-for-(the)-badness (of) the-luck not we-know the-much about this the-heritage the-rich in (the) lands (of) the-West for-(the)-lack (of) existence (of) translations of-them in-the-languages the-foreign.

7 And-on the-generality /so/-indeed (the) people (of) the-West they-are-ignorant (about) the-literature the-Arabic (an) ignorance complete with-(the)-exception (of the) book (a) Thousand Night and (a) Night and-it (is a) collection of the-stories and-the-fables the-oriental.

8 And-as-for the-writers and-the-critics the-Arab /so/-not is-considered this the-collection (a) book possessor (of) value with-them in-the-spite of that-it /*past marker*/ inspired (a) number great of-the-works the-literary and-the-artistic in the-West.

9 And-/*past marker*/ reached this the-influence even to the-culture the-popular and of (the) examples (of) that (the) play (of) the-children the-known Aladdin and-the-Lamp the-Magic which we-witnessed-it all and-we (were) young.

10 And-/*past marker*/ arrived this the-story the-Chinese (of) /the/-origin to-us by way (of) Thousand Night and-Night.

11 And-not stopped the-writing and-the-composition with the-Arabs during (the) Ages (of) the-Darkness in Europe.

12 And-contributed the-writers the-Arab /with/-their-works on the-sciences and-the-philosophy and-the-mathematics and-the-chemistry and-(the)-science (of) the-astronomy which were-translated some-(of)- them from the-Greek and-if not that/*conditional marker*/-were-lost these the-books the-precious.

13 And-after the-century the-fourth ten (i.e. fourteenth) approximately took (i.e. began) the-literature the-Arabic it-declines (a) declining gradual until its-renaissance in the-century the-twenty.

Background to text

This is not the place for a history of Arabic literature, but a few brief remarks are in order because the Arabs are very proud of their literary tradition. 'Culture' and 'heritage' are perhaps two of the most overworked words in their language.

As in most societies, literature appears to have begun among the Arabs with poetry. This was a strong enough tradition among the tribes for some of the works of the Age of Ignorance to survive into the Islamic period which began in the early seventh century. The best known of these poems are the Seven Moallaqat or 'Golden Odes', unruly works of great evocative charm describing life in the desert. Tribes appear to have had semi-professional poets whose job it was to sing the praises of their own tribes and insult their enemies.

The Holy Koran is the first major document in Arabic, and the coming of Islam brought with it the need for much codification of law, religious interpretation and practice and so on. Poetry continued to flourish, and by the mid-eighth century true artistic prose – in the sense of writing for entertainment rather than instruction – began to develop. Undoubtedly the 'Golden Age' of Arabic literature in most respects was witnessed in the courts of the Abbasid Caliphs in Baghdad. After this period a general decline set in but, as mentioned in the text, many classical Greek works were saved to the world by Arab translators. The fact that Arabic literature has

had a *continuous* tradition since the seventh century is very important, as also is the fact that the language of the early period can be
read almost as easily as modern material.

The novel in its true sense, and the writing of drama, are new
skills in Arabic, imported from the West in the twentieth century,
but now firmly established and thriving in the Arab world.

Analysis of text and grammar

1 يبتدىء – Form VIII of the verb بدأ (third radical *hamza*). The
carrier for *hamza* has to change because of the vowel altering from
a **bada'** to *i* **yabtadi'**.

2 حينئذ Note the spelling of this word. The **-in** ending should be
pronounced .... يفتخرون بها is a relative clause with indefinite antecedent شعراء.

يفتخر is a Form VIII verb, and يتنافس a Form VI, the latter
illustrating a common meaning pattern of VI, that of reciprocal
action, to do something to each other (here 'compete against each
other').

3 جمعت For this and all passive forms, see pp. 205–8. Since many
passives in Arabic are identical in writing to their equivalent active
forms, the vowelling has been given in this text. In practice it is
necessary to work out from the context whether such forms are
active or passive.

أحسن قصائد شعراء الجاهلية is a quadruple possessive: 'the best
of the poems of the poets of the Ignorance'.

ديوان has two separate meanings: the registry or chancellery of a
government (the term is still used in many modern states, especially
on the Arabian Peninsula), and an anthology of poetry (usually by
the same poet – 'Collected Works of ...').

يسمّى is the present tense passive of a Form II verb with third
radical *y* (see Table 9).

المعلّقات السبع is a term of doubtful origin. The most obvious
meaning of the word معلّق is 'hung, suspended', and one explanation is that the poems were so highly acclaimed that they were

'hung up' on public display in Mecca. Believe that if you like. The 'Golden Odes' (another title), however, still continue to fascinate, despite having been dismissed as forgeries by the most eminent Arab literary critic of the twentieth century.

لم يزل expresses the English 'still' (see page 178).

4 ازدهرت is a Form VIII verb from the root زهر . The infixed *t* changes to *d* under the influence of the preceding *z* (see Table 2 and notes).

العبّاسيين – after the death of the Prophet Muhammad, the Classical Age of Arabic history is divided into three caliphates (the caliph being the appointed head of the Islamic state). These are the Orthodox Caliphs (632–661) who ruled from Arabia, the Omayyad (or more correctly Umayyad) Caliphate (661–750) based in Damascus, and the Abbasids (750–1258) whose seat was Baghdad.

دامت is a Hollow verb (Table 5).

7 فانّ – the **fa** here is idiomatic.

يجهلون . . . جهلا تامّا again demonstrates this favourite device of Arabic which makes up for its lack of adverbs. We would say 'were completely ignorant of . . .'. Remember the Biblical 'They rejoiced a great rejoicing' which really means 'they rejoiced greatly'.

ألف ليلة وليلة – this rather quaint turn of phrase is the correct way to say '1001 Nights' in Arabic. The work unfortunately does not enjoy the same popularity and esteem in Arab lands as it does in Europe (except perhaps among the humbler classes, part of whose folk heritage it really is). The reason for this disdain is presumably the popular nature of the work, its style of language and occasional obscenity.

8 تعتبر is a Form VIII verb (passive). ذا is the accusative of ذو (see page 176) agreeing with كتابا : *A book* (possessor) *of value.*

ألهم is a Form IV verb.

9 مسرحية الاطفال is, of course, 'pantomime".

جميعا is the adverbial accusative form of جميع *the whole of something, all.*

ونحن صغار *when we were young.*

10 الصينية الأصل – technically this is a special kind of adjectival possessive construction 'Chinese of origin'. Because the first element is an adjective, it is allowed – contrary to the normal rules – to take the definite article in agreement with القصّة . Translate as 'This story of Chinese origin'.

11 يتوقّف is a Form V verb. التأليف والتصنيف are both verbal nouns of Form II (see Table 2). It is another favourite device of Arabic to place together two words of virtually the same meaning – all the better if they are of the same word-pattern as they are here. The idea is to decorate rather than to add to the meaning.

12 أسهم , a Form IV verb, requires the preposition **bi** before its object.

الكيمياء is the origin of our word 'alchemy' which preserves the Arabic definite article.

ترجم is a four-radical verb (Table 2, notes to Form II), here passive.

ولو **law** is the Arabic word for 'if' in unfulfilled (or unfulfillable) conditions (see pp. 217ff.). Its use requires the introductory word **la** (here in **la-fuqidat**) in the following clause.

13 الرابع عشر *fourteenth*. See ordinal numbers, Appendix 2.

تقريبا is the adverbial accusative 'approximately'. The **-an** ending should be pronounced.

أخذ – this verb, which we have already met as 'to take', is frequently used in Arabic in the sense of 'to begin'. In these cases it is followed by a present tense verb (here **yanHaTT**). The idea is not too far removed from the English idiom 'He *took* to visiting her regularly'.

انحطاطا تدريجيا – see remarks to line 7 above. The verbal noun **inHiTaaT** could have been left out, leaving the perfectly acceptable **tadriijiyyan** *gradually*. Hence the origin of the Arabic adverb.

العشرين – see ordinal numbers, Appendix 2.

EXERCISE 16.1 Read the Arabic text aloud and translate it into idiomatic English.

EXERCISE 16.2 Are the following statements concerning the text True or False?

١   ابتدأ الأدب العربي بعد مجيء الاسلام

٢   لم يكن الشعراء يتنافسون في أشعارهم

٣   جمعت أحسن قصائد الجاهلية في ديوان

٤   لم يكن عند العرب تأليف في عهد العبّاسيين

٥   اعتبر كتاب ألف ليلة وليلة كتابا ذا قيمة عند الأدباء العرب

٦   لم يكن العرب يعرفون الفلسفة والكيمياء

٧   الأوربّيون يعرفون كثيرا عن الأدب العربي

٨   ازدهر الأدب العربي بعد القرن الرابع عشر

٩   كتاب ألف ليلة وليلة هو مجموعة من القصائد

١٠ قصّة «علاء الدين والمصباح السحرى» صينية الأصل

١١ توقّف التأليف عند العرب خلال عصور الظلام

١٢ دامت الخلافة العبّاسية أكثر من ثلاث مائة سنة

The passive of the verb

The term *passive* comes from the Latin word 'to suffer', so it is used to describe verbs which express the 'suffering' of the action rather than its execution. In English the passive is formed by using the verb 'to be' with a past participle, e.g. 'He *is regarded* as a good worker', 'The new chairman *was elected* last week'. Other people are doing the regarding and electing – not the grammatical subject of the sentence ('He' and 'The new chairman').

The Arabs call the passive verb (described below) 'the unknown', and this is rather important because, in Arabic, the passive is *never* used if the person or persons carrying out the action are mentioned. For instance, in the sentences above, it would be quite in order in English to add this information:

'He is regarded *by his employers* as a good worker'
'The new chairman was elected *by the committee* last week'.

In Arabic, if this information is to be provided, it is necessary to use the ordinary active verb and say:

'His employers *regard* him as a good worker'
The committee *elected* the new chairman last week'

In general, the use of the passive is less frequent than it is in English. This is because Arabic verbs often have the option not available in English of using one or other of the derived stems which may have a 'passive' meaning, for example علّم (stem II) *to teach*, and تعلّم (stem V) *to be taught, to learn*. In spoken Arabic the use of the true passive is rare.

The main difficulty of the Arabic passive is that, in the usual unvowelled texts, it looks identical to the active in most verbs and reference has to be made to the context to see which makes sense.

Rules for forming the passive
Note that the fact that a verb is passive has no effect on the verb *endings* in both tenses, which are identical to those of the active. The passive forms are given throughout the verb tables, but the following rules are given to help you work them out for yourself.

Past tense
The middle radical of the root is vowelled *i* and all preceding letters *which have a vowel in the active* have this vowel changed to *u*. Short vowels become short *u*, long vowels become long *u*. Examples:

Active		Passive	
جمع	**jama:** *he collected*	**jumi:** *he (it) was collected*	
اعتبرت	**i:tabarat** *she considered*	**u:tubirat** *she was considered*	
أخذوا	**akhàdhuu** *they took*	**ukhidhuu** *they were taken*	
شاهد	**shaahad** *he witnessed, saw*	شوهد **shuuhid** *he (it) was seen*	

You will see from the above that both active and passive forms are identical in writing except when long vowels are involved (*shuuhid*). Many anomalies occur due to the presence of *hamza*, weak letters and other undesirable elements in the root. Reference should be made to the verb tables for these, and attention will be drawn to them as they occur. Perhaps it is worth noting the following at this stage:

1 **Hamza verbs** Verbs with *hamza* as first radical cause no problem as the carrier letter is always an *alif*, but where it is second or third radical, the carrier letter has to be changed:

أَكَل **'akal/'ukil** *he ate/was eaten*

سَأَل **sa'al/** سئِل **su'il** *he asked/was asked*

قَرَأ **qara'/** قُرِىء **quri'** *he read/he (it) was read*

2 **Doubled verbs** The uncontracted forms follow the rule given above, and the contracted forms all take a u-vowel:

رَدَّت **raddat/ruddat** *she gave back/she (it) was given back*

3 **Four-radical verbs** There is no 'middle' radical, so the third radical takes the i-vowel. Otherwise the rule applies:

ترجمت **tarjamat/turjimat** *she translated/she (it) was translated*

Present tense
The prefix takes a u-vowel, and all other letters vowelled in the active take an a-vowel (long or short as appropriate). Again the endings are unaffected (see note above).

Active		**Passive**	
يفقد **yafqid** *he loses*		**yufqad** *he (it) is lost*	
تطلب **taTlub** *she requests*		**tuTlab** *she (it) is requested*	
يحدّد **yuHaddid** *he defines*		**yuHaddad** *he (it) is defined*	
يشاهد **yushaahid** *he witnesses*		**yushaahad** *he (it) is witnessed*	

Again here are a few irregular forms:

Hamza verbs The most noticeable thing this time is the change of the carrier letter on verbs with *first* radical *hamza:*

يأخذ **ya'khudh/** يؤخذ **yu'khadh** *he takes/is taken*

Middle and *third* radical hamzas are written on *alif:*

يسأل **yas'al/yus'al** *he asks/is asked*

يقرأ **yaqra'/yuqra'** *he reads/he (it) is read*

Doubled and four-radical verbs are fairly straightforward, in the present tense, but these and the weak-radical verbs should be studied in the tables.

EXERCISE 16.3   Change the following sentences from active to passive (remembering that the agent, if mentioned, must be omitted in the passive form). Example:

The Arab writers translated thousands of books.	ترجم الأدباء العرب آلافا من الكتب
——*Thousands of books were translated.*	←— ترجمت آلاف من الكتب

١   جمع العرب أحسن القصائد في ديوان

٢   لا يعتبر النقّاد كتاب ألف ليلة وليلة كتابا هامًّا

٣   ألهم هذا الكتاب عددا كبيرا من الأعمال الأدبية

٤   وظّفتني الحكومة في وزارة التعليم

٥   ستجد هذا الكتاب في المكتبة

٦   سألني عن تاريخ الأدب العربي

٧   أرسلوها الى أمريكا لتدرس الرياضيات

EXERCISE 16.4   Try to translate the following passage, which describes a well-known figure in the cinema.

اذا تَرَكْنا رجال السياسة فَرُبَّما وجدنا أنّ الممثّل عمر الشريف من أَشْهَر العرب في الغرب . وقد وُلد هذا الكَوْكَب السينمائي في مصر وعمل مدّة في المَسْرَح هناك قبل أن يهاجر الى انجِلْتَرّا حَيْثُ أصبح مشهورا جدّا في عالم السينا . وقد لعب أدوارا عديدة في الأفْلام الانجليزية والامريكية أشهرها دوره الرئيسي في فلم «الدكتور جيفاكو» . ويعرف أَيْضاً بمَهارته في لعبة البريدج .

Unit Seventeen

أبو نواس وهارون الرشيد

١ كان أبو نواس شاعرا ونديما للخليفة العبّاسي هارون الرشيد

٢ واشتهر أبو نواس بذكائه ومزاحه كما اشتهر بشعره

٣ وتكثر في الفولكلور العربي القصص والخزافات عن مغامرات الشاعر مع الخليفة

٤ ومنها أنّ هارون قال لأبي نواس ذات يوم — وكان ذلك في الشتاء —

٥ يا أبا نواس ، ان قضيت ليلتك على سطح البيت وأنت عريان وليست لديك نار تتدفّأ منها ، أعطيتك ألف دينار

٦ فاتّفقا على ذلك وقلع أبو نواس ثيابه وصعد الى السطح وبات هناك

٧ وجاءه الخليفة في الصباح ولقيه بردانا جدّا وجسمه يرتجف

٨ قال الشاعر — هات المال ، قال الخليفة — لا ، قال — لِمَ ؟

٩ فأشار الخليفة الى نار على مبعدة قد ولّعها بعض البدو وقال — قد تدفّأت ، واللّه ، من تلك النار التي تراها هناك . ورفض أن يعطيه الدنانير

١٠ وبعد أيّام قليلة خرج الخليفة ومعه أبو نواس للصيد

١١ وعند الظهر قال هارون للشاعر — واللّه قد جعت — فقال أبو نواس — اجلس هنا واسترح . سأطبخ لك شيئا لذيذا تأكل منه . وذهب عنه .

١٢ وانتظر الخليفة زمنا طويلا واشتدّ جوعه ولم يرجع أبو نواس اليه

١٣ وفي آخر الأمر قام الخليفة ليبحث عن طعامه . ولقي أبا نواس جالسا عند نار قد أوقدها في أسفل شجرة ولم ير على النار قدرا فدهش من ذلك . ثمّ رفع عينيه الى الشجرة ورأى القدر قد عُلِّق في أعلاها

١٤ فقال وهو غضبان جدّا — فكيف يُطْبَخ الأكل والقدر في أعلى الشجرة والنار على الأرض ؟

١٥ قال أبو نواس — كما تدفّأت أنا تلك الليلة على سطح البيت

١٦ فضحك الخليفة وأعطاه الدنانير .

209

Vocabulary

Nouns

أَبُو نُواس *Abu Nuwas*	هارون الرَشيد *Harun al-Rashid*
نَديم (نُدَماء) *crony, boon companion*	ذَكاء *cleverness, shrewdness*
مُزاح *joking, wit*	فُولْكْلُور *folklore*
مُغامَرة (ـات) *adventure*	الشِتاء *winter*
الصَيْف *summer*	الخَريف *autumn*
الرَبيع *spring*	سَطْح (سُطوح) *roof, surface*
نار (نيران) *fire*(f)	دينار (دَنانير) *Dinar (currency unit)*
ثَوْب (ثِياب) *garment, pl. clothes*	جِسْم (أَجْسام) *body*
مال (أَمْوال) *money, wealth, goods*	بَدَويّ (بَدْو) *bedouin*
صَيْد *hunting, hunt*	الظُهْر *noon*
زَمَن ، زَمان (أَزْمِنة) *time*	جُوع *hunger*
أَسْفَل *base, lowest part*	قِدْر (قُدُور) *cooking pot*
عَيْن (عُيون) *eye* (f)	أَعْلَى *top, highest part*
طَعام (أَطْعِمة) *food*	أَكْل *eating, food*

Adjectives

عُرْيان (عَرايا) *naked*	بَرْدان *cold*
جالِس *sitting*	غَضْبان (غَضْبَى .f) *angry*

Verbs

اِشْتُهَر ، يَشْتُهِر (VIII) *become famous,* | كَثُر (u) *be many, numerous*
be famous

قَضَى ، يَقْضِي *pass, spend (time)* | تَدَفَّأ ، يَتَدَفَّأ (V) *get warm*

اِتَّفَق ، يَتَّفِق (VIII) *agree* | قَلَع (a) *strip off, take off*

صَعَد (a) *ascend, climb* | بات ، يَبِيت *spend the night*

لَقِيَ ، يَلْقَى *find, meet* | اِرْتَجَفَ ، يَرْتَجِف (VIII) *tremble,*
shiver

أَشار ، يُشِير (IV) *point, indicate* | وَلَّع ، يُوَلِّع (II) *light, kindle*

خَرَج (u) *go out, exit* | جاع ، يَجُوع *be/become hungry*

جَلَس (i) *sit* | اِسْتَراح ، يَسْتَرِيح (X) *rest*

اِنْتَظَر ، يَنْتَظِر (VIII) *wait, expect* | اِشْتَدّ ، يَشْتَدّ (VIII) *be/become strong,*
violent

بَحَث عَنْ (a) *search for* | أَوْقَد ، يُوقِد (IV) *light, ignite*

دَهِش (a) *be surprised* | رَفَع (a) *raise, lift*

عَلَّق ، يُعَلِّق (II) *hang, suspend* | قال ، يقول *say*

Other words

كَمَا *like, just as* | ذاتَ يَوْمٍ *one day*

لَدَى *with* | عَلَى مَبْعَدةٍ *in the distance*

وَاللّٰهِ *By God!* | في آخر الأَمْر *finally*

Literal translation

Abu Nuwas and-Harun al-Rashid

1   Was Abu Nuwas (a) poet Arab and-crony to-the-Caliph the-Abbasid
    Harun al-Rashid.

2   And-was-famous Abu Nuwas for-his-cleverness and-his-joking like-what
    he-was-famous for-his-poetry.

3   And-are-numerous in the-folklore the-Arab the-stories and-the-fables
    about (the) adventures (of) the-poet with the-Caliph.

4   And-of-them that Harun said to-Abu Nuwas *one day* (see vocabulary) –
    and-was that in the-winter –

5   O Abu Nuwas, if you-spent your-night on (the) roof (of) the-house and-
    you naked and-is-not with-you fire (which) you-get-warm from-it, I-gave-
    you (i.e. I will give you) thousand Dinar.

6   So-they-two-agreed on that and-stripped-off Abu Nuwas his-clothes and-
    ascended to-the-roof and-spent-the-night there.

7   And-came-(to)-him the-Caliph in the-morning and-he-found-him cold very
    and-his-body it-trembles.

8   Said the-poet 'Give the-money' Said the-Caliph – 'No' He-said – 'For-
    what?' (i.e. Why?)

9   So-pointed the-Caliph to (a) fire in distance (which) /*past marker*/ lit-it
    some (of) the-Bedouins and-he-said – '/*past marker*/ You-got-warm, by-
    God, from that the-fire which you-see-it there.' And-he-refused that he-
    give-him the-Dinars.

10 And-after days few went-out the-Caliph and-with-him Abu Nuwas to-the-
    hunt.

11 And-at the-noon said Harun to-the-poet – 'By-God /*past marker*/ I-
    became-hungry' So-said Abu Nuwas – 'Sit here and-rest. /*future marker*/-I-
    cook to-you (a) thing delicious (which) you-eat from-it.' And -he-went
    from-him.

12 And-waited the-Caliph (a) time long and-became-violent his-hunger and-
    not returns Abu Nuwas to-him.

13 And-in (the) last (of) the-matter (i.e. finally) stood-up the-Caliph to-search
    for his-food.
    And-he-found Abu Nuwas sitting at (a) fire (which) /*past marker*/ he-lit-it
    in (the) base (of a) tree and-not he-sees on the-fire (a) pot so-he-was-
    astonished from that. Then he-raised his-two-eyes to-the-tree and-he-saw
    the-pot /*past marker*/ was-hung in its-top.

14 And-he-said and-he angry very – 'How is-cooked the-food and-the-pot (is)
    in (the) top (of) the-tree and-the-fire on the-ground?'

15 Said Abu Nuwas – 'Like-what got-warm I that the-night on (the) roof (of)
    the-house.'

16 So-laughed the-Caliph and-gave-him the-Dinars.

Background to text

The heroes of this story are two of the most colourful characters in Arab history. Harun al-Rashid was Caliph, or leader of the Islamic State, in Baghdad from 786 to 809, and his rule seems to have been marked by the abundance of wealth and patronage of the arts. Abu Nuwas, who died in 810, was a great poet, a boon companion of the Caliph and one of the recipients of his generous patronage.

On the literary side, Abu Nuwas wrote some of the finest poetry in the Arabic language, although its subjects – frequently bawdy and much concerned with the consumption of alcohol – have not always been acceptable to the more conservative. However, the two figures, the Caliph and his witty adversary, have become firmly established in Arab folklore, partly because they feature in the Arabian Nights, but perhaps more because of the abundance of orally transmitted tales about them – no doubt most of them apocryphal. Abu Nuwas, with his over-developed sense of humour, is always either receiving vast amounts of wealth when his jokes work, or about to be thrown in prison when they misfire.

In general, the Arabs are very fond of telling stories and jokes and are very good at it. The better raconteurs love their language and know how to use it, extracting maximum effect from its rich vocabulary and decorative turns of phrase. A lot of this comes through in the Arabian Nights. This is available in many translations, but as usual far richer rewards come from reading the original.

Analysis of text and grammar

Title أَبو نواس **Abuu** is, of course, 'father (of)' and is a common feature in Arabic names. It is one of the nouns (see page 175) which show their grammatical case by varying the long vowel **-uu**, to **-aa** (accusative) and **-ii** (genitive). هارون , also written هٰرون , is equivalent to the Biblical Aaron.

1 شاعرا , etc., all show the accusative indefinite marker after the verb **kaan**.

2 اشتهر is a Form VIII verb, from the same root as مشهور *famous*.

ذكائه – the placing of the *hamza* on a dotless *yaa* shows that the case ending vowel, if pronounced, is *-i*.

3 تكثر – verbs with such meanings as 'to be/become many, (few, far, near, etc.)' sound strange to the English ear, but are relatively common in Arabic. Many of them (including this example) take the comparatively rare u-vowel on the middle radical in the past tense (see Table 2). فولكلور is, of course, a borrowing from English.

4 ومنها أنّ We would have to say something like 'One of these is ...'.

أبي is in the genitive case after the preposition **li-** (see note to title above).

ذات يوم is a literary idiom meaning simply 'One day'. Pronounce it with the full literary endings, viz. **dhaata yawmin**. The normal meaning of **dhaat** is something like 'essence, self', which is of no help here.

5 يا أبا نواس illustrates a rule which only shows up in print with words like **abuu** which show their original cases by long (therefore written) vowels. The rule is not of great importance but, for completeness, it states that if the phrase which follows the vocative particle *yaa* (see page 196) is a possessive construction, the first element of this construction must go into the accusative case. **Abuu nuwaas**, although a name, is such a construction, meaning originally 'Father *of* ...'.

ان *If* – see pp. 217ff. on conditionals, also for the tense of the verbs قضيت and أعطيتك in the following line.

ليلتك with the suffixed **-ak** *your night* is idiomatic.

وليست لديك ... and وأنت عريان ... are what the Arabs call 'clauses of circumstance', i.e. they describe the circumstances obtaining at the time the main verb (here **qaDayt**) is, or is to be, performed. They are usually translated by using the English 'While', but here, because of the conditional, we would have to say something like 'If you spend the night on the roof of the house, naked and without a fire ...'.

لدى means the same as عند. It is a literary form, still widely used, and behaves exactly like **:alaa** and **ilaa** when pronoun suffixes are added (see page 121, note 3).

تتدفّأ منها is a relative clause with the antecedent نار, indefinite and therefore requiring no relative pronoun. Translate as 'a fire from which you might get warm'.

تدفّأ is a Form V verb from a final *hamza* root (Table 2).

دينار , with the strange plural دنانير (magically acquiring an extra *n*), is a currency unit, originally gold, still used in some countries.

6 اتّفق is a Form VIII verb from the root وفق , the *waaw* being assimilated to the infixed **t** (Table 4). The verb here has the long **-aa** ending of the dual past tense, because two people are being referred to. بات is a hollow verb, original root **b-y-t**. Compare بيت *house* (presumably a place where you spend your nights).

7 جاءه – note again that the Arabic verb 'to come' takes a direct object 'he came *him*'. In English we have to say 'he came *to* him'.

8 هات is the imperative form 'Give! Bring!' (see page 194). Note that Arabic does not usually use inverted commas for direct speech. Most Arabic punctuation has been imported from Western sources, and its use is often idiosyncratic.

لم is the shortened interrogative form of **li-** plus **maa** (see page 134. An alternative form is لماذا **li-maadhaa**.

9 أشار is a Form IV hollow verb.

على مبعدة is a literary idiom meaning something like 'on (at) a distance'.

. . . قد ولّعها , etc., is a relative clause with indefinite antecedent **naar** 'a fire'.

بدو – of course we get our English 'bedouin' from a variant form of this word.

والله is a very frequent form of oath both in literary and spoken Arabic, where it is often pronounced with the classical genitive ending *-i* **wallaahi**.

تراها – the **-haa** of course refers to the feminine noun **naar**.

يعطيه is a Form IV verb from the root **:-T-y**. Note that this verb in Arabic takes two direct objects. If one of these is a pronoun, it is attached to the verb as here. If both are pronouns, one is attached to the verb and the other to a special 'carrying word' (meaningless) ايّا **iyyaa**, e.g. أعطيته ايّاه *I gave him it*. This does not occur very frequently in modern Arabic.

11 جعت is a hollow verb, root **j-w-:**.

اجلس and استرح are imperative forms, the latter from a Form X hollow verb showing the short vowel of the jussive.

12 زمنا طويلا are accusatives of time.

اشتدّ is a Form VIII verb from the doubled root **sh-d-d**.

13 قام is a hollow Form I verb, root **q-w-m**.

أبا is an accusative form; see above.

يـر – be careful with this shortened jussive (after **lam**) form of رأى *to see*, normal present tense يرى (see Table 8, notes).

عينيه is in the dual accusative case with *nuun* omitted before the pronoun suffix (page 220).

علّق is the past tense passive of a Form II verb: 'it had been hung'.

14 وهو غضبان is another 'circumstantial clause' meaning 'He said, being angry'; we would say perhaps 'He said in anger', 'He said angrily'.

يطبخ is a passive present tense, vowel **yuTbakh**.

والقدر . . . etc., is yet another circumstantial clause, and should be translated this time with 'when': 'How will the food cook when the pot is in the top of the tree ...'

15 تدفّأت أنا shows the use of **anaa** *I* for effect, the pronoun having been already expressed in the verb.

EXERCISE 17.1   Read the text aloud, and translate it into idiomatic English.

EXERCISE 17.2   True or false?

١   كان أبو نواس خليفة عباسيّا

٢   تكثر القصص عن أبي نواس وهارون الرشيد في الفولكلور العربي

٣   بات أبو نواس على سطح البيت في الصيف

٤   تدفأ أبو نواس من النار التي ولّعها البدو

٥   جاء الخليفة في الصباح وأعطاه الفلوس

٦   خرج الشاعر مع الخليفة للصيد

٧   كان ذلك بعد مدّة طويلة

٨   جاع هارون الرشيد في الصباح

٩   وضع أبو نواس القدر على النار

١٠   كان الأكل مطبوخا

Conditional sentences – 'If X, then Y'

Conditional sentences are composed of two separate parts. The first part is a proposition (supposition, hypothesis), usually introduced in English by the word 'if'. Exceptions to this are sentences like '*Should* it rain, the match will be cancelled', really meaning '*If* it rains ...'. We shall call this first part the *if-clause*.

The second part of such sentences states what happens (would or will happen etc.) if the proposition contained in the if-clause is fulfilled. Although not always introduced by this word in English, we shall call it for convenience the *then-clause*, on the pattern '*If* it rains, *then* the match will have to be cancelled'.

Arabic has three words for *if*, and there are certain restrictions on their use:

لو **law** is used for propositions which, in the opinion of the speaker, are unlikely to be fulfilled, or cannot possibly be fulfilled, e.g. 'If he had saved his money, he could have bought that new car' (the condition cannot be fulfilled, because presumably he has *not* saved his money); 'If I had the wings of a dove I would fly' (obviously impossible); 'If I became prime minister, I would abolish all taxes' (not impossible, but extremely unlikely). When **law** is used in the if-clause, the then-clause *must* be introduced by the prefixed particle **la-** (see examples below).

ان **in** and اذا **idhaa** have more or less the same function in modern Arabic, and either may be used in conditional sentences where the proposition contained in the if-clause is capable of re- alisation, e.g. 'If you pay cash you get a 10% discount' (it is quite possible that you will pay cash and realise the proposition); similarly 'If we see him we'll tell him', 'If you go out in the rain, you'll get wet'. Certain types of then-clause, after **idhaa** only, must be introduced by the particle **fa-**.

In the majority of Arabic conditional sentences, the verb is in the *past tense*, *regardless of what time is referred to*, which must be worked out from the meaning and the context. For instance line 5 in the text says (translating literally) 'If you *spent* the night on the roof ... I *gave* you a thousand dinars', but it is obvious that the event has not yet happened and Harun is merely making a proposal. Common sense provides the translation 'If you spend ... I shall give'. Sometimes in Arabic the present tense (usually jussive mood) is used, but this does not really affect the meaning. The golden rule is to ignore the tense of the Arabic verb and translate as the context requires. You will not go far wrong either if you always use the past tense verb when translating into Arabic.

The above account necessarily contains some generalisations (in the name of simplicity), but emphasises the basic principles:

1 Select the correct word for 'if', guided by whether the condition is likely or unlikely to be fulfilled.

2 Keep all Arabic verbs in the past tense until you gain more experience.

3 Remember to introduce the then-clause with **la-** after **law**, and with **fa-** after **idhaa** as described below.

لَوْ

لو كنت مدير الشركة لوظّفتك فيها *If I were the manager of the company, I would employ you in it.* (Impossible or unlikely since I am not the manager.)

لو جاءت لكلّمتها *If she were to come, I would speak to her* (The implication is that she is not likely to come. Contrast 'If she comes I'll speak to her'.)

لو كنّا قرأنا الجريدة لفهمنا *If we had read the newspaper we would have understood.* (Obviously we have not read the newspaper. Note the use of the compound tense **kaan** with the past tense of the main verb. This is common with **law** and definitely puts the action in the past.

لو لم يأمره أبوه بالذهاب لما ذهب *If his father had not ordered him to go, he would not have gone* (Again, obviously his father *had* ordered him to go. The negatives with **lam** and **maa** are usual in the if- and then-clauses respectively.)

إن

إن فتّشت وجدته *If you search, you will find it*
إن رأيته أعطيته الكتاب *If I see him, I'll give him the book*

The general impression is that the use of **in** is becoming less frequent in modern Arabic, and any difference in implication between it and **idha** is becoming eroded. Some grammar books say that it can take **fa-** in the then-clause in the same way as **idhaa**.

اذا

اذا سافر صديقي سافرت معه   *If my friend goes* (*travels*) *I shall go with him.*

اذا جعت أكلت شيئا   *If I get hungry, I'll eat something.*

The most usual circumstances when the then-clause is introduced by the particle **fa-** are when its verb is imperative (a command, see first example), and when it is a noun sentence, having no verb at all (second example):

اذا أردت أن تكسب فاشتغل   *If you wish to earn, work.*

اذا عملنا ذلك فالأمر فاشل   *If we do that, the thing won't work* (Lit. the matter is futile)

Masculine plurals and duals in possessive constructions

There are two types of external plural formations in Arabic which consist of a long vowel plus the letter *nuun*. These are:

1   The external masculine plural ending which is **-uun** in the nominative case, and **-iin** in the accusative and genitive (strictly speaking **-uuna** and **-iina**, the final vowel usually being omitted; see page 101);

الموظّفون   *the officials*   من الموظّفين   *from the officials*

2   The dual ending, to express two of anything, which is **-aan(i)** in the nominative and **-ayn(i)** in the accusative and genitive (see page 108).

يومان   *two days*   بعد يومين   *after two days*

Also with feminine nouns:

سنتان   *two years*   قبل سنتين   *before two years* (i.e. two years ago)

These two types of endings have the special characteristic of dropping the *nuun* when they occur as the first (property) part of a possessive construction. Such possessive constructions can of course have either nouns or pronoun suffixes as the owner part. Thus we get:

موظّفو الشركة	*the employees of the company*
من موظّفي الشركة	*from the employees of the company*
موظّفوها	*its employees*
من موظّفيها	*from its employees*

Duals are quite commonly used to refer to parts of the body which occur in pairs:

يدا الولد	*The boy's hands*	(the two hands of the boy)
بين يدى الولد	*In front of the boy*	(an idiom, Lit. 'between the two hands of the boy')
يداه	*His (two) hands*	بين يديه *In front of him* (between his two hands)

Notes:

1 As usual, the first person singular suffix **-ii** *my* becomes **-ya** when attached to words ending in long vowels (see page 121). Thus we get:

:aynaaya عيناى *my (two) eyes* (nominative)

:aynayya في عينيّ *in my (two) eyes* (genitive, note spelling with *shadda*)

When this suffix is applied to masculine external plurals, the noun *always takes the accusative/genitive form*, due to assimilation:

mudarrisiyya مدرّسيّ *my teachers* (nominative; again note spelling)

من مدرّسيّ *from my teachers* (genitive).

The form **mudarrisuuya** does *not* exist.

2 When the endings **-hu**, **-hum** and **-hunna** follow **-ii** or **-ay** they change their u-vowels to *i* (see page 121).

EXERCISE 17.3 Try to translate the following story about Joha, another comic character from Middle Eastern folklore. **Jallaabiyya** (galabiyya) is the name given in Egypt to the long shirt or gown worn by men.

جلّابية جحا

ذات يوم وجد جحا جلابيته وسخة جدًّا فأمر زوجته بأن تَغْسِلَها . فغسلتها وعلّقتها
to wash

على حَبْل كان على سطح البيت . واشتدّت الريح في ذلك اليوم وأطارَت الجلابية
cause to fly rope; wind

فوقعت في الشارع . وجاء الناس وَدَاسُوا عليها حتى تَوَسَّخَت وتَمَزَّقَت وأصبحت
become torn get dirty tread

لا تَنْفَع لشىء . وبعد مدّة نَزَل جحا من البيت وخرج الى الشارع فرأى جلابيته
be of use come down

على الأرض وقد توسّخت وتمزّقت . فرفع يديه الى أعلى وقال — الحمد والشُكْر
thanks

لله . فَتَعجَّب الناس من ذلك وقالوا له — يا جحا لماذا تقول «الحمد والشكر
be amazed

لله» وجلابيتك على الأرض وقد أصبحت لا تُساوى شيئا ولن تَقْدِر أن تَلْبَسها مرّة
wear, put on be able be worth

أخرى . قال جحا — واللّٰه لو كنت لابسها لكنت أنا وقعت من السطح وكان
الناس داسوا علىَّ أنا ووَسَّخُونِي وَمزَّقُونِي فالحمد للّٰه والشكر على ذلك .
to tear to make dirty

Unit Eighteen

Text

السياحة في مصر

١   انّ موسم الشتاء في مصر لطيف جدّا ليس فيه حرّ شديد ولا برد قارس

٢   ولذلك سيجد السائح الجوّ صحوا مناسبا للفسح بعد مغادرته سموات أوربّا الرمادية

٣   وعند هبوط الطائرة في مطار القاهرة وبعد القيام بالاجراءات الرسمية يخرج المسافر من باب المطار ويركب سيارة أجرة تنقله الى المدينة

٤   ويكون قد اختار أحد فنادق القاهرة الكثيرة الممتازة للاقامة فيه ولربما يريد أن يستريح قليلا بعد رحلته الطويلة

٥   فينام . . . ويستيقظ بعد فترة قصيرة كانت أو طويلة . . . . . فيخرج الى البلكون ليلقي نظرته الأولى على هذه العاصمة الضخمة ومبانيها الفخمة التي تنبسط أمام عينيه تحت سماء افريقيا الزرقاء

٦   ويكون كل سائح قد تعلّم وهو تلميذ في المدرسة الابتدائية شيئا عن الآثار الفرعونية التي تُوجَد في مصر وحدها

٧   ومن الممكن أن يزور أوّلا أبا الهول والاهرام الواقعة في الجيزة على طرف الصحراء الخالدة

٨   وبعد ذلك فلا بدّ له من أن يرى شيئا من الآثار الاسلامية الكبرى التي توجد في هذه المدينة المؤسسة قبل ألف عام

٩   فهناك مساجد وجوامع تستحقّ المشاهدة ، من أشهرها جامعا السلطان حسن ومحمّد علي اللذان يقعان بالقرب من قلعة صلاح الدين على جبل المقطّم

١٠   ولعلّ أشهر الآثار الاسلامية هو جامع الأزهر الذى أُسِّسَت فيه أوّل جامعة في العالم

١١   ومن الخصائص التي يتميّز بها أهل السياحة — ولا سيّا السيدات — أنّهم لا يحبّون الرجوع الى الوطن بدون غنيمة — أعنى الهدايا والأشياء

222

التي تذكّرهم في المستقبل برحلتهم السعيدة

١٢ ولأجل ذلك فليقصدوا أسواق خان الخليلي التي لا تبعد عن الأزهر الّا بخطوات بسيطة والتي يجد السائح فيها ما يملأ قلبه سرورا ، كمصنوعات النحاس الأصفر ومنسوجات القطن والسجادات الملوّنة وألف شيء غيرها

١٣ ومن عجائب مصر الطبيعية نهر النيل الذى تقع على ضفتيه مطاعم وملاه كثيرة يستطيع الزائر أن يتذوّق فيها طبيخ الشرق الأوسط بأشكاله المتنوّعة وأصنافه المتعدّدة

١٤ وبينما يتغدّى أو يتعشّى مكنه أن يستمع الى نغمات الموسيقى العذبة ويتفرّج على عروض الرقص البلدي

١٥ حقّا . . . لقد صدق المثل المصرى الذى يقول «اللي يشرب من ميّة النيل مرّة لازم يرجع لها تاني»

Vocabulary

Nouns

سِياحَة	*tourism*	مَوسِم (مَواسِم)	*season*
حَرّ	*heat*	بَرْد	*cold*
سائِح (سُوّاح)	*tourist*	فُسْحَة (فُسَح)	*outing, excursion*
مُغادَرة (ـات)	*leaving, departing from*	سَماء (سَمَوات)	*sky (f)*
هُبوط	*descent, landing*	قِيام بـ	*carrying out, performing*
الإجْراءاَت الرَسْميّة	*formalities*	أحَد	*one thing, one person*
فُنْدُق (فَنادِق)	*hotel*	لُوكَنْدَة (ـات)	*hotel*
إقامَة	*residence*	فَتْرة (فَتَرات)	*period, while, time*

نَظْرة (نَظَرات) glance, look	بَلْكُون (ـات) balcony
آثار antiquities	مَبْنى (مَبانٍ) building
هَرَم (أَهْرام) pyramid	أَبُو الهَوْل the Sphynx
طَرَف (أَطْراف) edge	الجِيزة Giza
عَام (أَعْوام) year	صَحْراء (صَحَارَى) desert
سُلْطان (سَلاطين) sultan	مُشَاهَدة witnessing, looking at
صَلاَح الدين Saladin	قَلْعة (قِلاع) citadel, fort
المُقَطَّم Mukattam	جَبَل (جِبال) mountain, hill
خَصِيصة (خَصَائِص) characteristic	الأَزْهَر the Azhar
هَدِيَة (هَدايا) gift, present	غَنِيمة booty, plunder
خان الخَليلي Khan al-Khalili	المُسْتَقْبَل the future
قَلْب (قُلوب) heart	خَطْوة (خَطَوات) step, pace
مَصْنوعات manufactured articles	سُرُور joy, happiness
نُحَاس أَصْفَر brass (Lit 'yellow copper')	نُحاس copper
قُطْن cotton	مَنْسُوجات woven articles
عَجيبة (عَجائِب) wonder	سَجّادة (ـات) rug, prayer mat
النيل the Nile	نَهْر (أَنْهُر، أَنْهار) river
مَطْعَم (مطاعِم) restaurant	ضَفّة (ضِفاف) bank
طَبِيخ cuisine, cookery	مَلْهَى (مَلاهٍ) night club
صَنْف (أَصْناف) kind, type	شكْل (أَشْكال) form, shape, kind
غَداء lunch	فُطور breakfast

عَشاء dinner

نَغَمة (ـات) tone, tune

موسيقَى music

عَرْض (عُروض) show, exhibition

رَقْص dance

Adjectives

لَطيف (لِطاف) pleasant, kind

قارِس biting

صَحْو clear, bright

رَمادِيّ grey

مُمْتاز excellent

ضَخْم huge

فَخْم magnificent

أَزْرقَ (زُرْق) blue

اِبْتِدائيّ elementary (school)

فَرْعونيّ pharaonic, Ancient Egyptian

واقِع situated

خالِد eternal

مُؤَسَّس founded

سَعيد (سُعَداء) happy

أَصْفَر (صُفْر) yellow

بَسيط (بُسَطاء) simple; few

مُلَوَّن coloured

مُتَنَوِّع assorted

مُتَعَدِّد numerous

عَذْب sweet (of music, etc.)

بَلَديّ local, native, folkloric

لازِم necessary

Verbs

نَقَل (u) transport, convey

اِخْتار ، يَخْتار (VIII) choose

نام ، يَنام sleep

اِسْتَيْقَظ ، يَسْتَيْقِظ wake up

أَلْقَى ، يُلْقِي (IV) throw, cast

اِنْبَسَط ، يَنْبَسِط (VII) stretch out

226 Arabic

رَأَى ، يَرَى   see

أَسَّس ، يُؤَسِّس (II) found

تَمَيَّز ، يَتَمَيَّز بِـ (V) be distinguished by

ذَكَّر ، يُذَكِّر (II) remind

قَصَد (i) seek out, make for

تَذَوَّق ، يَتَذَوَّق (V) taste

تَعَشَّى ، يَتَعَشَّى (V) dine

أَمْكَن ، يُمْكِن (IV) be possible (for someone to do)

صَدَق (u) be truthful, tell the truth

تَعَلَّم ، يَتَعَلَّم (V) learn

اِسْتَحَقّ ، يَسْتَحِقّ (X) deserve

أَحَبّ ، يُحِبّ (IV) love, like

عَنَى ، يَعْنِي   mean

مَلأَ (يَمْلأ) (a) fill

اِسْتَطاع ، يَسْتَطِيع (X) be able

تَغَدَّى ، يَتَغَدَّى (V) lunch

اِسْتَمَع ، يَسْتَمِع إلى (VIII) listen to

تَفَرَّج ، يَتَفَرَّج عَلَى (V) look at, watch

Other words

لا بُدَّ مِنْ أَنْ ...   it is necessary that ...

بدون   without

رُبَّا and لَعَلّ   perhaps (for the **la-** on **rubbamaa** see notes)

بَيْنَما   while

وَحْد (with following pronoun suffix) alone

أَوَّلاً   firstly

بالقُرْب مِنْ   in the vicinity of, near

لا سِيَّما   especially

لأَجْل   for the purpose of

حَقّا   truly

Colloquial words

(ثَانِياً) تَاني again (for   مِيَّة water (for ماء)   اللِّي he who (for الذي)

Literal translation

The-Tourism in Egypt

1 Indeed (the) season (of) the-winter in Egypt (is) pleasant very, is-not in-it heat extreme and-not cold biting.

2 And-for-that /*future marker*/-finds the-tourist the-weather bright suitable for-the-excursions after his-leaving (the) skies (of) Europe the-grey.

3 And-at (the-) descent (of) the-plane in (the) airport (of) Cairo and-after the-execution /to/-the-proceedings the-official goes-out the-traveller from (the) gate (of) the-airport and- boards (a) car (of) hire (which) transports-him to the-city.

4 And-he-will-be /*past marker*/ he-chose (i.e. he will have chosen) one (of) hotels (of) Cairo the-many the-excellent for-the-residence in-it and-indeed-perhaps he-wants that he-rests (a) little after his-journey the-long.

5 So-he-sleeps ... and-he-wakes after (a) while short it-was or long ... and-he-goes-out to the-balcony so-that-he-casts his-glance the-first on this the-capital the-huge and-its-buildings the-magnificent which it-stretches before his-two-eyes beneath (the) sky (of) Africa the-blue.

6 And-he-will-be every tourist /*past marker*/ he-learned (i.e. will have learned) and-he pupil in-the-school the-elementary (i.e. while a pupil in ...) thing about the-antiquities the-pharaonic which are-found in Egypt its-singularity (i.e. alone).

7 And-of the-possible that he-visits firstly Father (of) the-Terror (i.e. the Sphinx) and-the-pyramids the-situated in Giza on (the) edge (of) the-desert the-eternal.

8 And-after that so-no escape to-him from that he-see (i.e. he must see) thing of the-antiquities the-Islamic the-great which are-found in this the-city the-founded before thousand year (i.e. 1000 years ago).

9 So-there (are) mosques and mosques (which) deserve the-seeing, of their-most-famous (the) two-mosques (of) the-Sultan Hassan and-Muhammad Ali, which they-two-are-situated in-the-vicinity of (the) citadel of Saladin on (the) mountain (of) Muqattam.

10 And-perhaps (the) most-famous (of) the-antiquities the-Islamic he (is) Mosque (of) al-Azhar which was-founded in-it first university in-the-world.

11 And-of the-characteristics which are-distinguished by-them (the) people (of) tourism – and-especially the-ladies – that-they not like the-return to the-homeland without plunder – I-mean the-gifts and-the-things which remind-them in-the-future of-their-journey the-joyful.

12 And-for-(the)-purpose (of) that so-/*exhortative marker*/-they-make-for (i.e. so let them make for) (the) markets (of) Khan al-Khalili which not they-are-distant from al-Azhar except by-steps few and-which finds the-tourist in-them what fills his-heart (with) joy, like-manufactured-articles (of) the-copper the-yellow (brass) and-woven-articles (of) the-cotton and-the-prayer-mats the-coloured and thousand thing other-(than)-them.

13 And-of (the) wonders (of) Egypt the-natural (is the) river (of) the-Nile

which are-situated on its-two-banks restaurants and-night-clubs many
(which) is-able the-visitor that he-tastes in-them (the) cuisine (of) the-East
the-Middle in-its-forms the-assorted and-its-types the-numerous.

14   And-while he-lunches or he-dines it-is-possible-for-him that he-listens to
(the) tones (of) the-music the-sweet and-he-watches /on/ (the) displays (of)
the-dance the-local.

15   Truly ... /*emphatic past marker*/ was-truthful the-proverb the-Egyptian
which it-says 'Who drinks of (the) water (of) the-Nile (it is) necessary (that)
he-returns to-it again'.

Background to text

The text is an imaginary tourist brochure for Egypt, written in the
flowery style of such pieces. The proverb at the end is given in its
original colloquial Egyptian form.

Although the official word for Cairo is **al-qaahira**, in common
usage the word **miSr** is applied both to the country and its capital.
Giza (the Arabic *jiim* pronounced as a hard 'g', the way the
Egyptians do) is a part of Cairo on the west of the city, and well
known as the site of the Sphinx and the pyramids.

There are of course Islamic remains all over the city, but perhaps
the central point is the complex of the Citadel of Saladin, on the
slopes of Mukattam (several spellings) in the south of the city. The
mosque of Muhammad Ali is in the complex, and that of Sultan
Hassan nearby. The famous teaching mosque of al-Azhar and the
bazaars of Khan al-Khalili are in another quarter of the city not far
away from the Citadel. The original religious teaching institution at
al-Azhar has now developed into a full-scale modern university.

Analysis of text and grammar

1   Note the use of ولا (Lit. 'and not') after the negative verb ليس.

2   جو , literally meaning 'air', is frequently used for 'weather'.

سموات (also spelled سماوات) – words which end in ـاء often put in
this intrusive *waaw* before feminine suffix plural and dual endings,
but not always. See اجراءات below.

3   القيام بـ is a verbal noun from the expression قام (يقوم) بـ. The
verb on its own means 'to stand up.'

4   يكون قد اختار is the future perfect tense 'He will have chosen',
formed by using the present tense of **kaan** (which usually has a

future meaning) plus the past tense of the main verb, usually with the past marker **qad** in between. If the subject of the verb is stated, it is usually placed between **kaan** and **qad** (see page 93).

اختار – be careful with these Form VIII hollow verbs, which preserve the long *aa* in the present, contrary to the usual *a/i* alternation in the pattern (see Table 5).

لرمّيا – the prefixed **la-** is said by the Arabs to be emphatic, but in fact does little to change the meaning. Its use is rather stylistic, giving a 'literary' or 'poetic' flavour.

يستريح is a Form X hollow verb. The *aa/ii* alternation *does* take place in this form, contrary to what was said above concerning Form VIII. Form VII, incidentally, behaves in the same way as VIII. Consult the relevant Tables.

5 قصيرة كانت أو طويلة is again literary, poetic: 'Were it short or long', 'Be it short or long'.

ليلقي   *So that he might cast, to cast.* For this **li-** see page 177.

عينيّة   *His two eyes,* see page 220 for the omission of the *nuun* of the dual ending.

زرقاء is a colour adjective (see section below) qualifying the feminine noun سماء .

6 يكون . . . قد تعلّم is the future perfect again – see remarks to line 4 above.

وهو تلميذ is a circumstantial clause introduced by **wa-**. Translate as 'While (or 'when') he was a pupil . . .'

توجد is the passive present tense of وجد وحد is used with a following pronoun suffix to mean 'alone'. وحدى *I alone, on my own,* وحدك *You alone,* etc.

7 أبا الهول – for **abuu**, see page 175. Here it is accusative, being the object of the verb **yazuur**.

8 لا بدّ له من أن means literally 'There is no escape to him from that he . . .'. It is a common idiom, used when we would say 'must, has to'.

الكبرى is technically a feminine superlative (see pp. 147–8). It is, however, used more as an intensive than as a literal superlative and is better translated 'great'.

مؤسّس is the passive participle from the verb أسّس. The change in *hamza*-carrier is caused by the preceding u-vowel. Note the use of **qabl** *before* where we would say 'ago'.

9 مساجد وجوامع – Arabic is rather fond of using two words of virtually identical meaning placed together for effect. (The same thing occurs in the Bible 'He slumbers not nor sleeps'.) A **jaami:** is a major mosque (from the root **j-m-:** 'to gather together') and a **masjid** is a lesser mosque or prayer place (from the root **s-j-d** 'to bow down in prayer').

تستحقّ is a Form X verb from the doubled root **H-q-q** (Table 3).

جامعا is a dual with *nuun* omitted in the possessive construction (see page 220).

اللذان is a dual relative pronoun. The feminine form is اللتان .

يقعان is a dual verb agreeing with the preceding dual subject **jaami:aa**. The verb **waqa:** loses its *waaw* in the present (Table 4).

10 لعلّ *Perhaps*. This word behaves like **'inna** (see page 92) and *must* be followed by a noun or a pronoun suffix.

أُسِّسَت is the passive of أَسَّسَت (root **'-s-s**, Form II).

11 أهل السياحة *People of tourism, tourists.*

يحبّون is a Form IV verb of root **H-b-b**.

12 فليقصدوا – see section below.

لا . . . الّا *Not ... except* is a very common construction in Arabic, where we would use 'only'.

سرورا shows an adverbial use of the indefinite accusative which the Arabs call 'the accusative of distinction', i.e. it distinguishes (here) what his heart will be filled with. ما is used in this sentence as a relative, 'The tourist will find in them *that which* fills his heart, etc.' This is quite common, also with من *who, he who* referring to persons. In most cases, the usual الذي can be used instead.

أصفر – see section on colours below.

13 ملاه is one of the class of words which take (in Classical Arabic) the ending **-in** (ملاه) in the indefinite, and a *yaa* ending in the definite (الملاهي). In speech it is always pronounced as if the *yaa* were present: **malaahii** (see also page 142, note to line 2). The word comes from rather an interesting root **l-h-w** which carries the meaning of 'diversion, pleasure, wasting time', the formation being a noun of place.

يستطيع is a Form X hollow verb. Arabic has two verbs 'to be able', this one and the simple verb **qadar**. Note also the verb **amkan** in line 14 which has a similar meaning.

14 يتغدى is a Form V verb from a root with the third radical weak (Table 9). يتعشى is the same type of verb.

يمكنه أن is rather a difficult construction to explain and perhaps best interpreted as an 'impersonal verb': 'It is possible for him that he listens, i.e. he can listen'.

15 حقّا is an adverbial accusative, 'Truly, in truth, really'. The colloquial forms used in the proverb are explained in the vocabulary.

لازم *It is necessary* (*that*) ... is the universal colloquial way of saying 'must'. It is admissible, but not so frequent in written Arabic.

EXERCISE 18.1 Read the text aloud and translate it into idiomatic English.

Adjectives of colour and physical disability

It is difficult to imagine why such adjectives should behave differently from others, but apparently something in the ancient Arab mind distinguished them, for not only is there a special adjective pattern used with the main colours and physical defects, but there is also a special verb form (IX). The latter, however, is quite rare in use and has been confined in this book to the verb tables, without further discussion.

The adjective forms must, however, be learned. The basic schematic is given below, along with a few examples.

Masculine Singular		Feminine Singular		Plural		
$aC^1C^2aC^3$		$C^1aC^2C^3aa'$		$C^1uC^2C^3$		
أحمر	'aHmar	حمراء	Hamraa'	حمر	Humr	*red*
أصفر	'aSfar	صفراء	Safraa'	صفر	Sufr	*yellow*
أخضر	'akhDar	خضراء	khaDraa'	خضر	khuDr	*green*
أزرق	'azraq	زرقاء	zarqaa'	زرق	zurq	*blue*
أسود	'aswad	سوداء	sawdaa'	سود	suud	*black*
أطرش	'aTrash	طرشاء	Tarshaa'	طرش	Tursh	*deaf*
أعرج	'a:raj	عرجاء	:arjaa'	عرج	:urj	*lame*

'White', because it has *yaa*' for its middle radical, has a slightly irregular plural:

أبيض **'abyaD**   بيضاء **bayDaa'**   بيض **biiD**   *white*

Words with a weak third radical (*waaw* or *yaa*') take the following forms:

أعمى **'a:maa**   عمياء **:amyaa'**   عميان **:umyaan**   *blind*

Notes:

1   Neither of the two singular forms takes the accusative indefinite marker, but the plural does.

2   The dual of the feminine form changes its final *hamza* to a *waaw*, e.g. سوداوان **sawdawaan**.

3   Many less basic colours are formed by adding the relative adjective ending (**-ii**) to the name of some natural object, e.g. رمادي *ash-coloured*, *grey* (from رماد **ramaad**, *ashes*), وردي *rose-coloured*, *pink* (from ورد **ward**, *roses*), بنفسجي *violet*. These, of course, do not behave like the adjectives given above, but take regular endings.

The exhortative use of the jussive

The jussive verb can be used on its own, usually in the third person, to express exhortation (cf. in English 'let him speak now or forever hold his peace' in the wedding ceremony). More commonly, however, it is prefixed by the particle **li-**, or the compound of particles **fal-** (for **fali-**). This all sounds rather rhetorical in English, but is quite common in Arabic, e.g. فليقصدوا أسواق خان الخليلي *Let them make for the markets of Khan al-Khalili* in the text.

The above usage is easily confused with the use of **li-** with the *subjunctive* verb to express purpose, as the subjunctive of most verbs is identical to the jussive in writing. However, the context usually helps.

For really strong exhortations, the so-called 'energetic' mood of the verb is still sometimes used. This formation was common in old Arabic, and is basically formed by adding **-anna** to the requisite part of the verb. It is mostly found in the two singular forms يكتبنّ **yaktubanna** *Let him write!* and تكتبنّ **taktubanna** *Let her write!*

EXERCISE 18.2 Here is a piece from a newspaper about Egypt's problem in feeding a rapidly growing population. It contains many terms which will be useful to those working on agricultural projects. New words are given and the idea is to see if you can work out how the Arabic fits together.

nutritional   crisis   solution

حَلّ لِلأَزْمَة الغِذائِيَّة في مصر ؟

suggestions   State Council

أعلن رئيس مَجْلِس الشورَى أمس اقْتِراحَات قد تحلّ الأزمة الغذائية في مصر ،

be more   animals

قال — قد بلغ عدد سكّان مصر ٤٣ مليونا وانّ رؤوس الحَيَوانَات يَزيد عددها

produce   vegetable   nutrition   principally   than

على عشرة ملايين . وتعتمد هذه الحيوانات أَساساً على الغِذاء النَباتيّ الذى تُنْتِجُه

humans   supplying   incapable   wealth   return

أرض مصر . والعائِد من ثَرْوَتنا الحيوانية ما زال عَاجِزا عن تَزْويد البَشَر

about   annually   sow   needs

باحْتِيَاجَاتِهم الغذائية من لحم وغيره . نحن نَزْرَع في مصر سَنَوياً نَحْو ٢,٨ مليون

harvested — total quarter represent area — lucerne acre

فَدَّان بَرْسيماً للحيوانات وهذه المَسَاحَة تُمَثِّل رُبْع جُمْلَة المساحة المَحْصُوليّة في

equals — whole

مصر . وُتَوازى — إن لم تكن تزيد قليلا — على مَجْمُوع المساحة التي نزرعها

wheat corn structure ponder

بالقَمْح والذُّرَّة معا . واذا تَأَمَّلنا تَرْكيب ثروتنا الحيوانية ووظيفتها نجد انَّ حيوانات

economic — some — riding draught burden

الحَمْل والجَرّ والرُّكُوب يبلغ عددها بِضْعَة ملايين . فانَّ الحيوانات الاقتصاديّة لا

heritage — agricultural — production — breed

يُربُّونها من أجل الإنْتاج منها ولكن من أجل العمل الزراعيّ . وهذا تُرَاث قديم

saying in need of — peasant inherit

ورثه الفَلَّاح المصرى عن ابائه وأجداده ولسنا بحَاجَة الى القَوْل بأنّ هذه

in an amount milk — overworked

الحيوانات المُجْهَدَة بالعمل الزراعي لا تعطي لحما أو لَبَنا بقَدْر اقتصادى . ومعنى

thinking — review — production

هذا أنّ ثروتنا الحيوانية وإنْتاجنا الحيواني في حاجة الى إعَادة النَظَر .... الى فِكْر

strategy — lines

جديد .... الى اسْتراتَجية جديدة . وانّي أضع بعض الخُطُوط الرئيسية لهذه

specialisation

الاستراتجية أمام أهل الاخْتِصَاص .

be rid of — mechanisation expansion

أوّلا — التَوَسُّع في المَيْكَنة الزراعية حتى نَتَخَلَّص تدريجيا من حيوانات الحمل

liberate food gobble save

والجرّ والركوب لكي نُوَفِّر ما تَلْتهمه من غِذاء وحتى نحَرِّر الحيوانات

agriculture field

الاقتصادية من أعمال الحَقْل والزراعة .

fields technology scientific methods newest subjection

ثانيا — إخْضَاع انتاجنا لأحْدَث الأسَاليب العِلْميّة والتِكْنُولُوجيّة في مَجَالات

by treatment by protection health care feeding strains improvement

تَحْسِين السُلَالَات والتَغْذِيَة والرعَايَة الصحّيّة وقائيّة وعلاجيّة .

vast — thirdly

ثَالثاً — اعادة النظر في التركيب المحصولي حتي نوفّر المساحة الشَاسِعَة

التي تزرع برسيا .

Appendices

Appendix 1 The Arabic Verb

The Arabic verb is best considered from three distinct points of view – grammatical, phonetic and stem-modification.

Grammar

The grammatical variations of the verb in any language are there to convey such information as who is carrying out the action, the time of the action and so on.

Subject markers Arabic distinguishes three persons in the verb:

First person (the speaker, English 'I', 'we')

Second person (the person spoken to, English 'you')

Third person (the person spoken about, English 'he', 'she', 'they')

This is the same system as in English. However, Arabic makes finer distinctions in gender (the sex of persons) and number (how many). Thus we have separate forms for masculine and feminine in both singular and plural of the second and third persons (not the first), and special forms for the dual, used when addressing/speaking about two people/objects. Thus any finite verb has thirteen parts, as set out below. (The persons are traditionally given in the reverse order in Arabic, because the third person masculine form is the simplest form of the verb.)

	Singular	**Dual**	**Plural**
Third person	he she	they two (m) they two (f)	they (m) they (f)
Second person	you (m) you (f)	you two (m or f)	you plural (m) you plural (f)
First person	I (m or f)	—	we (m or f)

Pronouns are not usually used with the Arabic verb, as the subject markers are prefixes/suffixes added to the verb stem.

Tense The next thing to consider is *when* the action of the verb takes place. This is known in grammar as *tense*, and Arabic has only two distinct forms, present and past.

236

Mood The present tense only has three variant forms, technically called *moods*, although this term is not very apt for describing their function in Arabic. For the most part, they are used automatically after certain conjunctions. The unaffected form of the present tense is called the *indicative*, and the other two moods are the *subjunctive* and *jussive*. Strictly speaking there are two more moods, the command form or *imperative*, and the so-called '*energetic*'. To avoid clutter, these have been left out of the verb tables and dealt with in the units.

Voice *Voice* means active or passive, i.e. whether the subject of the sentence is carrying out the action (he strikes) or suffering it (he is struck). All the above tenses and moods of the verb may be either active or passive.

Non-finite parts All Arabic verbs have two participles (active and passive) and a verbal noun which are given in the tables.

Phonetics

Phonetic means relating to the sound of a word, or more particularly here, to the nature of the consonants which go to make up an Arabic verb stem. Most of these stems are based on series of three consonants, and verb parts diverging from the standard forms occur when one or more of the following are present in the stem:

1 The letter *hamza*. This causes mainly spelling difficulties in the selection of the carrier letter for *hamza*. No special verb tables are given.

2 The second and third consonants of the stem are the same, e.g. d-l-l, m-r-r. This causes the appearance of contracted verb forms.

3 The occurrence of either of the so-called 'weak letters' *waaw* or *yaa'* as one of the stem consonants. These cause the most trouble of all, mainly due to their being elided (i.e. omitted) in many parts of the verb. Further complications are caused by Arabic's aversion to the proximity of the sounds *i/ii/y* and *u/uu/w*.

Stems not showing any of the above features are regarded as sound, and provide the basis for learning the Arabic verb system.

Stem modification

Arabic has a system of internal and external modification to the verb stem, which is best considered and learned along with the grammatical and phonetic aspects. The modified stems are traditionally known as *derived forms*, and referred to by means of the Roman numerals I to X, I being the unmodified base form.

Table 1   Prefixes and Suffixes of the Verb

This table gives all the prefixes and suffixes which, when applied to the relevant verb stem, form the parts of the Arabic verb. It should be studied in conjunction with the following notes.

		Past tense	Present tense	Subjunctive	Jussive
Singular	he	STEM	STEM يَ	No written change except for parts given	All parts written as subjunctive
	she	ـَتْ ___	تَ		
	you (m)	ـْتَ ___	تَ		
	you (f)	ـْتِ ___	تَ ـ ـِينَ	تَ ___ ـِي	
	I	ـْتُ ___	أَ ___		
Dual	they two (m)	ـَا ___	يَ ___ ـَانِ	يَ ___ ـَا	
	they two (f)	ـَتَا ___	تَ ___ ـَانِ	تَ ___ ـَا	
	you two	ـْتُمَا ___	تَ ___ ـَانِ	تَ ___ ـَا	
Plural	they (m)	ـُوا ___	يَ ___ ـُونَ	يَ ___ ـُوا	
	they (f)	ـْنَ ___	يَ ___ ـْنَ		
	you (m)	ـْتُمْ ___	تَ ___ ـُونَ	تَ ___ ـُوا	
	you (f)	ـْتُنَّ ___	تَ ___ ـْنَ		
	we	ـْنَا ___	نَ ___		

Notes

1 Table 1 gives all the prefixes and suffixes which, when applied to the correct verb stem, give all the parts of all Arabic verbs with the following minor exceptions:

(*a*) With derived stems II, III and IV (see Table 2) and all passive stems (also in Table 2), the present tense prefixes are vowelled *u* instead of *a* (i.e. **yu-**, **tu-**, etc.)

(*b*) With certain types of verbs whose third radical is one of the weak letters *w* and *y*, the vowelling of some of the suffixes is modified, although there is no change in the written form (see Tables 6–9).

2 Certain *short final vowels* are habitually omitted in speech. These are:

Past tense The **-u** and **-a** of the *I* and *you* (m, sing.) (but *not* the **-i** of the *you* f, sing.) Resultant ambiguities are usually cleared up by context.

Present tense The **-i** of the dual forms, and the **-a** of the *you* (f, sing. and m, pl.) and *they* (m, pl.) (but not the **-a** of the *they* and *you* f, pl.)

3 Note carefully the *alif* which is conventionally written (but not pronounced) after all verb forms which end in long *u* (**-uu**).

4 The parts of the subjunctive and jussive which show no written change were originally differentiated by vowelling the final radical of the stem **-a** for subjunctive and **sukuun** for jussive where no other suffix is added. The feminine plurals ending in **-na** never showed any change for mood, and the parts given in the table form both subjunctive and jussive by simply dropping the final *nuun* of the indicative (and adding an *alif* where necessary, as indicated in 3 above).

Table 2 Verb stems, Participles and Verbal Nouns deriving from sound roots

Root l-m-s (Form I = 'to touch')

Active	Past stem	Present stem	Active participle	Passive participle	Verbal noun
I	لَمَس	لْمِس	لَامِس	مَلْمُوس	see notes
II	لَمَّس	لَمِّس	مُلَمِّس	مُلَمَّس	تَلْمِيس
III	لَامَس	لَامِس	مُلَامِس	مُلَامَس	مُلَامَسَة
IV	أَلْمَس	لْمِس	مُلْمِس	مُلْمَس	إِلْمَاس
V	تَلَمَّس	تَلَمَّس	مُتَلَمِّس	مُتَلَمَّس	تَلَمُّس
VI	تَلَامَس	تَلَامَس	مُتَلَامِس	مُتَلَامَس	تَلَامُس
VII	اِنْلَمَس	نْلَمِس	مُنْلَمِس	مُنْلَمَس	اِنْلِمَاس
VIII	اِلْتَمَس	لْتَمِس	مُلْتَمِس	مُلْتَمَس	اِلْتِمَاس
IX	see notes		مُحْمِرّ	none	اِحْمِرَار
X	اِسْتَلْمَس	سْتَلْمِس	مُسْتَلْمِس	مُسْتَلْمَس	اِسْتِلْمَاس

Notes

1 *General* Table 2 contains the bones of the Arabic verb system and must be mastered thoroughly. It should be used in conjunction with Table 1 which gives the prefixes and suffixes which have to be applied to the stems in order to make up or identify actual parts of the verb. The active and passive participles and the verbal nouns are also given. The table will work for any sound stem in Arabic,

Passive	Past stem	Present stem
I	لُمِس	لْمَس
II	لُمِّس	لَمَّس
III	لُومِس	لَامَس
IV	أُلْمِس	لْمَس
V	تُلُمِّس	تَلَمَّس
VI	تُلُومِس	تَلامَس
VII	انْلُمِس	نْلَمَس
VIII	الْتُمِس	لْتَمَس
IX	no passive	
X	أُسْتُلْمِس	سْتَلْمَس

i.e. any one *not* displaying any of the features already noted in the section on phonetics in the General Description.

Although passives have been given in full for reference, there is an easy rule for their formation. This is given on pp. 206–7.

2 *Derived forms* The root l-m-s has been chosen to illustrate these because it is easy to pronounce (the Arabs use f-:-l which is very difficult for us to pronounce and hence to remember words made up from it). Remember that the stems and derivatives given are for learning the *patterns*, and therefore must be given in full. I know of no Arabic root which admits of *all* derivatives, so inevitably some of the creations of Table 2 do not actually exist. The whole concept of derived forms and their allotted numbers is no more than a convenient shorthand (incidentally not used by the Arabs) for what would otherwise be a cumbersome system.

The remainder of these notes deal with the derived forms in turn in an attempt to point out special characteristics and give helpful hints for learning. The concept of 'meaning patterns' for Forms II to X is a delicate subject. While it is impossible to assess how conscious an Arab is of the relationship between the derived forms and the basic root meanings, most European books tend to be overenthusiastic on the subject and make sweeping – and inaccurate – generalisations. The policy adopted in the following notes on the forms has /been to mention only such connections which have proved fairly generally useful in practice. There is no doubt, for instance, that it is frequently helpful to know that IV is likely to be causative. On the other side of the coin, the meaning of VIII cannot often be deduced from a knowledge of the meaning of the base root.

Form I is the bare three-consonant root, with nothing added to it. However, it does present some difficulties, in that the vowelling of both tense-stems in the active is not predictable, nor is the shape of the verbal noun. Reference has already been made to this feature on page 114 and ultimately resort must be made to a dictionary. However, here are a few more useful guidelines.

1   The majority of Form I verbs take an a-vowel on the middle radical of the past stem. This usually gives a present stem with **u** or **i** on the middle radical, and in fact many verbs can take either. Present stems with an a-characteristic also occur, usually due to the influence of a guttural such as **H** or **:** as second or third radical of the root.
2   The second most common Form I type is that with an i-characteristic in the past, giving an **a-** in the present, e.g. **fahim/fham** *to understand*. Again there are exceptions, but not many.
3   The least common type is **u/u** like **qarub/qrub**.
4   No help at all can be given with the verbal noun, which must be ascertained from a dictionary.

To sum up, the only truly predictable parts of I are the two passive stems and the two participles. *Forms II to X are predictable in all parts*, so learn them systematically and carefully. A thorough knowledge of the behaviour of the sound roots is invaluable in dealing with the defective roots which deviate from this norm.

Note that all spoken dialects of Arabic take liberties with the vowelling of Form I stems, so you will probably be understood whether you say **yaktub**, **yaktab** or **yaktib**. It is only in very formal speech that special care is taken to use the correct literary form.

Form II is formed by doubling the middle radical of the root (see Table for vowelling). This is one of the forms which causes the prefixes of the present tense to take a u-vowel instead of an **a**. (The rule for this, by the way, is that it occurs in forms which increase the base-root by the addition of *one* additional letter. II adds an extra middle radical, shown by a *shadda*, and the other two in the category are III which adds an *alif* and IV which prefixes a *hamza*.)

Note now that all the participles of II–X begin with the prefix **mu-**. There is, in fact a rule for their formation (with the exception of the rare Form IX, for which see Table 3):

Active participle: **mu-** plus the present stem, but always with an i-vowel on the middle radical of the root. (V and VI have to be altered.)

Passive participle: exactly the same, but with an a-vowel on the middle radical. (All altered except V and VI.)

II has two useful meaning patterns:

1 *Causative:* **kabur** I *to be large;* **kabbar** II *to make big, enlarge;* **:alim** I *to know;* **:allam** II *to cause to know, teach.*

2 *Forming verbs from nouns:* **si:r** *price,* **sa::ar** II *to price, put a price on;* **miSr** *Egypt,* **maSSar** II *to Egyptianise.*

Quadriliteral roots, which always have a series of two consonants in the middle, are conjugated exactly like II, e.g. تَرْجَمَ , present tense يُتَرْجِم *to translate.* The verbal noun, however, is تَرْجَمَة .

Form III Again the present tense prefixes take **u** (see above). Note the long u-vowel in the past tense passive.

This form has an alternative shape for the verbal noun $C^1iC^2aaC^3$ which is sometimes used.

Form IV increases the base-root by a prefixed *hamza*, written over an *alif*. Although this disappears in the present tense, the prefix is still vowelled **u**. In all parts of the past tense, and in the verbal noun, this *hamza* is always pronounced, never elided (it is the 'cutting' *hamza*, see page 19). It is worth noting here that this is the only such *hamza* which occurs in the derived forms of the verb. The others (in VII–X inclusive) can all be elided.

IV is quite a common derivative and, like II, is frequently causative, e.g. **jalas** I *to sit,* **'ajlas** IV *to cause to sit, to seat;* **SalaH** I *to be good, right,* **'aSlaH** IV *to put right, mend, reform,* etc.

Form V is II with a prefixed **ta-**, but *note carefully the difference in vowelling*, which is **a** all through the present stem. VI is the only other form which behaves in this way, all the rest alternating past **a**/present **i** on the middle radical. *Quadriliterals:* The so-called second form of the quadriliteral verb behaves exactly like V, e.g. تَتَلْمَذَ, present tense يَتَتَلْمَذُ *to be a pupil.*

Form VI, like V, has both stems identical. Note the long u-vowel on the past stem passive (although this, in fact, rarely occurs). VI is not a very common form, but when it occurs it very often has the meaning of doing something in association with or in competition with someone else, e.g. **tanaafas** *to compete, vie with each other*, **taHaawar** *to carry on a discussion.*

Form VII is formed by prefixing **in-** to the Form I stem. In this and the remainder of the derived forms, the initial *alif* of the past stem is only there to satisfy the Arabic rule that no word may begin with a vowelless consonant. The i-vowel can therefore be elided, and disappears in the present stem and the participles, reappearing only on the verbal noun. Form VII is not all that common and is usually intransitive, with a passive or reflexive meaning, e.g. **inkasar** *to become broken, to break.*

Form VIII   The variation from the base form here is an infixed **t** after the first radical. Since the latter is vowelless, the same remarks regarding initial *alif* as in VII apply.
    The infixed **t** suffers some phonetic variations due to assimilation. These all concern the nature of the first radical of the root and may be summarised as follows:

(*a*) If the first radical of the root is one of the emphatic letters **S,D,T,DH**, the infixed **t** becomes **T**, e.g. root **Sn:** gives **iSTana:,Drb** gives **iDTarab**. **T** and **DH** are totally assimilated and written with *shadda*, e.g. **Tl:** gives **iTTala:, DHlm** gives **iDHDHalam**.

(*b*) If the first radical is **d,dh** or **z** the infixed **t** becomes **d** and the same pattern evolves: **iddarak** (drk), **izdaHam** (zHm), **idhdhakar** (dhkr).

(*c*) If it is *waaw* or *yaa'* this assimilates to the *taa'*, e.g. **ittaHad** (wHd). Also *hamza* on the root **'khdh** (Form I **'akhadh** *to take*) gives VIII **ittakhadh** *to take up for oneself.*

Form VIII is very common, but offers no helpful or easily traceable pattern of meaning.

Form IX As the structure of this form involves the doubling of the final radical of the base root, it will be dealt with in Table 3 along with the Doubled Verb, whose behaviour it follows. It is quite rare, and only used to form verbs from the special adjectives of colour and physical defect described on pp. 231–2.

Form X The prefix here is **sta-**, but Arabic orthography requires a prefixed *alif* as in the preceding three derived forms.

X often means to 'seek or ask for the action of the root', e.g. **:alim** I *to know*, **ista:lam** X *to seek or ask to know, to enquire*; **khadam** I *to serve, work*, **istakhdam** X *to seek or ask to work, to employ, use*.

Another common meaning pattern is 'to consider (something/-someone) as possessing the meaning of the root', e.g. **Hasun** I *to be good, nice, beautiful*, **istaHsan** X *to consider good, nice*, etc.

Concluding remarks

As has already been said, it is essential to master the forms in this table thoroughly, as they form the basis for the whole Arabic verb system. All the material in the ensuing tables will be concerned with *deviations from this master pattern* caused by unsoundnesses and other features in the roots.

Table 3   The Doubled Verb

دَلَّ 'to point, show'
In most forms, the doubled verb has two stems for each tense, a contracted stem (CS) written with a *shadda* and a regular stem (RS). See the notes to this table.

Notes

General   Doubled roots are those whose second and third radicals are the same letter. The main distinguishing feature in their conjugation is that, in both tenses, they have a *contracted stem*. This is used in all parts of the verb where either there is no written suffix, or the suffix begins with a vowel – e.g. **-at** for 'she' in the past tense, **-uun** for 'they' (m) in the present. If the suffix begins with a consonant, then the regular stem is used – e.g. before **-tum** for 'you' (m. pl.) in the past tense, and **-na** for the two feminine plurals in the present tense). In the present tense, the changes in ending for

Active	**Past stem**	**Present stem**	**Active participle**	**Passive participle**	**Verbal noun**
I CS	دَلّ	دُلّ	دَالّ	مَدْلُول	irregular
RS	دَلَل	دُلُل			
II	No irregularity, refer to Table 2				
III CS	دَالّ	دَالّ	مُدَالّ	مُدَالّ	دِلَال
RS	دَالَل	دَالِل			
IV CS	أَدَلّ	دِلّ	مُدِلّ	مُدَلّ	إِدْلَال
RS	أَدْلَل	دْلِل			
V	No irregularity, refer to Table 2				
VI CS	تَدَالّ	تَدَالّ	مُتَدَالّ	مُتَدَالّ	تَدَالّ
RS	تَدَالَل	تَدَالَل			
VII CS	اِنْدَلّ	نْدَلّ	مُنْدَلّ	مُنْدَلّ	اِنْدِلَال
RS	اِنْدَلَل	نْدَلِل			
VIII CS	اِمْتَدّ	مْتَدّ	مُمْتَدّ	مُمْتَدّ	اِمْتِدَاد
RS	اِمْتَدَد	مْتَدِد			
IX CS	اِحْمَرّ	حْمَرّ	مُحْمَرّ	none	اِحْمِرَار
RS	اِحْمَرَر	حْمَرَر			
X CS	اِسْتَدَلّ	سْتَدِلّ	مُسْتَدِلّ	مُسْتَدَلّ	اِسْتِدْلَال
RS	اِسْتَدْلَل	سْتَدْلِل			

subjunctive and jussive are as shown in Table 1. Unsuffixed parts are the same for all three moods.

As a general rule, when the contracted stem is used, the vowel which would have been on the second radical (now included under the *shadda*) is thrown back and goes on the first radical, but this does not happen in VII and VIII, where the i-vowel of the middle radical is lost altogether and the first radical takes its usual a-vowel.

Form I permits the same variation of second radical vowel as the sound root (see Table 2), but in the past tense this appears in the uncontracted forms only, the contracted forms always having **a**. In the present tense, the uncontracted form is again regular, and in the case of the contracted forms, its characteristic vowel is thrown back to the first radical according to the principle mentioned above. Thus there are the following possibilities (in various combinations):

Past	**Present**
CaCC (for *CaCaC*)	*CuCC* (for *CCuC*)
CaCC (for *CaCiC*)	*CiCC* (for *CCiC*)
CaCC (for *CaCuC*)	*CaCC* (for *CCaC*)

Forms II and V are completely regular, as the doubling of the middle radical makes it impossible for contracted stems to occur.

Forms III, IV, VI, VII, VIII and X Attention is drawn to the following point:
the active and passive participles differ only in the case of IV and X (**i**-vowel for active, **a** for passive). The remainder, which are identical, either are not used at all, or at least not in contrast, so no difficulty should be encountered in practice. (The root m-d-d has been used for Form VIII in the table, as d-l-l would assimilate – see Table 2, notes to Form VIII.)

Form IX is not a true doubled verb, but since the formation of IX from the sound root involves the doubling of the final radical, the form behaves exactly like a doubled verb. It is in any case quite rare, being derived only from roots which mean colours or bodily defects (see pp. 231–2). The verb illustrated in the table is from the root H-m-r, 'to be or become red, blush'.

The passive The two tenses of the passive are formed in accordance with the rules given on pp. 206–7 for the changes in vowelling. Like the active forms, they have contracted and uncontracted stems, the former observing the rule of throwing back the vowel described above.

III and VI (if it ever occurs) do not contract in the past tense:

$$\text{دُولِل ، تُدُولِل}\cdot$$

Summary
The doubled verb, in all its ramifications, is quite tricky to master. In printed Arabic – where the *shadda* of the contracted stems is usually omitted – it has to be 'detected', starting from the clue of an apparently missing radical. The derived forms have been given in full for completeness, but some occur rarely or never.

Quadriliteral roots The so-called fourth form of the quadriliteral verb (of which there is only one common example) has a doubled final radical, and so conjugates like the doubled verb. The main parts of **iTma'ann** *to be quiet, at ease* are:

	Past tense	Present tense	Active participle	Passive participle	Verbal noun
CS	اِطْمَأَنّ	طْمَئِنّ	مُطْمَئِنّ	(مُطْمَأَنّ)	اِطْمِئْنَان
RS	اِطْمَأْنِن	طْمَأْنِن			

Table 4 First-Weak Verbs

Notes
First weak verbs are those which have *waaw* or *yaa'* as their first radical. First-*y* verbs are more or less regular except for some smoothing out of clashes between the sounds *u* and *y*, but first-*w* roots show more irregularity. None of these changes affect the suffixation of the stems for person, mood, etc.

1 Verbs with first radical *waaw*: وَصَل *to arrive*

Active	Past stem	Present stem	Active participle	Passive participle	Verbal noun
I	وَصَل	صِل	وَاصِل	مَوْصُول	irregular
IV	أَوْصَل	وُصِل[ْ]	مُوصِل	مُوصَل	إيصَال
VIII	اِتَّصَل	تَّصِل	مُتَّصِل	مُتَّصَل	اِتِّصَال
X	Regular except for verbal noun				اِسْتِيصَال

Passive	Past stem	Present stem
I	وُصِل	وصَل[ْ]
IV	أُوصَل	وصَل[ْ]

First *waaw* verbs

I Almost all first *waaw* verbs lose this *waaw* completely in the present stem. The middle radical in the present stem is very frequently vowelled *i*, although other combinations exist, as is the case with all Form I verbs.

Apart from this, and the assimilation in Form VIII (see Table 2), all other irregularities can be summed up in the following two rules:

1. When vowelless *waaw* is preceded by a short u-vowel, the two fuse together to form a long *uu*. According to the conventions of Arabic orthography, this *waaw* is not then marked with a *sukuun* in vowelled texts.

2. When vowelless *waaw* is preceded by a short i-vowel, it is changed into a *yaa'* and the two fuse together in the same way as above, this time forming a long *ii*.

(It is as well to point out again here that Arabic in general avoids the close proximity of *u/y* and *i/w*.)

Derived forms   *The forms not mentioned in the table are regular.*

IV   Form IV demonstrates rule 1 above in the present stem, and rule 2 in the verbal noun.

VIII   *waaw* assimilates to give a doubled *taa'*.

X   Regular except for the verbal noun which has *ii* for *iw* as laid down in rule 2.

Passives are regularly formed, bearing in mind rule 1.

2   Verbs with first radical *yaa'*: يَبِس *to be dry*

Active	Past stem	Present stem	Active participle	Passive participle	Verbal noun
I	يَبِس	يْبَس	يَابِس	مَيْبُوس	irregular
IV	أَيْبَس	وْبِس [ه]	مُوبِس	مُوبَس	إيبَاس
VIII	اِتَّبَس	تَّبِس	مُتَّبِس	مُتَّبَس	اِتِّبَاس

Passive	Past stem	Present stem
I	يُبِس	وْبَس [ه]

First *yaa'* verbs

These do *not* lose their first radical in the present stem of I, and their conjugation is governed by the following two rules:

1   Short *i* followed by a vowelless *yaa'* becomes long *ii*.
2   Vowelless *yaa'* preceded by a short u-vowel changes to *waaw* and the two fuse to form long *uu*.

Both principles are illustrated in Form IV:

Verbal noun: **iibaas** for theoretical **iybaas** (rule 1).
Active participle: **muubis** for theoretical **muybis** (rule 2).

Passive   Again formed regularly, but subject to the rules above.

Derived forms   VIII again shows assimilation.

Table 5   Hollow Verbs

I قَال *to say,* سَار *to go,* نَام *to sleep*
IV أَقَام *to set up, reside*   **VII** اِنْقَاد *to be led*
VIII اِخْتَار *to choose*   **X** اِسْتَقَام *to be straight*

Active		Past stem	Present stem	Active participle	Passive participle	Verbal noun
I	1 LS	قَال	قُول	قَائِل	مَقُول	قَوْل
	SS	قُل	قُل			
	2 LS	سَار	سِير	سَائِر	مَسِير	سَيْر
	SS	سِر	سِر			
	3 LS	نَام	نَام	نَائِم	مَنُوم	نَوْم
	SS	نِم	نَم			
IV	LS	أَقَام	قِيم	مُقِيم	مُقَام	إِقَامَة
	SS	أَقَم	قِم			

Active		Past stem	Present stem	Active participle	Passive participle	Verbal noun
VII	LS	اِنْقَاد	نْقَاد	مُنْقَاد	مُنْقَاد	اِنْقِيَاد
	SS	اِنْقَد	نْقَد			
VIII	LS	اِخْتَار	خْتَار	مُخْتَار	مُخْتَار	اِخْتِيَار
	SS	اِخْتَر	خْتَر			
X	LS	اِسْتَقَام	سْتَقِيم	مُسْتَقِيم	مُسْتَقَام	اِسْتِقَامَة
	SS	اِسْتَقَم	سْتَقِم			

Passive		Past stem	Present stem
I	LS	قِيل	قَال
	SS	قِل	قَل
IV		أُقِيم	قَام
VII		اُنْقِيد	نْقَاد
VIII		اُخْتِير	خْتَار
X		اُسْتُقِيم	سْتَقَام

Notes

General Hollow verbs are those whose roots have middle radical *waaw* or *yaa'*. Since this frequently disappears because of elision, the verb is left without a middle, hence the name hollow. The problem throughout is which long or short vowel to substitute for this elided middle radical.

Form I, as usual, causes the most problems because of its vowel variations. For the purposes of the hollow verb we have to consider three distinct types.

1 Type 1 is exemplified in the table by **qaal**. This was originally **qawal** with middle *waaw*.
2 Type 2, illustrated by **saar**, originally **sayar**.
3 Type 3 is illustrated by **naam**. This type includes roots whose middle radical is either *waaw* or *yaa'*, the important thing being that in the original form, *the middle radical had an i-vowel*. Thus **naam** was originally **nawim**, and you will remember that verbs with a characteristic i-vowel in the past tense take an a-vowel on the middle radical in the present. This is important in learning the hollow verb.

The other principle which we must grasp is that which we have already met with in the doubled verb; that is, the idea of two stems for each tense.

The *long stem* (LS) is used in parts of the verb which have a suffix beginning with a vowel (**-at**, **-uun**, etc.) and in parts which have no written suffix at all (with the exception of the jussive; see below).

The *short stem* (SS) is used in all parts of the verb which have a suffix beginning with a consonant (**-tum**, **-naa**, **-na**, etc.) and additionally *in unsuffixed parts of the present tense jussive*. Thus the ordinary present tense 'he says' would be **yaquul** (long stem), but if we use the jussive, the form becomes **yaqul** – a difference which obviously shows in writing: يقل/يقول .

In Type 1 verbs (middle radical originally *waaw*) the past stems are LS **aa**, SS **u**; present tense LS **uu**, SS **u**.

Type 2 (middle radical *yaa'*) has past tense LS **aa**, SS **i**; present LS **ii**, SS **i**.

Type 3 (the rarest of the three; middle radical either *waaw* or *yaa'*) has past tense LS **aa**, SS **i**; present LS **aa**, SS **a**.

The verbal noun of I is, for once, more or less predictable in the form $C^1aC^2C^3$.

Note that many parts of these verbs, when they appear in texts, give no clue as to their original root form. The only answer is to check both the middle *waaw* form and the middle *yaa'* form in a dictionary. If, as sometimes happens, both exist you will have to select the one which makes most sense.

Derived forms Those not included in the Table (II, III, V, VI and IX) behave regularly, as the weak middle radical does not occur where it can be elided.

As usual, there is no permitted variation in vowelling in the derived forms, so, unlike I, the short stem vowel is always merely a shortened version of the vowel in the long stem. In addition, the derived forms given are identical no matter whether the original root had *waaw* or *yaa'*.

IV Note that the verbal noun has the feminine ending.

VII and VIII Note that the same a-vowel occurs in past and present stem. One would have expected an alternation *a/i* (as in X). VIII appears rarely as a regular form, the weak radical being treated as sound.

X The verbal noun again has the feminine ending, and there is a vowel distinction in the two tense stems and the two participles.

Passive As usual, the vowelling is standard for all forms. The full forms of both long and short stems have been given only for I as the SS always merely shortens the vowel of the LS.

Table 6   Third-Weak Verbs – 1

Third radical *waaw*, characteristic *a*

Notes

Third-weak verbs are those which have *waaw* or *yaa'* as their last radical. They occur in three distinct types, and as these are the most difficult verbs to master in Arabic, they have been set out in full in separate tables.

Type 1, as illustrated in Table 6, has third radical *waaw* and characteristic *a* – that is, originally the form was **nadaw**.

The passive of this type of verb is dealt with in the notes to Table 8, and its derived forms are in Table 9.

نَدَا to call, *invite*

		Past tense	Present tense		
			Indicative	*Subjunctive*	*Jussive*
Singular	he	نَدَا	يَنْدُو	Parts not given written as indicative	يَنْدُ
	she	نَدَتْ	تَنْدُو		تَنْدُ
	you (m)	نَدَوْتَ	تَنْدُو		تَنْدُ
	you (f)	نَدَوْتِ	تَنْدِينَ	تَنْدِي	
	I	نَدَوْتُ	أَنْدُو		أَنْدُ
Dual	they two (m)	نَدَوَا	يَنْدُوَانِ	يَنْدُوَا	
	they two (f)	نَدَتَا	تَنْدُوَانِ	تَنْدُوَا	
	you two	نَدَوْتُمَا	تَنْدُوَانِ	تَنْدُوَا	
Plural	they (m)	نَدَوْا	يَنْدُونَ	يَنْدُوا	Parts not given written as subjunctive.
	they (f)	نَدَوْنَ	يَنْدُونَ		
	you (m)	نَدَوْتُمْ	تَنْدُونَ	تَنْدُوا	
	you (f)	نَدَوْتُنَّ	تَنْدُونَ		
	we	نَدَوْنَا	نَنْدُو		نَنْدُ

Past tense The parts of the past tense which have suffixes beginning with a consonant are in fact regular, the *waaw* taking full consonantal status. The remainder of the forms show various elisions and deviations which are best learned by rote.

Present tense Only the three dual parts and the two feminine plural parts are anything like regular.

The subjunctive varies in writing from the indicative in the usual parts, which are also used for the jussive. In the unsuffixed parts of the jussive, the final weak radical disappears all together. This feature is common to all types of the third-weak verb, and can be confusing when encountered in print. In unvowelled texts, the jussives of unsuffixed parts of the doubled, hollow and third-weak verbs look exactly the same (as if they had a letter missing) and sometimes all possible variations have to be checked in the dictionary.

Active participle   This is the same for all types of third-weak verb, and is written:

Definite   نَادِى   *Indefinite*   نَادٍ

This type of irregular noun/adjective is discussed on page 142, note to 1.2.

Passive participle   This is in fact regular if the first *waaw* included under the *shadda* is regarded as a vowel lengthener and the second as a consonant. The form is مَنْدُوّ .

Verbal noun   نَدْو **nadw**, but not really a predictable form.

Table 7   Third-Weak Verbs – 2

Third radical *yaa'*, characteristic *a*

Notes

Type 2 of the third-weak verb has third radical *yaa'*, and characteristic *a*, i.e. original form **ramay** (a-vowel on middle radical).

For the passive see notes to Table 8; for derived forms see Table 9.

Past tense   Again the parts of the past tense which have suffixes beginning with a consonant are regular (cf. Table 6), and the rest, except for one dual, have various elisions.

Present tense   The long vowel this time on the unsuffixed parts is **-ii** (cf. **-uu** in Table 6) and this is again reduced to a short vowel in the unsuffixed parts of the jussive. The duals and the feminine plurals are regular, but in the parts where the long **ii** vowel would clash with a long **uu** in a suffix, the former is dropped all together (e.g. **yarmuun**).

رَمَى *to throw*	Past tense	Present tense		
		Indicative	*Subjunctive*	*Jussive*
Singular he	رَمَى	يَرْمِي	Parts not shown written as indicative	يَرْمِ
she	رَمَتْ	تَرْمِي		تَرْمِ
you (m)	رَمَيْتَ	تَرْمِي		تَرْمِ
you (f)	رَمَيْتِ	تَرْمِينَ	تَرْمِي	
I	رَمَيْتُ	أَرْمِي		أَرْمِ
Dual they two (m)	رَمَيَا	يَرْمِيَانِ	يَرْمِيَا	Parts not shown written as subjunctive
they two (f)	رَمَتَا	تَرْمِيَانِ	تَرْمِيَا	
you two	رَمَيْتُمَا	تَرْمِيَانِ	تَرْمِيَا	
Plural they (m)	رَمَوْا	يَرْمُونَ	يَرْمُوا	
they (f)	رَمَيْنَ	يَرْمِينَ		
you (m)	رَمَيْتُمْ	تَرْمُونَ	تَرْمُوا	
you (f)	رَمَيْتُنَّ	تَرْمِينَ		
we	رَمَيْنَا	نَرْمِي		نَرْمِ

Active participle   This is رَامٍ, definite رَامِي. See notes to Table 6.

Passive participle   This is مَرْمِيّ, preserving the long **ii**.

Verbal noun رَمْى **ramy** or رِمَايَة **rimaaya**. These two shapes are common with this type of verb.

Table 8   Third-Weak Verbs – 3

Third radical either *waaw* or *yaa'*, characteristic *i*

رَضِيَ *to be pleased*

		Past tense	Present tense		
			Indicative	*Subjunctive*	*Jussive*
Singular	he	رَضِيَ	يَرْضَى	Parts not shown written as indicative	يَرْضَ
	she	رَضِيَتْ	تَرْضَى		تَرْضَ
	you (m)	رَضِيتَ	تَرْضَى		تَرْضَ
	you (f)	رَضِيتِ	تَرْضَيْنَ	تَرْضَيْ	
	I	رَضِيتُ	أَرْضَى		أَرْضَ
Dual	they two (m)	رَضِيَا	يَرْضَيَانِ	يَرْضَيَا	Parts not shown written as subjunctive
	they two (f)	رَضِيَتَا	تَرْضَيَانِ	تَرْضَيَا	
	you two	رَضِيتُمَا	تَرْضَيَانِ	تَرْضَيَا	
Plural	they (m)	رَضُوا	يَرْضَوْنَ	يَرْضَوْا	
	they (f)	رَضِينَ	يَرْضَيْنَ		
	you (m)	رَضِيتُمْ	تَرْضَوْنَ	تَرْضَوْا	
	you (f)	رَضِيتُنَّ	تَرْضَيْنَ		
	we	رَضِينَا	نَرْضَى		نَرْضَ

Notes

Type 3 of the third-weak verb has (original) third radical *waaw* or *yaa*'. However, the form is written with a *yaa*' whatever the original letter, because of the influence of the characteristic i-vowel on the middle radical (remember *i*'s and *w*'s don't mix). This type is the least common of the third-weaks, but there are still quite a few around.

Past tense In fact if *ii* is regarded the same as *iy* (which it is in Arabic) all parts of this tense are regular except the *they* (m, plural) where the theoretical **-iyuu** ending is cut to **-uu** to avoid the i-y-u clash.

Present tense The long vowel this time is **-aa**, presumably reflecting the tendency of i-characteristic verbs to form their present tenses with **a** on the middle radical. This **a** causes the masculine plural endings to be rendered **-aw (n)**.

Active participle This is راضٍ, definite راضِي, according to the usual pattern for these verbs.

Passive participle This is مَرْضِيّ, on the same pattern as type 2.

Verbal noun This is رِضًى, but this shape is by no means predictable.

Passive of third-weak verbs The passive is the same for all three types and takes the following form:

Past tense

نُدِيَ

رَضِيَ conjugated like رمى

رضي

Present tense

يُنْدَى

يُرْضَى conjugated like يَرْمَى

يُرْضَى

The verb رَأَى **'to see'**   This is a hybrid verb, technically belonging to the third-weak category. It is conjugated as follows:

Past tense   رَأَى like **ramaa** (Table 7).

Present tense   يَرَى the *hamza* and its carrier are omitted and the remainder conjugated like **yarDaa** in this table. The distinct parts of the jussive consist of only the letter *raa'* and the prefix: يَرَ **yara**.

Other parts   The participles are used rarely, and the imperative not at all.

Note that there are a few other verbs which conjugate in the past tense as Table 7 and in the present as Table 8, e.g. سعى **sa:aa** *to run, hurry*, present tense يسعى **yas:aa**.

Table 9   Third-Weak Verbs – Derived Forms

Notes

All types of third-weak verbs form their derived stems in exactly the same way.

Forms II, III, IV, VII, VIII and X are conjugated like **ramaa** (Table 7) in both tenses.

The remaining two forms, V and VI, are conjugated like **ramaa** in the past tense, and **yarDaa** (Table 8) in the present tense.

Passive   The stems for the passive are vowelled according to the rule given in Note 1 to Table 2, and conjugated like **raDiy(a)** in both tenses.

	Past tense	Present tense	Active participle	Passive participle	Verbal noun
II	رَمَّى	رَمِّي	مُرَمِّي [1]	مُرَمّى	تَرْمِيَة
III	رَامَى	رَامِي	مُرَامِي	مُرَامَى	مُرَامَاة
IV	أَرْمَى	رْمِي	مُرْمِي	مُرْمَى	إِرْمَاء
V	تَرَمَّى	تَرَمَّى	مترَمِّي	مترَمّى	تَرَمِّي [1]
VI	تَرَامَى	تَرَامَى	مُتَرَامِي	مُتَرَامَى	تَرَامِي [1]
VII	اِنْرَمَى	نُرمِي	مُنْرَمِي	مُنْرَمَى	اِنْرِمَاء
VIII	اِرْتَمَى	رْتَمِي	مُرْتَمِي	مُرْتَمَى	اِرْتِمَاء
X	اِسْترْمَى	سْترْمِي	مُسْترْمِي	مُسْترْمَى	اِسْتِرْمَاء

[1] The active participles of all Forms, and the verbal nouns of V and VI are given in the definite form (with final *yaa*'). See notes.

Participles The active participle has been given in its *definite* form, with final **-ii**, as this is how it is usually pronounced in speech. When it is used indefinitely, the final *yaa*' is omitted unless the word is accusative (see page 142, note to line 2).

The passive participles end in long **-aa**.

Verbal nouns The verbal nouns of V and VI are also given with the final *yaa*' of the definite.

Appendix 2
The Arabic Numerals

The correct grammatical use of the numerals in Arabic is a complicated business and, as has already been suggested, if you intend to stick to reading and speaking Arabic, rather than writing it, the colloquial forms will be quite sufficient. The following account, however, may be useful for reference.

Cardinal numbers
(These are split up into groups according to their syntactical behaviour.)

	Masculine	*Feminine*	
1	أَحَد وَاحِد	إِحْدَى وَاحِدَة	A noun, not used as a numeral in spoken Arabic. An adjective which follows the noun in the usual way.
2	اِثْنَان	اِثْنَتَان	A dual form which must be declined (see page 108). It is used only alone or for emphasis, as the dual noun is usually sufficient.
3	ثَلَاثَة	ثَلَاث	3–10 form a group with the following characteristics:
4	أَرْبَعَة	أَرْبَع	(a) The feminine ending here marks the *masculine* form.
5	خَمْسَة	خَمْس	(b) these numbers take their noun in the *plural* (technically genitive case).
6	سِتَّة	سِتّ	Note the feminine form of the number 8 which behaves as described on page 142, note to line 2.
7	سَبْعَة	سَبْع	
8	ثَمَانِيَة	ثَمَان	
9	تِسْعَة	تِسْع	
10	عَشَرَة	عَشْر	

	Masculine	Feminine
11	أَحَدَ عَشَرَ	إِحْدَى عَشْرَةَ
12	اِثْنَا عَشَرَ	اِثْنَتَا عَشْرَةَ
13	ثَلَاثَةَ عَشَرَ	ثَلَاثَ عَشْرَةَ
14	أَرْبَعَةَ عَشَرَ	أَرْبَعَ عَشْرَةَ
15	خَمْسَةَ عَشَرَ	خَمْسَ عَشْرَةَ
16	سِتَّةَ عَشَرَ	سِتَّ عَشْرَةَ
17	سَبْعَةَ عَشَرَ	سَبْعَ عَشْرَةَ
18	ثَمَانِيَةَ عَشَرَ	ثَمَانِيَ عَشْرَةَ
19	تِسْعَةَ عَشَرَ	تِسْعَ عَشْرَةَ
20	عِشْرُونَ	
21	أَحَدٌ وَعِشْرُونَ	إِحْدَى وَعِشْرُونَ
22	اِثْنَانِ وَعِشْرُونَ	اِثْنَتَانِ وَعِشْرُونَ
30	ثَلَاثُونَ	
40	أَرْبَعُونَ	
50	خَمْسُونَ	
60	سِتُّونَ	
70	سَبْعُونَ	
80	ثَمَانُونَ	
90	تِسْعُونَ	

The numerals 11–99 inclusive take their noun in the indefinite accusative *singular*.

Notes

(a) *The teens.* Note that the *ten* part has reverted to normal gender pattern with the feminine ending on the feminine. However the *unit* part retains its perversion. The unit part of 12 behaves like a dual in a possessive construction, losing its final *nuun*.

(b) *The tens.* These are external masculine plurals, so the ending alternates **-uun/-iin** according to grammatical case (page 101). In spoken Arabic only the **-iin** ending is used.

(c) *In compounds*, the unit comes before the ten: three and twenty, five and sixty, etc.

100	مِائَة	Hundreds, thousands and millions, when used directly with a noun, take the *singular* (technically in the genitive case). However, in compounds of these +tens/units, *the noun is governed by the last part of the numeral.*
200	مِائَتَان	
300	ثَلَاث مِائَة	
1,000	أَلْف	
2,000	أَلْفَان	Note the irregular spelling of **mi'a** – the *alif* being ignored in pronunciation. Contrary to the rule given above, it does not go in the plural after the units (three hundred, etc.).
5,000	خَمْسَة آلَاف	
100,000	مِائَة أَلْف	
1,000,000	مَلْيُون	Zero is صِفْر (**Sifr**), whence we get our word 'cipher'.

Ordinal numbers

	Masculine	*Feminine*	
1st	الأَوَّل	الأُولَى	Special forms exist only for the units. Apart from 'first', which behaves like a superlative adjective, these have the shape $C^1aaC^2iC^3$ – but note the change of root used in 6th (some dialects use **saatit**). For the tens the cardinal form is used, but if this is accompanied by a unit the latter is in the ordinal form (see 11th, 25th).
2nd	الثَّانِي	الثَّانِيَة	
3rd	الثَّالِث	الثَّالِثَة	
4th	الرَّابِع	الرَّابِعَة	
5th	الخَامِس	الخَامِسَة	
6th	السَّادِس	السَّادِسَة	
7th	السَّابِع	السَّابِعَة	
8th	الثَّامِن	الثَّامِنَة	
9th	التَّاسِع	التَّاسِعَة	
10th	العَاشِر	العَاشِرَة	

	Masculine	Feminine
11th	الحَادِي عَشَر	الحَادِيَة عَشْرَة
12th	الثَانِي عَشَر	الثَانِيَة عَشْرَة
13th	الثَالِث عَشَر	الثَالِثَة عَشْرَة
20th		العِشْرُون
25th	الخَامِس والعِشْرُون	الخَامِسَة والعِشْرُون

Fractions

The word-shape for the fractions is $C^1uC^2C^3$, but 'half' is an exception. Note that again the root s-d-s is used for 6.

half	نِصْف	*seventh*	سُبْع
third	ثُلْث	*eighth*	ثُمْن
quarter	رُبْع	*ninth*	تُسْع
fifth	خُمْس	*tenth*	عُشْر
sixth	سُدْس		

The plural pattern for these fraction words is $'aC^1C^2aaC^3$.

Appendix 3
Internal Plural Shapes

There are only two reasonably consistent correlations between singular/plural shapes in Arabic – the two four-radical patterns given in Unit 9 – but there are a number of plural shapes which may be said to derive with some frequency from specific singular shapes. It is emphasised that the correlations given in the following list are not 'rules', but merely helpful hints which may aid you in acquiring a feel for the language. *The ultimate reference for any plural is the dictionary.*

1 $C^1uC^2C^3$ is the standard plural pattern for colour and physical disability adjectives (see Unit 18). Also used on some nouns, but not common.

2 $C^1iC^2aC^3$ is very common, with singular shape $C^1iC^2C^3a$ (with feminine ending):

قِطْعة pl قِطَع *piece, bit*

مِهْنة pl. مِهَن *trade, craft*

3 $C^1uC^2aC^3$ is equivalent to (2) above from singulars with a u-vowel ($C^1uC^2C^3a$):

لُعْبة pl. لُعَب *toy, game*

صُورة pl. صُوَر *picture*

It also occurs with singular shape $C^1aC^2C^3a$ when the middle radical is *waaw*:

دَوْلة pl. دُوَل *state, nation*

4 $C^1uC^2uC^3$ is quite common, but with no consistently occurring singular shape:

مَدِينة pl. مُدُن *town, city*

كِتَاب pl. كُتُب *book*

طَرِيق pl. طُرُق *way, road* (f)

266

5 $C^1iC^2aaC^3$ is a common pattern for adjectives with the singular shape $C^1aC^2iiC^3$:

صَغير pl. صِغَار *small*

كَبير pl. كِبَار *big*

It occurs also with nouns of various shapes:

رَجُل pl. رِجَال *man*

جَبَل pl. جِبَال *mountain*

جَمَل pl. جِمَال *camel*

كَلْب pl. كِلاَب *dog*

6 $C^1uC^2uuC^3$ is a very common pattern, usually from singular $C^1vC^2C^3$ (*v* meaning any of the three vowels, the important thing being that the middle radical is unvowelled):

قَلْب pl. قُلُوب *heart*

عِلْم pl. عُلُوم *science*

جُنْد pl. جُنُود *troop, army*

7 $C^1uC^2C^2aaC^3$ occurs frequently as the plural of singular shape $C^1aaC^2iC^3$ (active participle, Form I) when it refers to human beings:

سَاكِن pl. سُكَّان *resident, inhabitant*

سَائِح pl. سُوَّاح *tourist*

An alternative shape used with some such nouns is $C^1aC^2aC^3a$. For instance, طَالِب *student* can take either طُلَّاب or طَلَبَة.

8 ʾaC¹C²uC³ is not all that common. It occurs with the same sort of shapes as (6) above, and in fact often has (6) as an alternative plural:

شَهْر pl. أَشْهُر or شُهُور *month*

بَحْر pl. أَبْحُر or بُحُور *sea*

9 ʾaC¹C²aaC³ is one of the most common patterns. Again it is usually from the singular pattern C¹vC²C³ as in (6) above:

فِلْم pl. أَفْلَام *film*

شَكْل pl. أَشْكَال *shape, form, type*

لَوْن pl. أَلْوَان *colour*

Note also the rather unusual:

صَاحِب pl. أَصْحَاب *friend*

10 ʾaC¹C²iC³a is usually the plural of words which have a long a-vowel in the second syllable, and no feminine ending (cf. 14 below):

سُؤَال pl. أَسْئِلَة *question*

طَعَام pl. أَطْعِمَة *food*

قُمَاش pl. أَقْمِشَة *cloth, fabric*

11 ʾaC¹C²iC³aaʾ is from the singular shape C¹aC²iiC³:

صَدِيق pl. أَصْدِقَاء *friend*

غَنِيّ pl. أَغْنِيَاء *rich*

Note the slightly different shape for doubled roots:

طَبِيب pl. أَطِبَّاء *doctor*

Note that this and the following three shapes do not show the final *alif* in the indefinite accusative.

12 $C^1uC^2aC^3aa$' is common, from the singular shape $C^1aC^2iiC^3$ when it denotes male human beings:

	pl.		
أَمِير	pl.	أُمَرَاء	*prince*
وَزِير	pl.	وُزَرَاء	*minister*
سَفِير	pl.	سُفَرَاء	*ambassador*

It is also used with some adjectives:

	pl.		
عَظِيم	pl.	عُظَمَاء	*great, mighty*
فَقِير	pl.	فُقَرَاء	*poor*

13 $C^1awaaC^2iC^3$ is from the singular $C^1aaC^2iC^3(a)$ (masculine or feminine):

	pl.		
سَاحِل	pl.	سَوَاحِل	*coast*
قَاعِدَة	pl.	قَوَاعِد	*rule, principle, base*

14 C^1aC^2aa'iC^3 is from nouns with the feminine ending, and having a long vowel in the second syllable:

	pl.		
جَرِيدَة	pl.	جَرَائِد	*newspaper*
رِسَالَة	pl.	رَسَائِل	*article, essay*

15 $C^1aC^2aaC^3iC^4a$ is an alternative to the pattern $C^1aC^2aaC^3iiC^4$ or (less commonly $C^1aC^2aaC^3iC^4$ (pp. 100–1) used on some quadriliterals referring to people:

	pl.		
أُسْتَاذ	pl.	أَسَاتِذَة	*teacher*
تِلْمِيذ	pl.	تَلاَمِذَة	*pupil*

Appendix 4

Hints for Further Study

Arabic Grammars

Of the many Arabic grammar books on the market, the following two are recommended as providing the best material for progression beyond the scope of the present work. Both deal with modern literary Arabic, as opposed to the older or 'classical' language.

David Cowan, *An Introduction to Modern Literary Arabic*, Cambridge (University Press), 1964 (also available in paperback). This concise and accurate grammar provides a handy reference.

Farhat J. Ziadeh and R. Bayly Winder, *An Introduction to Modern Arabic*, Princeton (University Press), 1957. Written according to roughly the same inductive principles as this book, it contains a wealth of useful textual material.

Dictionaries

There is really only one Arabic–English dictionary worth considering:

Hans Wehr, *A Dictionary of Modern Written Arabic*, ed. J. Milton Cowan, Wiesbaden (Otto Harrassowitz), 1966 (also available in paperback).

If you can read German, the Langenscheidts *Taschenwörterbuch Arabisch–Deutsch, Deutsch–Arabisch*, Berlin and Munich, 1976, is useful for the beginner, as it is arranged strictly in alphabetical order, and not according to roots as all other dictionaries are, which can save a lot of time.

English–Arabic dictionaries tend to be written for Arabs, and hence do not make any effort to explain the exact meanings and usages of the Arabic words given. The most useful of them is probably *al-Mawrid*, by M. Baalbaki, Beirut (Dar al-Ilm li-l-Malayin), 1967.

Spoken Arabic

The Arabic vernaculars vary so much from place to place that unless you know exactly where you are going, some compromise has to be made. The Arabic taught in this book is literary, but trimmed of many of its grammatical trappings, and will be understood by educated people in all Arab countries. However, if you want to understand the locals, you will have to learn a dialect. Although not always the most popular, there is no doubt that Egyptian is still the most widely understood, due to the influence of Egyptian radio, TV and films.

Key to the Exercises

EXERCISE 0.1 Two-letter transliterations have been italicised here to avoid confusion

brk – fqd – lms – *sh dh dh* – : fw – Tlb – *khzn* – *th gh* r – hlk – Syt –
bhl – krh – mDy – l *gh* m – fhm – brqwq – b *gh* l – *kh* rj – jrH –
Hmd – mdH – D *gh* T – brnmj – jmhwr – *DH* n n – *sh* k k – Hmlq –
brbr – nbt – *th* q f – zlzl – HmD – *gh*rnT – rbl – b *gh* D – n : s –
Tlsm – hbhb – : dw – wmD – syTr – Hzn – bl*gh* – *th* l *th* – mkn – ryS –
zndq – skn – nhD – *dh* l l – bdr – b *dh* r – rHm – brTm – *gh* m D –
lstk – tlfn – *kh* l *kh* l – r : d – d r : – H *sh* y – THn – qfz.

EXERCISE 0.2

قرد — ممكن — ضبط — ذلل — دهن — مكتب — رمي — سقط — بعض —
بغض — وهم — سرطن — شمس — غفل — بيرم — ورور — رطن — ثني —
ربع — تلغرف — كتبن — حجج — خلف — رجز — فضض — ضفض —
خنفس — شخر — شكل — مزغ — زمرد — غلي — ثور — شبب — قلقل —
طحن — شغل — بنفسج — توت — حرمن — ثوب — فندق — نزك —
صرم — مرض — يلزم — خربش — جهنم — محلل — ضمن — ظهر —
جرجير — ضنق — فول — عنكبوت — زمخ — شمخ — حضرموت — نعنع —
برغث

EXERCISE 0.3 zamzam – markaz – farigh – qifl – hamaj – thulth –
Safar – Sarf – sharT – DHahara – ghariqa – marHab – nahr – balaH –
tharthara – waqr – fiqh – naHwa – yaman – maysar – Tarada – baghl –
jaHsh – sijn – jund – Sadaf – Sidq – quds – natin – makatha – bulbul –
shakhS

EXERCISE 0.4

بطَل — نخْل — مِنبَر — بُرج — حجَر — نقَدَ — حنْبَل — لعِبَ — رقَم —
حسُبَ — رُبْع — غزَز — لقَب — بقَر — ركِبَ — هبَطَ — شبْشِب — بشَر —
فِلْس — ربَطَ — طُرش — غزْل — سهْم — مكْر — مِلح

EXERCISE 0.5 raaghib – Taahir – SaaliH – faSiiH – Saghiir – rakhiiS –
kariim – baSiir – kulayb – ghafuur – Sanduuq – faanuus –
minkaar – qaabuus – bayram – muliiq – miizaan – fanaadiq – ghayr –

fawr – rukuub – Sawt – labiid – marHuum – Samiim – riiHaan –
ta:baan – baliid – fayruuz – naDHiir – naTruun – muniir – yaasir –
bayt – dhayl – diin – miSbaaH – baaruud – mawsim – samiir

EXERCISE 0.6

باطِن — جَميل — كامِل — صَحيح — جَواب — ريح — سَلام — هارِب —

ميثاق — هِلال — ضابِط — مَضْبوط — ظاهِر — غُراب — قِنْديل — صاروخ —

تَلْخيص — جاز — بَهْلول — مَوْج — في — يُقيم — سَفير — فيل — قَيْد —

قُيُود — ديك — خُرْطوم

EXERCISE 0.7 marra – mu:allim – mudarris – Sarraaf – tamazzaq –
Haadd – mumayyizaat – dabbaagh – khayyaam – Hammaal –
suwwaaH – rukkaab – khabbaaz – rattaba – sattaar – fannaan –
dabbuur – dalla – Dalla – Haqq

EXERCISE 0.8 jiddan – marHaban – mathalan – Tab:an – fi:lan –
sahlan – raghman – kathiiran – yawmiyyan – sanawiyyan.

EXERCISE 0.9 su'aal – ra'iis – 'amal – bi'r – juz' – 'ilhaam – mala'a –
mamluu' – ru'asaa' – qaa'il – ra's – 'asnaan – 'arba:aa' – Da'iil – ra'uuf –
'islaam – 'aghniyaa' – ya's – ba's – 'iimaan – 'udabaa' – mi'naath –
'asad – radii' – muta'assif – 'aHdaath – 'aHaadiith – 'uns – khunfusaa'.

EXERCISE 0.10 'aadaab – 'aabaar – 'aakhadha – 'aalaaf – 'aakala –
shuT'aan – 'aamaad – 'aamaal – 'aaHaad.

EXERCISE 0.11 fuSHaa – ghaDbaa – bilaadii – lii – 'ilaa – kitaabii –
ladaa – manzilii – kubraa – wusTaa – marsaa – darsii – :alaa – ukhraa –
yumnaa – mabnaa – mabnii.

EXERCISE 0.12 sayyaara – maktaba – majalla – jariida – wizaara –
tarbiyya – namla – nakhla – qarya – tarjama – Saghiira – ishtiraakiyya –
diimuuqraaTiyya – marwaHa – Taa'ira – riwaaya – mas'ala – aSliyya –
makka.

EXERCISE 0.13 dhaalik – haadhaa – allaah – haadhihi – haadhaan –
haa'ulaa'.

EXERCISE 0.14 jibáal – khabíir – izdiháar – arqáam – musta:ídd –
mutanáwwa:a – aráanib – :aSaafíir – yamúrr – yámsik – manshuuráat –
káa'in – baáriz – fatíila – aSdiqáa' – kútibat – katábnaa – sáafaruu –
dhí kraa – qaatalúunii – tájriba – Táawila – istá:lamat – fanaajíin –

zumúrrud – banáfsaj – dháalik – muusíiqaa – qanáabil – marHúum – ma:lúum – ma:luumaát – mu:allimúun – taláamidha – fátaHa – Sabíyy – taqáddum – máshat – qúmnaa – ta:áshshaa – Sádaqat – lá:ibuu – fáqaT – lámmaa.

EXERCISE 1.1

A 1 al-mudiir   2 al-waasi: 3 ash-shubbaak   4 al-maTaar
5 an-naDHiif   6 aS-Saghiir   7 al-kitaab   8 an-naafi: 9 al-qaSiir
10 ar-rajul.

B 1 an-naHiif   2 al-ba:iid   3 al-bayt   4 aT-Tawiil   5 ash-shaari:
6 al-:ariiD   7 al-mashghuul   8 ar-rajul   9 al-maTaar   10 al-walad

EXERCISE 1.2

١ رجل مشغول   ٢ كتاب صغير   ٣ باب عريض   ٤ ولد طويل

٥ شارع طويل   ٦ شبّاك نظيف   ٧ مطار بعيد   ٨ رجل مشهور

٩ مكتب واسع   ١٠ مدير صغير

EXERCISE 1.3

١ الرجل المشغول   ٢ الكتاب الصغير   ٣ الباب العريض

٤ الولد الطويل   ٥ الشارع الطويل   ٦ الشبّاك النظيف   ٧ المطار البعيد

٨ الرجل المشهور   ٩ المكتب الواسع   ١٠ المدير الصغير

EXERCISE 1.4

1 maTaar kabir waasi: *A large, spacious airport.*
2 ash-shubbaak al-:ariiD an-naDHiif   *The wide, clean window.*
3 al-walad aT-Tawiil an-naHiif   *The tall, thin boy.*
4 rajul mashghuul mashhuur   *A busy, famous man.*
5 al-baab al-kabiir al-:ariiD   *The big, wide door.*
6 shaari: Tawiil naDHiif   *A long, clean street.*

EXERCISE 2.1

A

١ الصندوق ثقيل   ٢ الصحن مكسور   ٣ الحاكم عادل

٤ الكاتب مشغول   ٥ الكلب سمين   ٦ التاجر غائب   ٧ المتحف قريب

٨ السكرتير حاضر   ٩ الدولاب واسع   ١٠ الطالب شاطر

B 1 The fat driver.   2 The busy employee.   3 The present ruler.
4 A beautiful museum.   5 The honest merchant.   6 A light box.

١ السائق سمين   ٢ الموظّف مشغول   ٣ الحاكم حاضر   ٤ المتحف جميل

٥ التاجر عادل   ٦ الصندوق خفيف

EXERCISE 2.2

١ عمر جميل ٢ أحمد غائب ٣ سليم سمين ٤ روبرت صغير

٥ رشيد شاطر ٦ جون عادل

EXERCISE 2.3

١ هو نحيف ٢ أنا مشغول ٣ أنت سمين

٤ هو مشهور ٥ أنت مريض ٦ أنا طويل

EXERCISE 2.4

١ هل الدولاب مملوء ؟ لا ، هو فارغ ٢ أمحمّد حاضر ؟ لا ، هو غائب

٣ هل المتحف بعيد ؟ لا ، هو قريب ٤ هل الصندوق خفيف ؟ لا ، هو ثقيل

٥ هل الشارع طويل ؟ لا ، هو قصير ٦ هل الولد طويل ؟ لا ، هو قصير

٧ هل المكتب صغير ؟ لا ، هو كبير ٨ أسليم نحيف ؟ لا ، هو سمين

٩ هل السائق حاضر ؟ لا ، هو غائب ١٠ أهو كبير ؟ لا ، هو صغير

EXERCISE 3.1

A ١ السائق المشغول ٢ السيّارة السريعة ٣ المكاتب الواسعة

٤ الأرض النظيفة ٥ الغرفة المقفولة ٦ الأمّ الحاضرة ٧ الكتابة الجميلة

٨ المسجد البعيد ٩ الحرب الطويلة ١٠ الطاولة الثقيلة

B 1 The busy driver. 2 The fast car. 3 The spacious offices.
4 The clean ground (earth). 5 The closed room.
6 The present mother. 7 The beautiful writing. 8 The distant mosque.
9 The long war. 10 The heavy table.

C ١ سائق مشغول ٢ سيّارة سريعة ٣ مكاتب واسعة ٤ أرض نظيفة

٥ غرفة مقفولة ٦ أمّ حاضرة ٧ كتابة جميلة ٨ مسجد بعيد

٩ حرب طويلة ١٠ طاولة ثقيلة

D ١ السائق مشغول ٢ السيّارة سريعة ٣ المكاتب واسعة

٤ الأرض نظيفة ٥ الغرفة مقفولة ٦ الأمّ حاضرة ٧ الكتابة جميلة

٨ المسجد بعيد ٩ الحرب طويلة ١٠ الطاولة ثقيلة

EXERCISE 3.2 1 The plate is on the table.
2 The chair is in the room. 3 Salim is in the mosque.
4 The sun is above the earth. 5 The secretary is with the manager.

6 Ahmed is from the town.   7 The books are in the library.
8 The manager and the secretary are in the airport.
9 The delegate is with the manager.   10 The tailoress is in the market.

EXERCISE 3.3   ١ هناك كتاب على المكتب   ٢ هناك بيوت كبيرة في المدينة
٣ هناك مكتبة في السوق   ٤ السيّارة الجديدة في الشارع
٥ الطالب من المدرسة

EXERCISE 4.1

A   ١ هذه المجلة   ٢ هذا المجلس   ٣ هذه الأقلام   ٤ هذا المصنع
٥ هذا الماء   ٦ هذه المنطقة   ٧ هذه السينما   ٨ هذه الوزارة
٩ هذا الجامع   ١٠ هذه الشوارع

B   ١ تلك المدينة   ٢ تلك المدن   ٣ تلك الجريدة   ٤ ذلك المتحف
٥ ذلك الكاتب   ٦ ذلك السائق   ٧ تلك الدواليب   ٨ ذلك المشروع
٩ تلك الطاولة   ١٠ تلك اليد

C 1 This magazine.   2 This council.   3 These pens.   4 This factory.
5 This water.   6 This region.   7 This cinema.   8 This ministry.
9 This mosque.   10 These streets.

1 That town.   2 Those towns.   3 That newspaper.   4 That museum.
5 That clerk.   6 That driver.   7 Those cupboards.   8 That project.
9 That table.   10 That hand.

D   ١ ذلك الاعلان الهامّ   ٢ هذه الحكومة الجديدة
٣ تلك المجلّات الاسبوعية   ٤ هذا المجلس العامّ   ٥ هذه الطائرات الحديثة
٦ ذلك القسم الرئيسي

EXERCISE 4.2

A   ١ هذه الشجرة صغيرة   ٢ ذلك العامل مجتهد   ٣ هذه الجريدة قديمة
٤ هذه المنازل واسعة   ٥ تلك السكرتيرة كسلانة   ٦ تلك المصانع كبيرة
٧ هذا الصندوق فارغ   ٨ هذا الباب مقفول   ٩ تلك البنت جميلة
١٠ ذلك الشارع عريض

B 1 This tree is small.   2 That workman is diligent.
3 This newspaper is old.   4 These houses are spacious.

5 That secretary is lazy.   6 These factories are big.
7 This box is empty.   8. This door is shut.   9 That girl is pretty.
10 That street is broad.

EXERCISE 4.3

A

١ تلك مطبعة قديمة   ٢ هذه منطقة كبيرة   ٣ ذلك قسم خاصّ
٤ هذه جرائد أسبوعية   ٥ تلك شبابيك وسخة   ٦ هذه يد نظيفة
٧ ذلك رجل عادل   ٨ تلك متاحف هامّة   ٩ هذه حكومة حديثة
١٠ تلك مصادر رئيسية

B

١ تلك هي المطبعة القديمة   ٢ هذه هي المنطقة الكبيرة
٣ ذلك هو القسم الخاصّ   ٤ هذه هي الجرائد الأسبوعية
٥ تلك هي الشبابيك الوسخة   ٦ هذه هي اليد النظيفة
٧ ذلك هو الرجل العادل   ٨ تلك هي المتاحف الهامّة
٩ هذه هي الحكومة الحديثة   ١٠ تلك هي المصادر الرئيسية

C 1 This is an old printing house.   2 This is a large region.
3 That is a special department.   4 These are weekly newspapers.
5 These are dirty windows.   6 This is a clean hand.
7 That is an honest man.   8 These are important museums.
9 This is a modern government.   10 These are major sources.

1 This is the old printing house.   2 This is the large region.
3 That is the special department.   4 These are the weekly newspapers.
5 These are the dirty windows.   6 This is the clean hand.
7 That is the honest man.   8 These are the important museums.
9 This is the modern government.   10 These are the major sources.

EXERCISE 4.4   1. as-saa:a sab:a illa rub: 2 as-saa:a :ashara wa-thulth
3 as-saa:a arba:a wa-rub: 4 as-saa:a thamaaniya wa-niSf wa-khamsa
5 as-saa:a sab:a wa-khamsa   6 as-saa:a ithna:shar illa thulth
7 as-saa:a thalaatha wa-:ashara   8 as-saa:a tis:a wa-niSf illa khamsa
9 as-saa:a ithna:shar illa :ashara   10 as-saa:a thamaaniya wa-niSf.

Unit 5   Transliteration
1 kitaab-ka   2 ghurfat-haa   3 maktab al-mudiir
4 wizaarat ad-daakhiliyya   5 bayt buTrus   6 jaami:at al-qaahira
7 qamiiS-ii al-jadiid   8 sayyaarat al-waziir al-kabiira
9 qiT:at laHm   10 riwaaya min riwaayaat tuumaas haardii
11 natiijat haadhihi as-siyaasa   12 Hukuumat-naa haadhihi.

EXERCISE 5.1

A ‏١ مدير البنك ٢ اعلان المجلس ٣ حديقتك ٤ وزير الداخليّة‏
‏٥ مجلّاته ٦ أمّنا ٧ سيّارة عمر ٨ فروع الشركة ٩ مطبعة الحكومة‏
‏١٠ رأسها‏

B ‏١ منزلكِ ٢ سيّارته ٣ طرودهنّ ٤ أختهم ٥ رواياتكَ ٦ ساعتكنّ‏

C ‏١ فساتين البنات ٢ حديقة البيت ٣ وظائف الوزراء‏
‏٤ نتائج السياسات ٥ رؤوسهم ٦ قميصك ٧ رواياتهنّ‏
‏٨ مكاتب السكرتيرات‏

EXERCISE 5.2

A 1 My cheap watch.   2 The manager's new car.
3 Salim's heavy parcel.   4 His dirty suit.
5 The important announcement of the newspapers (the newspapers' . . .).
6 The bank's diligent manager (the diligent manager of . . .).
7 The fat driver of the car.   8 Her old jokes.
9 The government's new factory.   10 Our spacious room.

B ‏١ ساعتي رخيصة ٢ سيّارة المدير جديدة ٣ طرد سليم ثقيل‏
‏٤ بذلته وسخة ٥ اعلان الجرائد هامّ ٦ مدير البنك مجتهد‏
‏٧ سائق السيّارة سمين ٨ نكتها قديمة ٩ مصنع الحكومة جديد‏
‏١٠ غرفتنا واسعة‏

EXERCISE 5.3

1 A kilogram of meat.   2 A piece of bread.   3 A man's return.
4 A branch of a company.   5 A kilogram of flour.

EXERCISE 5.4

A ‏١ فروع هذا البنك ٢ رأس هذا الولد ٣ دخول هذا المندوب‏
‏٤ سياسة هذه الشركة ٥ أخت هذه البنت ٦ سيّارة هذا السائق‏
‏٧ باب هذه الطائرة ٨ قلم هذه السكرتيرة ٩ يد هذا الرجل‏
‏١٠ غرفة هذا الزائر‏

1 The branches of this bank.   2 This boy's head.
3 The entry of this delegate.   4 The policy of this company.
5 This girl's sister.   6 This driver's car.   7 The door of this aeroplane.
8 This secretary's pen.   9 This man's hand.   10 This visitor's room.

B   ١ مدينتنا تلك   ٢ مشروع الحكومة ذلك   ٣ باب الجامعة ذلك
٤ كتابه ذلك   ٥ مصدر البترول ذلك

1 That town of ours.   2 That project of the government.
3 That gate of the university.   4 That book of his.
5 That source of oil.

EXERCISE 6.1   1 d-q-q   2 k-b-r   3 j-n-n   4 w-z-r   5 sh-j-r
6 sh-r-:   7 sh-gh-l   8 H-k-m   9 b-:-d   10 H-D-r   11 w-DH-f
12 s-y-r   13 sh-r-:   14 H-r-r   15 f-r-:   16 d-kh-l   17 H-d-q   18 r-w-y
19 kh-f-f   20 S-n-d-q   21 H-m-d   22 sh-T-r   23 s-w-q   24 m-l-'
25 j-l-s

Unit 7   Transliteration

1 saafar ilaa al-kuwayt thumma raja: ilaa al-baHrayn
2 fataHat al-baab wa-dakhalat   3 hal dafa:t al-fuluus? laa, rafaDt
4 'akalnaa wa-sharibnaa   5 kallam as-saa'iq ar-ra'iis
6 Tabakhat zawjatii aT-Ta:aam   .   7 'a:lanat al-jaraa'id natiijat al-intikhaab
8 rafaD al-:ummaal al-:alaawa wa-'aDrabuu
9 ijtama:at as-sakriteeraat wa-intakhabna manduubat-hunna
10 waDa:t-hu fii shanTatii fii aS-SabaaH (*pronounced*: fi S-SabaaH)
11 'adkhalat-nii al-bint wa-'ajlasat-nii
12 qad waSal ra'iis al-wuzaraa' ilaa ar-riyaaD (ila r-riyaaD) 'ams
13 maa wajadnaa at-taqriir fii ad-daftar (fi d-daftar)

EXERCISE 7.1   1 We wrote.   2 They (m) arrived.   3 She elected.
4 They (f) refused.   5 He cooked.   6 You (m, pl) went on strike.
7 You (f, pl) drank.   8 They (m) paid.   9 I put.   10 You (m, pl) ate.
11 We entered. 12 They (m) announced.   13 They (f) had a meeting.
14 You (m, pl) spoke to (addressed).   15 You (f) wrote.
16 You (m) arrived.   17 They (m) put.   18 We arrived.
19 She drank.   20 He ate.

EXERCISE 7.2

A   ١ أكل الولد الخبز   ٢ شربت السكرتيرة الماء   ٣ كلّمت الخيّاطة السائق
٤ أعلنت الجرائد النتيجة   ٥ دفع العمّال الفلوس
٦ سافرت الأمّ من المطار   ٧ وجدت البنت شنطتها
٨ فتحت الطالبة الباب   ٩ كتبت زوجته التقرير
١٠ وضع التجّار الصناديق في البيت

B 1 The boy ate the bread.   2 The secretary drank the water.
3 The tailoress spoke to the driver.
4 The newspapers announced the result.
5 The workmen paid the money.
6 The mother travelled from the airport.   7 The girl found her case.
8 The student (f) opened the door.   9 His wife wrote the report.
10 The merchants put the boxes in the house.

EXERCISE 7.3

A   ١ شربت البنت الماء ثمّ أكلت اللحم   ٢ اجتمع الوزراء وانتخبوا مندوبهم

٣ دخل الموظّفون وكلّموا المدير

٤ سافرت البنات الى الرياض ثمّ رجعن الى الكويت

٥ دخل التاجر الغرفة ووجد زوجته   ٦ اجتمع العمّال ورفضوا العلاوة

B 1 The girl drank the water then ate the meat.
2 The ministers met and elected their delegate.
3 The officials came in and spoke to the manager.
4 The girls travelled to Riyad, then returned to Kuwait.
5 The merchant entered the room and found his wife.
6 The workers met and refused the raise.

EXERCISE 7.4

A   ١ أدخلها   ٢ كلّمته   ٣ طبخناها   ٤ رفضناه   ٥ شربتها   ٦ أكلته

٧ كلّمتموهم   ٨ كتبته   ٩ دفعها   ١٠ أجلسناها

B 1 He let her in.   2 She spoke to him.   3 We cooked it
4 They (f) refused it.   5 You drank it.   6 I ate it.
7 You (m, pl) spoke to them.   8 You (f) wrote it.   9 He pushed her.
10 We gave her a seat.

EXERCISE 7.5   1 The manager put the file in the cupboard.
2 The minister spoke to his wife, then went (travelled) to the airport.
3 We did not speak to the boss yesterday.
4 They have drunk the water and eaten the meat.
5 She let her mother in and gave her a seat.
6 They (f) found her house in Riyad.
7 The employees (f) held a meeting yesterday in the factory.
8 Did you go to Bahrain?
9 The secretary wrote the long report and put it in the file.
10 They went to Kuwait and did not come back (did not return from it).

Unit 8   Transliteration

1 kaan jamal :abd an-naaSir qaa'id(an) :aDHiim(an)
2 kaan al-muhandis mashghuul(an) 3 kaanat 'umm-hu mariiDa.
4 kunt fii dubay yawm al-khamiis
5 kunnaa fii al-masraH (*pronounced*: fi l-masraH)
6 laysa haadha al-barnaamaj (haadha l-barnaamaj) munaasib(an) li-l-
'aTfaal
7 laysat 'ukht-haa jamiila 8 Saar al-malik jabbaar(an)
9 'aSbaHat al-'umuur mu:aqqada   10 inna ar-rajul jaahil
11 inna haadhihi (a)s-siyaasa la-faashila
12 inna muHammad(an) :aamil mujtahid
13 innahu dhakii 14 kaan al-wafd qad waSal
15 kaanuu qad 'akaluu

EXERCISE 8.1

A

١ كانت البنت جميلة   ٢ كانت السياسة فاشلة

٣ كان الصندوق الكبير ثقيلا   ٤ كان هذا صعبا   ٥ كان فستانها جميلا

٦ كان ذلك المهندس أجنبيّا   ٧ كانت بذلته رخيصة   ٨ كانت من دبي

٩ كانت البنت مع أمّها   ١٠ كان الوفد عند الوزير   ١١ كانت ذكية

١٢ كان التمرين سهلا

B 1 The girl was beautiful.   2 The policy was futile.
3 The big box was heavy.   4 This was difficult.
5 Her dress was pretty.   6 That engineer was foreign.
7 His suit was cheap.   8 She was from Dubai.
9 The girl was with her mother.
10 The delegation was with the minister.   11 She was clever.
12 The exercise was easy.

EXERCISE 8.2

A

١ ليس الولد جاهلا   ٢ ليست السكرتيرة في المكتب

٣ ما كانت في البحرين يوم السبت   ٤ ليست هذه المجلّة جديدة

٥ ليس باب البنك مقفولا   ٦ ما كنّا عند أختنا

٧ ليس الكتاب على الرفّ   ٨ ما كانت الأرض وسخة

٩ ليس هذا الكرسي ثقيلا   ١٠ ليس محمّد مدرّسا في المدرسة الجديدة

B 1 The boy is not ignorant.   2 The secretary is not in the office.
3 She was not in Bahrain on Saturday.   4 This magazine is not new.
5 The door of the bank is not shut.

6 We were not at our sister's house.   7 The book is not on the shelf.
8 The ground was not dirty.   9 This chair is not heavy.
10 Muhammad is not a teacher in the new school.

EXERCISE 8.3   (Mark yourself correct whichever of the two verbs you
have used, provided it has the correct ending.)

١ أصبحت الشمس حارّة   ٢ أصبح اللحم رخيصا

٣ أصبح قميصه وسخا   ٤ صارت مشهورة في الكويت

٥ صار التمرين سهلا   ٦ أصبحت وظيفته صعبة   ٧ أصبح قائدا عظيما

٨ أصبحت سكرتيرة في الحكومة   ٩ أصبحت تلك الجريدة الجديدة مشهورة

١٠ صارت سياستهم غريبة

EXERCISE 8.4

A

١ إنّ هذا الولد ذكي   ٢ إنّ المهندس المشهور أجنبي

٣ إنّ الجامعة بعيدة   ٤ إنّ البنك المركزيّ في المدينة

٥ إنّ وظيفة المفتّش لسهلة   ٦ إنّ هذه الرواية لغريبة

٧ إنّ المحرّر لرجل ذكي   ٨ إنّ تلك الشركة محلّية   ٩ إنّه من الكويت

١٠ إنّ المدير مبسوط

B 1 This boy is clever.   2 The famous engineer is foreign.
3 The university is far away.   4 The central bank is in the town.
5 The job of inspector (or of the inspector) is easy.
6 This story is strange!   7 The editor is certainly a shrewd man.
8 That company is local.   9 He is from Kuwait.
10 The manager is content.

EXERCISE 8.5
A 1 The delegate arrived at Bahrain airport (the airport of Bahrain).
2 The girl drank the water.   3 We ate the meat.
4 The engineer took the report from the secretary.
5 The student put her book in the case.
6 The merchant took the money on Monday.
7 The government rejected the report.
8 The secretary spoke to the manager of the new company.
9 The Prime Minister travelled to Riyad on Sunday.
10 The affairs of this useless government have become difficult and
complicated.

B

١ كان المندوب قد وصل الى مطار البحرين

٢ كانت البنت قد شربت الماء ٣ كنّا قد أكلنا اللحم

٤ كان المهندس قد أخذ التقرير من السكرتير

٥ كانت الطالبة قد وضعت كتابها في الشنطة

٦ كان التاجر قد أخذ الفلوس يوم الاثنين

٧ كانت الحكومة قد رفضت التقرير

٨ كانت السكرتيرة قد كلّمت مدير الشركة الجديدة

٩ كان رئيس الوزراء قد سافر الى الرياض يوم الأحد

١٠ كانت أمور هذه الحكومة الفاشلة قد أصبحت صعبة معقّدة

Unit 9   Transliteration

1 mudun kabiira   2 al-muhandisuun al-judad
3 al-mudarrisaat al-jadiidaat   4 waSal al-Haffaaruun 'ams
5 fattash muwaDHDHaf al-jamaarik al-musaafiriin al-mughaadiriin
6 dakhalat aT-Taalibaat jaami:aat kathiira
7 hum :ummaal fii maSna: as-sayyaaraat
8 naHnu tajjaar fii al-:aaSima (*pronounced* fi l-:aaSima)
9 'a-'antum miSriyyuun?
10 laysa haa'ulaa' al-'awlaad min tilka al-madaaris (tilka l-madaaris)
11 'uulaa'ik an-nisaa' khayyaaTaat maahiraat
12 kharaj aS-SaaHibaan min as-siinamaa
13 qara' maqaalatayn Tawiilatayn fi l-majalla

EXERCISE 9.1

A

١ أمر هامّ ٢ الملك العظيم ٣ كانت المدرّسة الجديدة غائبة

٤ أخذ الحمّال الصندوق الثقيل ٥ اشتغل الحفّار في دبي

٦ العامل مجتهد ٧ يوم طويل ٨ كان المشروع فاشلا ٩ خيّاطة ماهرة

١٠ رواية عجيبة ١١ الموظّف الجديد ١٢ الفرع المركزيّ الرئيسيّ

B

١ مقاولون مصريون ٢ النجّارون الخبراء ٣ مقالات كاملة

٤ محاسبون أذكياء ٥ رؤساء الشركات

٦ أخذت السكرتيرات الجميلات الدفاتر الفارغة

٧ كتب المديرون الاعلانات الهامّة ٨ أخواتي ممرّضات

٩ كلّم المفتّشون الركّاب المغادرين ١٠ أرسل الوزراء الموظّفين الى البنوك

١١ ذهب الضيوف المصريون الى المدن الكبيرة

١٢ سيّارات سريعة ودبّابات ثقيلة ١٣ ليست التمارين صعبة

١٤ وجدت المدرّسات المشغولات الأولاد الصغار في البيوت البعيدة

١٥ الشبابيك مقفولة والأبواب مكسورة .

C (A) 1 An important matter.   2 The mighty king.
3 The new teacher was absent.   4 The porter took the heavy box.
5 The driller worked in Dubai.   6 The workman is diligent.
7 A long day.   8 The project was futile.   9 A skilled tailoress.
10 A wonderful story.   11 The new employee.
12 The main central branch (the central main branch).

(B) 1 Egyptian contractors.   2 The expert carpenters.
3 Complete articles.   4 Shrewd accountants.
5 The bosses of the companies.
6 The beautiful secretaries took the empty files.
7 The managers wrote the important announcements.
8 My sisters are nurses.
9 The inspectors spoke to the departing passengers.
10 The ministers sent the employees to the banks.
11 The Egyptian guests went to the big towns.
12 Fast cars and heavy tanks.   13 The exercises are not difficult.
14 The busy teachers found the small boys in the remote houses.
15 The windows are closed and the doors are broken.

EXERCISE 9.2

A

١ هذه المرأة الجميلة ٢ هذه المجلّات الأجنبية

٣ هؤلاء الكهربائيون الماهرون ٤ هذه الجرائد اليوميّة

٥ هؤلاء الضيوف الكثيرون ٦ هذه الترتيبات الجديدة

٧ هؤلاء القوّاد العظماء ٨ هذه الأمور المعقّدة

٩ هؤلاء الممرّضات الجديدات ١٠ هؤلاء المصريون الفقراء

B

١ تلك العواصم المشهورة ٢ أولئك الخيّاطون الأجانب

٣ تلك الشوارع الطويلة ٤ أولئك الرجال السمان

٥ أولئك المدرّسات الحاضرات ٦ أولئك البنات الصغيرات

٧ تلك الطائرات الجديدة ٨ أولئك الأصحاب الغائبون

٩ تلك الصحون المكسورة ١٠ أولئك الحكّام الجبابرة

C (A) 1 This beautiful woman. 2 These foreign magazines.
3 These skilled electricians. 4 These daily newspapers.
5 These many guests. 6 These new arrangements.
7 These mighty leaders. 8 These complicated affairs.
9 These new nurses. 10 These poor Egyptians.

(B) 1 Those famous capitals. 2 Those foreign tailors.
3 Those long streets. 4 Those fat men.
5 Those present teachers (i.e. teachers who are present).
6 Those young girls. 7 Those new planes. 8 Those absent friends.
9 Those broken plates. 10 Those tyrannical rulers.

D

١ أنتم جهّال ٢ مكتبهم قريب ٣ نحن مصريون

٤ ليس الضيوف في بيتهم (بيوتهم) ٥ ان الخبّازين أصحابي (أصحابنا)

٦ هم محاسبون مشاهير ٧ انّها ثلّاجات جديدة ٨ أأنتنّ ممرّضات ؟

٩ هنّ مدرّسات في المدينة ١٠ انّهم رسّامون مشاهير

E 1 You (pl) are ignorant. 2 Their office is near.
3 We are Egyptians.
4 The guests are not in their house (their houses).
5 The bakers are my friends (our friends).
6 They are famous accountants. 7 They are new fridges.
8 Are you (f) nurses? 9 They (f) are teachers in the town.
10 They are famous artists.

EXERCISE 9.3

A

١ فتّش الموظّفان الراكبين المغادرين ٢ انّ المقاولين حاضران

٣ الدبّاستان على المكتبين ٤ قرأ الكتابين الأجنبيّين

٥ إنّ اللحّامين ماهران ٦ دخل الوزيران البيتين

٧ السائقان في السيّارتين الكبيرتين ٨ جريدتان يوميتان حديثتان

٩ كلّم المديران العاملين الجديدين ١٠ طفلان صغيران جميلان

B 1 The two officials inspected the two departing passengers.
2 The two contractors are present.
3 The two staplers are on the two desks.
4 He read the two foreign books. 5 The two welders are skilled.
6 The two ministers entered the two houses.
7 The two drivers are in the two big cars.
8 Two modern daily newspapers.
9 The two managers spoke to the two new workmen. 10 Two beautiful
little babies.

Unit 10   Transliteration

1 yaskunuun fii shaqqa kabiira fii landan
2 tanshur al-Hukuuma al-iHSaa'iyyaat ar-rasmiyya fii 'awwal ash-shahr
3 yadrus fii jaami:at al-qaahira   4 maadhaa ta'kul fi S-SabaaH?
5 sawfa yuqaddim al-fariiq al-qawmii barnaamaj(an) min ar-raqS
ash-sha:bii ghadan   6 sa-'adhhab yawm as-sabt
7 laa na:rif shay'(an) :an aS-Saadiraat wa-l-waaridaat
8 lan yarji:uu ilaa waTan-hum 'abadan
9 'a-lam tashrabii l-qahwa?   10 yaDHak :alay-naa
11 sa-'adfa: la-hu l-fuluus   12 'akhadh minnii junayhayn

EXERCISE 10.1

A ترقصين ٦   تفهم ٥   يحملن ٤   أضحك ٣   تكتبون ٢   يدرسون ١

تفتّش ١١   يدافعون ١٠   تقدّمون ٩   نصرف ٨   يسكنون ٧

تكون ١٧   يشتغل ١٦   يذهبن ١٥   نطلب ١٤   تقرئين ١٣   تسأل ١٢

تصلن ٢٢   يطبخن ٢١   تأخذون ٢٠   يصير ١٩   يصبحون ١٨

تدخلون ٢٥   نجتمع ٢٤   يجد ٢٣

B 1 They (m) study.   2 You (m, pl) write.   3 I laugh.
4 They (f) carry.   5 She understands.   6 You (f) dance.
7 They (m) dwell.   8 We spend.   9 You (m, pl) present.
10 They (m) defend.   11 You (m) inspect.   12 She asks.
13 You (f) read.   14 We request.   15 They (f) go.   16 He works.
17 She is (will be).   18 They (m) become.   19 He becomes.
20 You (m, pl) take.   21 They (f) cook.   22 You (f, pl) arrive.
23 He finds.   24 We meet.   25 You (m, pl) enter.

EXERCISE 10.2

سيكلّم المدير الموظّفين غدا ٢   يأكل الطعام ١

كان يشرب قهوة ٤   كانت تسكن في شقّة كبيرة في لندن ٣

سوف ينشرون الاحصائيات قبل يوم السبت ٥   نفهم اللغة العربيّة ٦

كان الحمّال يحمل صندوقا ثقيلا ٧   يسافر السفير كثيرا ٨

يفتّش العساكر الشنط في المطار ٩   يلعب الأطفال في الشارع ١٠

نكسب الفلوس ونصرفها ١١

EXERCISE 10.3

تدرّسي ٥   يكونوا ٤   تجدوا ٣   يرفضوا ٢   ترجعي ١

تضحكوا ١٠   يدافعوا ٩   تذهبي ٨   تسألوا ٧   يشتغلوا ٦

EXERCISE 10.4

A

١ لم يكونوا هنا أمس ٢ لن تعلن الجريدة هذه العلاوة غدا

٣ لم يقرأ رئيس الوزراء التقرير الطويل في مكتبه

٤ لا تدرس أختها اللغة الانجليزية في جامعة لندن

٥ لم ترجع زوجته الى وطنها

٦ لم تضع السكرتيرة الانجليزية التقرير في شنطتها

٧ لا يكسب كثيرا في وظيفته الجديدة

٨ لن أرسل الكهربائي الى المصنع غدا

٩ لا يشتغل المحاسب في مكتب الاحصائيات

١٠ لا يصرف البخلاء فلوسهم .

B 1 They were not here yesterday.

2 The newspapers will not announce this raise tomorrow.

3 The Prime Minister did not read the long report in his office.

4 Her sister does not study the English language in the University of London.

5 His wife did not return to her homeland.

6 The English secretary did not put the report in her case.

7 He does not earn much in his new job.

8 I shall not send the electrician to the factory tomorrow.

9 The accountant does not work in the statistics office (office of statistics).

10 Misers do not spend their money.

EXERCISE 10.5 ١ فِيكِ ٢ تَحتنا ٣ منكم ٤ عَنِّي ٥ اِلَيَّ ٦ بعده

٧ لَهُم ٨ لدَيْنا ٩ بِهِنّ ١٠ قبلي ١١ مِنِّي ١٢ علَيْهِم

EXERCISE 11.1

Muslim Festivals

John How many festivals do Muslims have?/**Ahmed** We have two important festivals./**J** What are they?/**A** The first one is the small festival, called the Fast-Breaking Festival./**J** And what month is it in?/**A** The small festival is on the first day of the month of Shawwal./**J** And what is the occasion for it?/**A** The occasion for it is that the month of Shawwal comes after the month of Ramadan, which is a month of fasting for the Muslims./**J** What is the meaning of 'fasting'?/**A** Fasting means that people don't eat or drink during the day. That is the meaning of 'fasting'./**J** And what is the other festival?/**A** It is the Great

Festival, or the Festival of the Sacrifice./**J**   And what is the occasion for
it?/**A**   Its occasion is the Pilgrimage, and it begins on the last day of the
Pilgrimage. 'Pilgrimage' means that people travel to Mecca and visit
the Kaaba./**J**   And how do they celebrate this Festival?/**A**   They
slaughter sacrifice animals./**J**   What is a sacrifice animal?/**A**   A sacrifice
animal is a sheep which they kill and eat at the end of the Pilgrimage.
This is a custom with the Muslims./**J**   So you only have two
festivals, then?/**A**   No, in some places they celebrate a third festival./**J**   And
what is it?/**A**   The Prophet's Birthday, in the month of Rabii:
al-Awwal./**J**   Yes, that's like Christmas with us Christians.

EXERCISE 11.2   (No hard and fast answers can be given to exercises like
this, but your answers should be something like the following.)

A   يسافرون الى مكّة   ٣   عيد الفطر في شهر شوال   ٢   يذبحون فيه ذبائح   ١

معنى الصوم أنّ الناس لا يأكلون ولا يشربون في النهار   ٤

العيد الثالث هو مولد النبي   ٥

B   كيف نفتح (تفتحون) الباب ؟   ٣   ما اسمك ؟   ٢   ماذا يأكلون ؟   ١

متى يسافر (في أيّ شهر يسافر) ؟   ٤   كم بيتا عندهم ؟   ٥   من هي ؟   ٦

من أين هذا الكتاب ؟ (من أيّ بلد هذا الكتاب)   ٧

شهر شوال يعقب أيّ شهر ؟   ٨   متى تقرأ الجريدة ؟   ٩

أين يشتغل (في أيّ مصنع يشتغل) ؟   ١٠

EXERCISE 11.3

A   عندنا سيّارة صغيرة   ٣   للبيت بابان   ٢   للمدير سكرتيرة جديدة   ١

لها أخت جميلة   ٤   للدولاب رفوف كثيرة   ٥   للشركة فرع في لندن   ٦

عنده بذلة جديدة   ٧   عندهم لحم وخبز   ٨   عند أحمد طفل صغير   ٩

عند الراكب شنطة ثقيلة   ١٠

B   كانت للمدير سكرتيرة جديدة   ١   كان للبيت بابان   ٢

كانت عندنا سيّارة صغيرة   ٣   كانت لها أخت جميلة   ٤

كانت للدولاب رفوف كثيرة   ٥

C   سيكون للشركة فرع في لندن   ٦   ستكون عنده بذلة جديدة   ٧

سيكون عندهم لحم وخبز   ٨   سيكون عند أحمد طفل صغير   ٩

ستكون عند الراكب شنطة ثقيلة   ١٠

EXERCISE 11.4

A

١ المسلمون عندهم عيد مهمّ في شهر شوال

٢ الأمير له بيوت في الرياض ولندن ونيو يورك

٣ المصريّون لهم عيد في شهر أبريل اسمه شمّ النسيم

٤ السفير له سيّاره كبيرة جدًّا ٥ الحكومة ليست لها سياسة جيّدة

B 1 The Muslims have an important festival in the month of Shawwal.
2 The prince has houses in Riyad, London and New York.
3 The Egyptians have a festival in the month of April called (its name is) Shamm al-Nasiim. 4 The ambassador has a very large car.
5 The government does not have a good policy.

EXERCISE 12.1   The Oil Age
In the last century, the Western world witnessed a great revolution, the Industrial Revolution. The new factories depended on mineral resources, most of which were to be found in Europe, such as coal and iron. Because of this, the western countries were independent to some extent. But in the year 1876, the famous German engineer Nikolaus Otto invented a machine of a new kind – the internal combustion engine. And the fuel of this wonderful engine was petrol. And petrol is one of the products of oil. As you know, there are only a few sources of oil in Europe, in the North Sea. Most of the sources are in the countries of the Middle East, such as the Kingdom of Saudi Arabia, Iraq, Libya and the nations of the Arabian Gulf like Kuwait and Qatar and the United Arab Emirates. Thus Europe began to depend to a great extent on importation from the Islamic World. And this dependence of the European countries on the Arabs increased greatly during the first half of the twentieth century. And the price of oil increased greatly in the seventies of this century, and the picture of Sheikh Zaki Yamani became a familiar one on European television screens. And this age of oil created strong connections between the people of the west and the Arab people. And one of the results of these connections was the interest of Europeans in the Arabs' language, culture and their Islamic religion.

EXERCISE 12.2

١ شهد العالم الغربي ثورة عظيمة في القرن الماضي

٢ الموارد المعدنية الموجودة في أوربّا هي الفحم والحديد

٣ اخترع نيكولوس أوتّو آلة الاحتراق الداخلي . كان ذلك في سنة ١٨٧٦

٤ لا ، ليس في أوربّا من مصادر البترول الّا قليلا

٥ نتائج هذه العلاقات هي اهتمام أهل أوربّا بلغة العرب وثقافتهم ودينهم

EXERCISE 12.3

١ هو مصريّ ٢ هي قطريّة ٣ هو أمريكي ٤ هم لبنانيون
٥ هنّ فرنسيات ٦ هم أردنيّون ٧ هو ليبيّ ٨ هم كويتيون
٩ هو عراقي ١٠ هو يمني

EXERCISE 12.4   1 This door is wider than that one.
2 Cairo is the biggest city in the Arab world.
3 The manager's car was the most beautiful and fastest of cars.
4 Bread is cheaper than meat.
5 The Arabic language is more difficult than the English language, and
the French language is the easiest of languages.
6 Morocco is the nearest of the Arab countries, and the furthest of them
is the Yemen.
7 Most oil is found in the Middle East.
8 Her dress is one of the cheapest of dresses.
9 This novel is one of the most strange of English novels.
10 The suitcase was heavier than the small box.

EXERCISE 13.1   The Islamic Conquests
The original homeland of the Arabs is the Arabian peninsula. After the
appearance of Islam, the Arab armies conquered many of the neighbouring
countries such as Syria and Iraq, and in Africa they conquered all the
countries of the North coast, from Egypt to Morocco. And they ruled
Spain for a period of four hundred years until the Christian forces expelled
them in the year 1492. The number of Arab states today has reached
eighteen, population about 130 million. The people of these numerous
lands use the Arabic language in their daily life, their work and their
worship. The cause of this spread of the Arabic language was the appearance of Islam. Before it, the Arabs were of no great importance. The
fact is that God revealed the Holy Koran to His apostle Muhammad in
the Arabic language, and ordered him to preach the new religion to his
people. That was in Mecca, whose people were worshipping idols. Some of
the powerful men of Mecca disliked the Prophet and the message he
brought. Because of that, the Apostle fled to Medina in the year 622. After
eight years, Muhammad and his Helpers returned from Medina to Mecca
and conquered it. The Prophet died in Medina in the year 632, and his
Caliphs continued the movement of conquest after him. And in the period
of eighty years, the Muslim armies reached the borders of Europe. And
that was the basis of the Islamic Empire, from which the modern Arab
countries are descended.

EXERCISE 13.2

١ موطن العرب الأصلي هو الجزيرة العربيّة

٢ فتحت جنود العرب ساحل افريقيا الشمالي

٣ طردت الجيوش المسيحيّة العرب من اسبانيا

٤ يستخدم سكّان الدول العربيّة اللغة العربيّة

٥ كان سبب انتشار اللغة العربيّة ظهور الاسلام

٦ كان أهل مكّة يعبدون الأصنام قبل الاسلام

٧ هاجر رسول اللّه الى المدينة في سنة ٦٢٢

٨ رجع محمّد الى مكّة بعد ثماني سنوات ، وجاء الأنصار معه

٩ مات النبي في سنة ٦٣٢   ١٠ وصلت الجيوش المسلمة الى حدود أوربّا

EXERCISE 13.3

١ الذي   ٢ ——   ٣ التي   ٤ الّتي   ٥ ——

٦ التي   ٧ الذي   ٨ التي   ٩ ——   ١٠ ——

EXERCISE 13.4   1 The factory in which I work is large.
2 A man (whom) I didn't know came.
3 This is the newspaper which we read yesterday.
4 The manager spoke to the (f) employees who arrived today.
5 Salim brought food which we ate.
6 The number of states which (are) descended from the Islamic Empire
   has reached (Ar. 'reaches') eighteen.
7 Muhammad, who died in Medina, was the Apostle of God.
8 The plane which arrived in the morning came from London.
9 He is a man who does not laugh much.
10 They sent a teacher (f) who doesn't know Arabic.

EXERCISE 13.5   1 The merchant travels to his homeland every year.
2 All the teachers met in the director's office.
3 Some of the papers published this important announcement yesterday.
4 Every pupil has a pen and a piece of paper.
5 The company paid all the money to the workmen.
6 Some of the boys were playing in the street.
7 All the guests were eating and drinking a lot.
8 Every door has its key.
9 Not all the sources of oil are in the Middle East.
10 Some of the windows are open, and some of them are closed.

EXERCISE 13.6

١ ٨٧   ٢ ٦   ٣ ٦٤   ٤ ٦٤   ٥ ٦١٧٦

٦ ٢٣٢٤   ٧ ٢٢٤   ٨ ١٢   ٩ ٨٠   ١٠ ٤٩

EXERCISE 14.1   Arab Social Structure

Naturally Arab social structure varies from country to country. Despite that, however, it has not gone far away from its original order about which we read in history books. And this is true even in the countries which have progressed most from the point of view of education, politics and material wealth. The tribe was the basis of Arab society in its earliest history, and it still plays an important role up till now. It is difficult for us to define precisely what a tribe is, and of what it consists. For there are large tribes of great importance, and at the same time small tribes which have no importance except in their own areas. The head of a tribe is its sheikh, and the sheikhs of some of these great tribes have become rulers of modern states. And the custom of the Arabs in their names is that a man carries the name of his father and his grandfather. And at the end of his name we find his *nisba*, that is the name of his tribe. An example of that is 'Hassan son of Ali son of Salim the Tamimi', which would be the name of a man whose father's name is Ali, whose grandfather's name is Salim and whose tribe is Tamim. The tribe is divided into families, and the family will be under the leadership of the eldest of its males. As for women, their position in the family, as well as in the tribe, is very weak, and their rights are not equal to the rights of the men. It is incumbent on the members of the family that they consult the head of the family on every important matter, such as marriage, divorce, or the buying and selling of land, for instance. And it is possible that the head of the family may consult the sheikh of the tribe if he himself is unable to resolve some matter. For this reason, every ruler or sheikh holds a daily council in which he receives the members of his tribe in order to listen to their requests and complaints.

EXERCISE 14.2

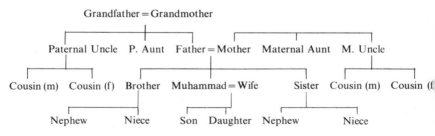

1 His mother is the wife of his father.
2 His maternal uncle is the brother of his mother.
3 His grandmother is the mother of his father or the mother of his mother.
4 His father is the grandfather of his son and the grandfather of his daughter.
5 His cousin (f) is the sister of his male cousin (father's side).

6 His grandfather is the husband of his grandmother.

7 His paternal uncle is the brother of his father.

8 His wife is the mother of his son.

9 His brother is the son of his father.

10 His nephew is the brother of his niece.

EXERCISE 14.3 1 He ordered him to go to the town to consult the experts in the factory.

2 He went to Bahrain to speak to the Minister of Education.

3 My brother Salim arrived in Mecca yesterday to celebrate the festival.

4 We asked them to pay today but they refused.

5 She was speaking Arabic so that her young son would not understand.

6 The workmen came to the capital to receive their leader.

7 The printing house refused to publish the new magazine.

8 It is up to the army to defend the homeland.

9 It is difficult for us to define exactly what socialism is.

10 I go to the library every day to read the papers.

EXERCISE 14.4 1 I am still studying the history of Arabia.

2 The company nearly employed her as secretary to the manager.

3 The merchants are still presenting requests and complaints. (still keep on presenting...)

4 The little girl kept on asking about her father.

5 Egyptian engineers are still earning a lot in the Gulf states.

6 The television programme had almost begun (was about to begin).

EXERCISE 15.1 At the Airport
Traveller (to taxi driver) Take me to the airport please./*Driver* Yes sir. Where will you be travelling to (God willing)?/*Traveller* To Khartoum./*Driver* Fine. What time does the plane leave?/ *Traveller* Half past ten./*Driver* Very good. We have time enough. (at the airport) Here we are. Where do you want me to stop?/*Traveller* Stop there, at the main gate./*Driver* (takes the bags out of the car and gives them to the porter) Take the bags, porter./*Traveller* How much is the fare?/*Driver* Five dinars, please./*Traveller* (gives him the money). Here's the money./*Driver* Thank you. Good bye./*Traveller* (to police officer) Where is the National Airlines office please?/*Officer* Go to the end of this big hall and turn to your right. After that go in the first door on the left, and you'll find the office in front of you/*Traveller* Thanks very much. (he goes off and the porter follows him carrying the bags. They arrive at the aviation company's office) Good morning./*Company Official* Good morning. (recognises the traveller) Ah, hello Mr Smith. How are you?/*Traveller* Fine, thanks. I'm booked on the 10.30 plane to Khartoum, first class./*Official* Yes, that's right. Flight number

257. Give me your ticket please./*Traveller* Here you are./*Official* Porter, put the cases on the scales. Thank you. (to the traveller) Here's your boarding card. Please go from here to the customs to have your luggage and passport checked. You will board the plane from gate number eight. Have a good trip./*Traveller* Thanks. (goes off towards the customs)/*Official* Just a moment, sir./*Traveller* Yes?/*Official* Unfortunately news has just come that your flight will be twenty minutes late. I'm sorry./*Traveller* Thank you. It doesn't matter. (gets to the Passport officer/*Passport Officer* Passport please. (takes the passport from the traveller, looks at it then gives him it back) Thank you. Please go to the Customs Officer there./*Customs Officer* Anything to declare?/*Traveller* No, nothing./*Customs Officer* Open this big case for examination please. (the traveller opens the case and the officer examines its contents) Thank you./*Announcement from the Airport Public Address System:* We request that passengers on flight number 257 for Khartoum proceed immediately to gate number eight for boarding. Thank you.

EXERCISE 15.2

اِتبع ، اِتبعي ، اِتبعوا — فَتّش ، فَتّشي ، فَتّشوا — كل ، كلي ، كلوا —

اِشرب ، اِشربي ، اِشربوا — اُرقص ، اُرقصي ، اُرقصوا — قُم ، قومي ،

قوموا — اِضحك ، اِضحكي ، اِضحكوا — قدّم ، قدّمي ، قدّموا — اِسمع ،

اِسمعي ، اِسمعوا — كُن ، كُوني ، كُونوا — رُدّ ، رُدّي ، رُدّوا — أعْطِ ، أعطي ،

أعْطُوا — اُطلب ، اُطلبي ، اُطلبوا — قِف ، قِفي ، قِفوا — تَعالَ ، تَعالي ،

تَعالُوا — اِستقبل ، اِستقبلي ، اِستقبلوا — اِدفع ، اِدفعي ، اِدفعوا — اِحتفل ،

اِحتفلي ، اِحتفلوا — لِفّ ، لفّي ، لفّوا — اِشتغل ، اِشتغلي ، اِشتغلوا — زُر ،

زوري ، زوروا — أرْسِل ، أرْسِلي ، أرْسِلُوا — عَلِّم ، علّمي ، علّموا — اِبْدأ ،

اِبْدَئي ، اِبْدَؤُوا .

EXERCISE 15.3   1 Enter the airport by the big gate and turn to your left at the customs office.

2 Arrange these books on the shelf please.

3 Ask (teacher) Abdullah about the history of the Arabs.

4 Ahmed, take this heavy case and put it in the car.

5 Please sit down. Help yourself to food and drink.

6 Ask the merchant to give you back the money right away.

7 Don't stop here, go to the end of the street and stop at the factory.

8 Don't speak to me in English. I only understand Arabic.

9 Write your name here and give the paper to the secretary.

10 Give me the passport please, sir, so that I may look at it.

EXERCISE 15.4

١ لا تلعب في الشارع يا ولد

٢ ردّ الجواز اليه فورا من فضلك   ٣ لا تضحكوا ، هذا أمر هامّ

٤ لا تتأخّرى ، يا فاطمة ، الطائرة تقوم الساعة أربعة ونصف (الرابعة والنصف)

٥ افتح الكتاب واقرأ ما فيه

EXERCISE 15.5

EGYPTAIR ORGANISES SPECIAL FLIGHTS TO BRING
EGYPTIANS FROM AMERICA AND CANADA
AT TOURIST PRICES

Egyptair has decided to organise special flights to both America and Canada at tourist rates to carry Egyptians during the summer season. It has also decided to fix the prices of air tickets and tourist services in Egypt.

EXERCISE 16.1   Arabic Literature

Arabic literature begins in the Age of Ignorance, that is before the coming of Islam. At that time the tribes had poets who would glorify their own tribes and compete against each other with their poems. The best of the odes of the pre-Islamic poets were collected together in an anthology called the Seven Mu'allaqat, which people still read and study today. Literature and the arts flourished in the age of the Abbasids, whose caliphate lasted from 750 to 1258. Thousands of books were written about history, religious sciences, poetry and artistic prose. Unfortunately we do not know much about this rich heritage in the Western countries because of the lack of translations of it in foreign languages. In general, the people of the West are totally ignorant of Arabic literature, with the exception of the Book of the Thousand and One Nights, which is a collection of oriental tales and fables. This collection is not considered a book of much worth among Arab writers and critics, despite the fact that it has inspired a large number of literary and artistic works in the West. This influence has even reached popular culture, an example of that being the well-known pantomime 'Aladdin and the Wonderful Lamp', which we have all seen as children. This story of Chinese origin came to us by way of the Thousand and One Nights. Writing and authorship did not come to a stop with the Arabs during the Dark Ages in Europe. Arab writers contributed their works on the sciences, philosophy, mathematics, chemistry and astronomy, some of which were translated from Greek, and, had it not been for this, these precious books would have been lost. After about the fourteenth century, Aribic literature began to decline gradually, until its renaissance in the twentieth century.

EXERCISE 16.2   1 F   2 F   3 T   4 F   5 F   6 F   7 F   8 F   9 F
10 T   11 F   12 T

EXERCISE 16.3

١ جُمِعَت أحسن القصائد في ديوان

٢ لا يُعْتَبَر كتاب ألف ليلة وليلة كتابا هامّا

٣ أُلهِم عدد كبير من الأعمال الأدبية   ٤ وُظِّفْت في وزارة التعليم

٥ سَيُوجَد هذا الكتاب في المكتبة   ٦ سُئِلْت عن تاريخ الأدب العربي

٧ أُرْسِلَت الى أمريكا لتدرس الرياضيات

EXERCISE 16.4
If we left out men of politics, perhaps we would find that one of the most famous Arabs in the West is the actor Omar Sharif. This film star was born in Egypt and worked for a time in the theatre there before emigrating to England, where he became very famous in the world of the cinema. He has played many parts in English and American films, the most famous of them being his leading role in the film 'Dr Zhivago'. He is known also for his skill at the game of bridge.

EXERCISE 17.1   Abu Nuwas and Harun al-Rashid
Abu Nuwas was an Arab poet, and a boon companion of the Abbasid caliph Harun al-Rashid. Abu Nuwas became famous for his cleverness and wit just as much as for his poetry. There are many stories and tales in Arabic folklore about the adventures of the poet with the Caliph. One of them is that Harun said to Abu Nuwas one day (and that was in the wintertime) 'Abu Nuwas, if you spend the night on the roof of the house, naked and without a fire to get warm from, I'll give you a thousand dinars.' So they agreed on that, and Abu Nuwas took off his clothes and went up on the roof and spent the night there. The Caliph came in the morning and found him very cold, his body shivering. The poet said, 'Give me the money.' 'No', said the Caliph. 'Why?' he said. The Caliph pointed to a fire in the distance which some bedouin had lit, and said 'By God, you got warm from that fire which you can see there.' And he refused to give him the dinars. After a few days the Caliph went out hunting and Abu Nuwas was with him. In the middle of the day Harun said to the poet 'By God, I'm hungry'. Abu Nuwas said, 'Sit down here and rest. I'll cook something nice for you to eat.' And he went away from him. The Caliph waited for a long time and got very hungry, and Abu Nuwas did not come back to him. In the end the Caliph got up to look for his food. He found Abu Nuwas sitting at a fire he had lit at the bottom of a tree, and he did not see any cooking-pot on the fire, and was surprised at that. Then he raised his eyes up to the tree and saw the pot hung at the very top of it. So he said in extreme anger, 'And how will the food get cooked when the pot is at the top of the tree and the fire on the ground?' Said Abu Nuwas, 'The same way as I got warm that night on the roof of the house!' So the Caliph laughed and gave him the money.

EXERCISE 17.2 1 F   2 T   3 F   4 F   5 F   6 T   7 F   8 F
9 F   10 F

EXERCISE 17.3   Joha's Jallabiyya
One day Joha found his jallabiyya very dirty, so he ordered his wife to
wash it. She washed it and hung it on a rope that was on the roof of the
house. The wind got strong that day and blew away the jallabiyya and it
fell in the street. People came along and trod on it until it became dirty
and torn and no good for anything. After a while Joha came down from
the house and went out into the street and saw his jallabiyya on the
ground, dirty and torn. So he raised his hands in the air and said, 'Praise
and thanks to God.' And the people were amazed at that and said to him,
'Joha, why do you say 'Praise and thanks to God' when your jallabiyya is
on the ground, worthless, and you will not be able to wear it again?' Said
Joha, 'By God, if I had been wearing it, *I* would have fallen from the roof
and people would have trodden on *me* and got *me* dirty and torn me up, so
praise and thanks to God for that.'

EXERCISE 18.1   Tourism in Egypt
The winter season in Egypt is very pleasant, with neither extreme heat nor
biting cold. So the tourist will find the weather clear, and suitable for
outings after leaving the grey skies of Europe. As the plane lands in Cairo
Airport, and after carrying out the formalities, the traveller will come out
of the airport gate and board a taxi which will take him to town. And he
will have chosen one of Cairo's many excellent hotels to stay in, and
perhaps he will want to rest a little after his long journey. So he sleeps ...
and wakes after a time, be it long or short ... and goes out to the balcony
to cast his first glance upon this vast capital with its magnificent buildings
which stretch out before his eyes under the blue sky of Africa. And every
tourist will have learned as a pupil in the primary school something about
the pharaonic antiquities which are to be found in Egypt alone. Perhaps he
will visit first the Sphinx and the Pyramids, sited in Giza on the edge of the
eternal desert. After that he must see something of the great Islamic
antiquities to be found in this city founded a thousand years ago. There are
mosques big and small worth seeing, among the most famous the two
mosques of Sultan Hassan and Muhammad Ali which stand near the
Citadel of Saladin on Mukattam hill. And perhaps the most famous
Islamic monument of all is the Azhar Mosque, in which was founded the
first university in the world. One of the characteristics by which tourists –
especially the ladies – are distinguished, is that they dislike returning to
their homeland without spoils – I mean presents and things which will
remind them in the future of their happy journey. To this end, let them
seek out the bazaars of Khan al-Khalili, only a few steps away from the
Azhar, in which the tourist will find something to fill his heart with joy,
such as articles of brass, woven things of cotton, coloured rugs and a

thousand things besides. One of the natural wonders of Egypt is the River Nile, on whose banks stand many restaurants and night clubs in which the visitor may taste Middle Eastern cuisine in its various forms and numerous types. And while he lunches or dines, he can listen to the sweet tones of music and watch displays of folk dancing. Indeed ... there is truth in the Egyptian proverb which says, 'He who drinks of the water of the Nile must return to it another time'.

EXERCISE 18.2
SOLUTION FOR THE NUTRITIONAL CRISIS IN EGYPT?

The chairman of the State Council announced yesterday suggestions which could solve the nutritional crisis in Egypt. He said, 'The number of inhabitants of Egypt has reached 43 million, and the number of head of stock exceeds 10 million. These animals depend principally on plant food produced by the Egyptian soil. The return from our animal assets is still not capable of supplying the human population with their nutritional needs in the way of meat and other things. We sow in Egypt about 2.8 million acres annually with lucerne for the animals, and this area represents a quarter of the total harvested area in Egypt. And it is equal to – if not a little bigger than – the total area which we sow with wheat and corn together. If we reflect on the structure of our animal assets, and their role, we find that the number of transport, draught and riding animals reaches a few million. Economically productive animals are not being raised in order that they might be produced from, but for the purpose of agricultural work. This is an ancient legacy which the Egyptian peasant has inherited from his fathers and grandfathers, and we have no need to say that these animals overworked in agricultural tasks do not give meat or milk in economic quantities. This means that our animal assets and our animal production are in need of review ... of re-thinking ... of a new strategy. I place a few main lines for this strategy before the specialists.

Firstly – expansion in agricultural mechanisation, so that we may be gradually rid of beasts of burden, draught and riding, so that we may save what they gobble up of food, and so that we may free the economic animals from the labours of the field and agriculture.

Secondly – the subjection of our production to the latest scientific and technological methods in the areas of improvement of breeds, feeding and health care both preventative and clinical.

Thirdly – A review of the structure of our cropping, so that we may save the huge area sown with lucerne.

Arabic–English Vocabulary

This concise Arabic–English vocabulary list is given for ease of reference. It contains all the words used in the exercises, and a few more of frequent occurrence. Arrangement is alphabetical (Arabic alphabet) according to the spelling of the actual word, and not the root. Plurals (with alternative forms), irregular feminines, etc., are given where appropriate. Vowelling for the imperfect of Form I verbs is given in an abbreviated form, and the placing of this vowel will vary according to the type of root (e.g. hollow, third-weak, etc.). Reference should be made to Appendix 1 in cases of difficulty.

أَحْمَد Ahmad (name)

أَحْمَر red

أَخ (إِخْوَان ، إِخْوَة) brother

أُخْت (أَخَوَات) sister

اِخْتَار (VIII) choose

اِخْتَرَع (VIII) invent

اِخْتَلَف مِن (VIII) differ, be different from

أَخَذ (u) take

آخَر (أُخْرَى .f) other, another

آخِر last

أَخْضَر green

أَدَب (آدَاب) literature

أَدَبِيّ literary

أَدْخَل (IV) cause to enter, admit

أَدِيب (أُدَبَاء) writer, author, literary man

إِذَا when, if

أَرَاد (IV) want, wish

أَب (آبَاء) father

اِبْتَدَأ (VIII) begin

أَبَدًا never, ever

أَبْرِيل April

اِبْن (أَبْنَاء) son

أَبْيَض white

اِتَّفَق (VIII) agree

اِتَّجَه إِلَى (VIII) go to, make for

اِجْتَمَع مَع (VIII) meet, have a meeting with

مِن ـــــــ (أَجْل) because of, for the sake of

أَجْلَس (IV) cause to sit, offer a seat

أَجْنَبِيّ (أَجَانِب) foreign; foreigner

أَحَبّ (IV) like, love

اِحْتَفَل بـ (VIII) celebrate

أَحْسَن better, best

إِحْصَائِيَّات statistics (pl.)

اِرْتَفَع (VIII) rise, go up

أَرْسَل (IV) send

أَرْض earth, ground, land

اِزْداد (VIII) increase

اِزْدَهَر (VIII) flower, flourish

أَزْمة (أَزَمات) crisis

اِسْبَانيا Spain

أُسْبوعيّ weekly

أُسْتاذ (أَساتِذة) teacher, professor

اِسْتَحَقّ (X) deserve

اِسْتَخْدَم (X) use, employ

اِسْتَمَع إِلَى (VIII) listen to

أُسْرة (أُسَر، ـات) family

اِسْم (أَسْماء) name

أَسْوَد black

اِشْتَدّ (VIII) become severe, strong

اِشْتِراكيّة socialism

اِشْتَغَل (VIII) work

أَشْهَر more famous, most famous

أَصْبَح (IV) become

أَصْليّ original

أَصيل pure, genuine

أَضْرَب (IV) go on strike

اِطَّلَع عَلَى (VIII) peruse, study

اِعْتَبَر (VIII) consider, be of the opinion

اِعْتَمَد عَلَى (VIII) depend on

أَعْطَى (IV) give

إِعْلان (ـات) announcement, advertisement

أَعْلَن (IV) announce

أَعْلَى higher, highest

اِفْريقيا Africa

أَكَل (u) eat

أَكْل food

إِلَّا except (adv.)

الاِثْنَيْن (يَوْم ———) Monday

الأَحَد (يَوْم ———) Sunday

الإِسْلام Islam

الآن now

الَّذي (الَّذين .pl ,الَّتي .f) which, who, that (relative)

أَلْف (آلاف) thousand

القُرْآن the Koran

اللّٰه God, Allah

أَلْهَم (IV) inspire

أُمّ (أُمَّهات) mother

أَمَام in front of

اِمْبِراطُورية empire

أَمَر (u) order, command

اِمْرَأة (المَرْأة with art.) woman

أَمْس yesterday

أَنْ that (conjunction)

إِنْ if

اِنْتِشار spreading

اِنْتَهَى (VIII) end, be finished

اِنْجِليزيّ (اِنْجِليز) English; Englishman

اِنْحَدَر مِن (VII) descend from

أَهْل (أَهالٍ) family, kin, people

أَهَمِّية importance, concern

أَوْسَط middle (adj.)

أَوَّل (أُولَى f) first

أَوَّلاً firstly, in the first place

باب (أَبْواب ، بِيبان) door, gate

بات (i) spend the night

بِتْرُول (crude) oil

بَحْر (بِحَار ، بُحُور) sea

البَحْرَين Bahrain

بَخِيل (بُخَلاء) mean, miserly

بَدَأ (a) begin

بَدَويّ (بَدُو) bedouin

بِدُون without

بَذْلة suit (clothes)

بَرْد cold, coldness

بَرْنامَج (بَرامِج) programme

بِطاقة (ـات ، بَطائِق) card; identity card

بَعْد after

بَعْض some

بَعيد far, distant

بَلَد ، بِلاد (بُلْدان) town, settlement; country

بَلَغ (u) reach, arrive at

بْن son of (in names)

بِنْت (بَنات) daughter, girl

بَنْك (بُنُوك) bank

بَوّابة (ـات) gate, gateway

بَيْت (بُيُوت) house

بَيْن between

بَيْنَما while

تاجِر (تُجّار) merchant businessman

تاريخ date; history

تَأْليف authorship, act of writing

تامّ complete, whole

تَبِع (a) follow	تَنَافَس (VI) compete with each other
تَحْت under, below	تَوَقَّف (V) halt, come to a stop
تَدْرِيجِيّاً gradually	
تَذْكَرَة (تَذاكِر) ticket	ثَالِث third (adj.)
تُراث heritage	ثَانِياً secondly
تَرْتِيب (ـات) arrangement	ثَقَافَة culture
تَرْجَم translate	ثَقِيل (ثِقَال) heavy
تَعَشَّى (V) dine	ثَلّاجة (ـات) fridge
تَعَلَّم (V) learn	ثُمَّ then
تَعْلِيم education	ثَمَن (أَثْمان) price
تَغَذَّى (V) lunch	ثَوْرة (ـات) revolution (political)
تَفْتِيش inspection	
تَفَرَّج عَلَى (V) watch, look at	جاء (i) come
تَفَضَّل (V, usually imperative) 'Please go ahead', 'After you'	جاء بِ (i) bring
تَقَدَّم (V) progress	جاع (u) be hungry
تَقْرِيباً approximately	جامِع (جَوامِع) mosque
تَقْرِير (تَقارِير) report (document)	جامِعة (ـات) university
تَكَلَّم (V) speak	جاهِل (جُهّال) ignorant
تَكَوَّن مِن (V) consist of	الجاهِلِيّة the Age of Ignorance (pre-Islamic era)
تِلِفِزْيون television	
تِلْكَ that (f.)	جَبّار (جَبابِرة) tyrant
تِلْمِيذ (تَلامِذة) pupil	جَبَل (جِبال) mountain
تَمْرِين (تَمارِين) exercise, drill (n.)	جَدّ (أَجْداد) grandfather
	جَدّة (ـات) grandmother

جِدّاً very	حَرْب (حُرُوب) war
جَرِيدة (جَرائِد) newspaper	خَاصّ special, private
جَزِيرة (جُزُر) island	خال (أَخْوال) maternal uncle
جَلَس (i) sit	خالة (ـات) maternal aunt
جُمْرُك (جَمَارك) customs (border)	خَبَّاز (ـون) baker
جَمَع (a) collect, gather	خَبَر (أَخْبار) news
جَمِيعاً all, all together	خُبْز bread
جَمِيل beautiful, handsome	خَبِير (خُبَرَاء) expert
جُنَيْه (ـات) pound (£)	خَرَج (u) go out
جَواز سَفَر passport	خُروج exit
جُوع hunger	خَفِيف light, not heavy
جَيِّد good	خِلافة Caliphate
جَيْش (جُيُوش) army	خِلال during
	خَلِيج (خُلْجان) gulf
حارّ hot	الخَلِيج العَرَبيّ the Arabian Gulf
حاضِر present (adj.)	خَلِيفة (خُلَفاء) caliph
حاكِم (حُكّام) ruler, head of state	خَيّاط (ـون) tailor
حَتّى until	خَيّاطة (ـات) tailoress
الحَجّ the Pilgrimage	
حَدّ (حُدُود) limit; (pl.) border, frontier	دافَع عَنْ (III) defend
حَدَّد (II) limit, define	دام (u) last, endure
حَدِيث new, modern	دَبّابة (ـات) tank (military)
حَدِيقة (حَدائِق) garden, park	دَبّاسة (ـات) stapler

دُبَيْ   *Dubai*

دَخَل   (u) *enter*

دُخُول   *entrance*

دَرَجة (ـات)   *class, degree*

دَرَس   (u) *study*

دَرَّس   (II) *teach*

دِرْهَم (دَراهِم)   *dirham* (currency)

دَفْتَر (دَفاتِر)   *file, folder, notebook*

دَفَع   (a) *push, pay*

دَقِيق   (adj.) *fine;* (noun) *flour*

دُنْيا   *world*

دَهِش   (a) *be astonished, surprised*

دَوْر (أَدْوار)   *role*

دُولاب (دَوالِيب)   *cupboard*

دَوْلة (دُوَل)   *state, nation*

دِين (أَدْيان)   *religion*

دِينار (دَنانِير)   *dinar* (currency)

دِيوان (دَواوِين)   *collection of poetry; chancelry*

ذاتَ يَوْمٍ   *one day*

ذاق   (u) *taste*

ذٰلِك (أُولائِكَ pl., تِلْكَ f.)   *that* (demonstrative)

ذَكِي (أَذْكِياء)   *clever*

ذَهَب   (a) *go*

ذُو   *possessor (of)...*

رَأْس (رُؤُوس)   *head (of body)*

راكِب (رُكّاب)   *passenger*

رَأْي (آراء)   *opinion*

رَئِيس (رُؤَساء)   *head, chief*

رَئِيس الْوُزَراء   *Prime Minister*

رَبّ (أَرْباب)   *lord, master*

رُبَّما   *perhaps*

رَتَّب   (II) *arrange*

رَجَع   (i) *return, come back*

رَجُل (رِجال)   *man*

رُجوع   *return* (n.)

رِحْلة (ـات)   *journey, trip*

رَخِيص   *cheap*

رَدّ   (u) *return, give back, reply*

رِسالة (رَسائِل)   *message, letter, article*

رَسّام (ـون)   *artist*

رَسْمِيّ   *official*

رَسُول اللّٰه   *the Messenger of God* (the Prophet Muhammad)

رَفّ (رُفُوف)   *shelf*

رَفَض   (i,u) *refuse*

رَفَع (a) raise, lift   سِحْرِيّ magical

رَقَص (u) dance   سَرِيع quick, fast

رَقْم (أَرْقام) number, figure   سَطْح (سُطُوح) roof, surface

رَكِب (a) ride   سِعْر (أَسْعار) price

رَمَضان Ramadan (month)   سِكْرِتَيْر، (سكرتيرة f) secretary

رِوَاية (ـات) story, tale, novel   سَماء (سَمَوات) sky

رِياضِيات mathematics   سَمِع (a) hear

الرِيَاض Riyaḍh   سَمَّى (II) name, call

     سَمِين (سِمان) fat

زائِر (زُوَّار) visitor   سَنة (سِنُون، سَنَوات) year

زاد (i) increase, add   سَهِل easy

زار (u) visit   سُوق (أَسْواق) market

زال (a) cease; (used in negative with other verbs) to keep on...   سِياحِيّ tourist (adj.)

زَمان، زَمَن (أَزْمِنة) time   سَيّارة (ـات) car

زَوْجة (ـات) wife   سِياسة (ـات) policy, politics

     سَيِّد (سادة) gentleman, Mr

سائِق (ـون) driver   سَيِّدة (ـات) lady, Mrs

سَأَل (a) ask   سِينَما cinema

ساحِل (سَواحِل) coast

ساعة (ـات) hour; clock, watch   شَأْن (شُؤُون) affair, matter

سافَر (III) travel   شارِع (شَوارِع) street

ساكِن (سُكَّان) inhabitant   شاطِر (شُطَّار) clever, smart

سَبَب (أَسْباب) cause   شاعِر (شُعَراء) poet

السَبْت (يَوْم ———) Saturday   شاهِد (III) see, witness

شاوَر (III) consult	صار (i) become
شُبّاك (شَبابيك) window	صَباح morning
شِتاء winter	صَحْن (صُحُون) plate
شَجَرة (أَشْجار) tree	صَحيح correct, right
شَرِب (a) drink	صَديق (أَصْدِقاء) friend
الشَرْق the East	صَرَف (i) spend (money)
الشَرْق الأَوْسَط the Middle East	صَعْب hard, difficult
شَرِكة (ـات) company (commercial)	صَغير (صِغار) small, young
شَعْب (شُعُوب) folk, people	صَناعيّ artificial; industrial
شِعْر (أَشْعار) poetry	صَنْدُوق (صَناديق) box, chest
شِكاية (ـات) complaint	صَوْم fast, fasting
شُكْراً thank you, thanks	صَيْد hunting
شكْل (أَشْكال) shape, form	صَيْف summer
شَمال north	صِينيّ Chinese
شَماليّ northern	بالضَّبْط exactly ضَبْط exactitude
شَمْس (شُمُوس) sun	ضَحِك (a) laugh
شَنْطة (شُنَط) bag, case, suitcase	ضَخْم huge
شَهِد (a) see, witness	ضَعيف (ضُعَفَاء ، ضِعاف) weak
شَهْر (شُهُور ، أَشْهُر) month	ضَيْف (ضُيُوف) guest
شَوّال Shawwal (month)	طائِرة (ـات) aeroplane
شَيْء (أَشْياء) thing	طالِب (طَلَبة ، طُلّاب) student
شَيْخ (شُيُوخ) sheikh, chief, elder	طالِبة (ـات) female student
صاحِب (أَصْحاب) friend, master	طَبَخ (u) cook

طَبِيعيّ   natural

طَرَد (u) expel

طَرْد (طُرُود)   parcel

طَرِيق (طُرُق)   way, road

طَعام (أَطْعِمة)   food

طِفل (أَطفال)   baby, child

طَلَب (u) ask for, request

طَلَب (ـات)   request (noun)

طَوِيل (طِوَال)   long, tall

طَيِّب   good, kind

طَيَران   aviation

ظَلام   darkness

ظُهْر   noon

ظُهُور   appearance

عائِلة (ـات ، عَوائِل)   family

عادة (ـات)   custom, habit

عادِل   just, honest

عاصِمة (عَواصِم)   capital (of a country)

عالَم   world

عِبادة   worship (n.)

عَبّاسيّ (ـون)   Abbasid

عَبْد   slave; worshipper

عَبْدُ الله   Abdullah

عَجِيب   wonderful, amazing

عَدَد   number, amount

عَدِيد   numerous

عَرَبيّ (عَرَب)   Arabic; Arab

العَرَبيّة   Arabic (language)

عَرَف (i) know

عَرِيض   broad, wide

عَشاء   dinner, supper

عَصْر (عُصُور)   age, era; mid afternoon

عَظِيم (عُظَماء)   mighty, powerful

عَقَب (u) come after, follow

عَلاء الدِّين   Aladdin

عَلاقة (ـات)   connection, relationship

عَلاوة (ـات)   increase, rise (n.)

عَلَّق (II) hang, suspend

عَلِم (a) know

عَلَّم (II) teach

عَلَى   on, upon, against, despite

عَمّ (أَعْمام)   paternal uncle

عَمّة (ـات)   paternal aunt

عَمِل (a) do, work

عَمَل (أَعْمال)   work (n.)

عَنْ *from, out of*

عِنْد *by, with, in the possession of*

عَنَى (i) *mean*

عَهْد (عُهُود) *age, era*

عِيد الأَضْحَى *Festival of the Sacrifice*

عِيد الفِطْر *Festival of the Fast-breaking*

غائِب (ـون) *absent*

غادَر (III) *leave, depart*

غَداً ، الغَد *tomorrow*

غِذاء *nourishment*

غِذائِيّ *nutritional*

غَرْب *west*

غَرْبِيّ *western*

غُرْفة (غُرَف) *room*

غَرِيب (غُرَباء) *strange; stranger*

غَيْر *other than*

فارِغ *empty*

فاشِل *unsuccessful, failing, futile*

فَتَح (a) *open; conquer*

فَتَّش (II) *inspect*

فَرْع (فُرُوع) *branch* (in all senses)

فَرَنْسِيّ *French, Frenchman*

فُسْتَان (فَساتِين) *dress, frock*

فَقَد (i) *lose*

فَقَطْ *only*

فَقِير (فُقَراء) *poor*

فِلْس (فُلُوس) *fils* (small currency unit); plural used vulgarly for 'money'

فَلْسَفة *philosophy*

فَنّ (فُنُون) *art, craft*

فُنْدُق (فَنادِق) *hotel*

فَهِم (a) *understand*

فَوْراً *immediately*

فَوْق *above*

فُولْكلُور *folklore*

فِي *in, at,* etc.

قائِد (قادة) *leader, commander*

القاهِرة *Cairo*

قال (u) *say*

قام (u) *stand up*

قَبْل *before*

قَدَر (i) *be able*

قَدَّم (II) *offer, present*

قَدِيم (قُدَماء) *old, ancient*

قَرَأ (a) *read*

القُرآن *the Koran*

قَرَّر (II) decide	كَثُر (u) be many, numerous
قَرْن (قُرُون) century	كَثِير many, much
قَرِيب near	كَثِيراً a lot (adv.)
قِسْم (أَقْسام) section, department	كُرْسِيّ (كَراسِي) chair
قِصّة (قِصَص) story	كَرِه (a) hate, dislike
قَصِيدة (قَصائِد) poem	كَرِيم (كُرَماء) noble, generous
قَصِير (قِصار) short	كَسَب (i) gain, earn, win
قُطْر (أَقْطار) region	كَسْلان (كَسالَى) idle
قِطْعة (قِطَع) piece	كُلّ all, each, every
قَلَم (أَقْلام) pen, pencil	كَلْب (كِلاب) dog
قَلِيل few, little	كَلَّم (II) speak to, address
قَلِيلاً a little (adv.)	كَلِمة (كَلِمات) word
قَمِيص (قُمْصان) shirt	كَمْ how many?
قَوِيّ (أَقْوِياء) strong, powerful	كَما just as
قِيمة value	كَنَدا Canada
	كَهْرَبائِي (ـون) electrician
كاتِب (كَتَبة ، كُتّاب) clerk	الكُوَيْت Kuwait
كاد (a) with other verbs 'to almost...'	كَيْ so as to, in order to
كامِل complete, perfect (adj.)	كَيْف how?
كان (u) be	كِيلُوغْرام kilogram
كَبِير (كِبار) big, old	كِيمْياء chemistry
كِتاب (كُتُب) book	
كِتابة writing	لِ to, for, because of, etc.
كَتَب (u) write	لِأَنّ because; in order to
	لا no, not

لابِس wearing, dressed in

لازِم necessary

لَحْم meat

لَحَّام (ون) welder

لِذلِك for this reason

لَعِب (a) play

لُعْبة game

لَعَلَّ maybe, perhaps

لُغة (ـات) language

لَفَّ (u) turn, wrap

لْكِن but

لِكَيْ in order to

لِماذا why?

لَنْدَن London

لَوْ if

لِيبْيا Libya

لَيْسَ (verb) is/are not

لَيْلة (لَيالٍ) night

ماء (مِياه) water

ما what; not

مِائة (ـات) hundred

مات (u) die

ماذا what?

مَبْسُوط (ون) content (adj.)

مَتْحَف (مَتاحِف) museum

مَتَى when?

مِثْل like

مَثَلاً for instance

مُجْتَهِد (ون) diligent, hard-working

مَجَلّة (ـات) magazine

مَجْلِس (مَجالِس) council; reception room

مَجْمُوعة (ـات) group, collection

مَجْنُون (مَجانين) mad

مَجِيء coming, arrival

مُحاسِب (ون) accountant

مُحَرِّر (ون) editor

مَحَلِّي local

مُدّة period of time

مُدَرِّس (ون) teacher

مَدْرَسة (مَدارِس) school

مُدير (ون ، مُدَراء) manager

مَرْأة woman (امرأة when used without definite article)

مَرّة (ـات) time, occasion

مَرْكَزِيّ central

مَريض (مَرْضَى) ill

مَسْجِد (مَساجِد) mosque

مُسْلِم (ون) Muslim

نَظِيف (نِظاف) clean

نَعَمْ yes

نَقَل (u) move, transport

نُكْتة (نُكَت) joke

نَهار daytime

نِهاية end (n.)

نَوْع (أنْواع) kind, type

هامّ important

هاجَر (III) emigrate

هٰذا (هٰؤُلاء .pl , هٰذِهِ .f) this

هَلْ (word used to indicate that the following sentence is a question)

هُنا here

هُناك there

هٰكَذا thus, in this way

واسِع spacious, roomy

وَاللهِ By God! (common oath used for emphasis)

وَجَد (i) find

وَراء behind

وَرَقة (أوْراق) paper, sheet of paper

وَزارة (ـات) ministry

وَزير (وُزَراء) minister

وَسِخ dirty

وَصَل (i) arrive at, reach

وَضَع (a) put, place

وَطَن (أوْطان) homeland, native land

وَظَّف (II) appoint, employ

وَظِيفة (وَظائِف) job, position

وَفْد (وُفُود) delegation

وَقَع (a) fall; be situated

وَقَف (i) stop, stand

وَلَد (أوْلاد) boy

وَلَّع (II) ignite

وَلٰكِن but

يَد (أيْدٍ ، أيادٍ) hand

يَسار left

يَمين right

يَناير January

يَوْم (أيّام) day

اليَوْم today

يَوْمِيّ daily